D1210069

WORRYING THE NATION

THEORY/CULTURE

General editors:
Linda Hutcheon, Gary Leonard, Jill Matus,
Janet Paterson, and Paul Perron

WORRYING THE NATION

Imagining a
National Literature
in English Canada

Jonathan Kertzer

UNIVERSITY OF TORONTO PRESS
Toronto Buffalo London

© University of Toronto Press Incorporated 1998
Toronto Buffalo London
Printed in Canada

ISBN 0-8020-4303-8 (cloth)

Printed on acid-free paper

Canadian Cataloguing in Publication Data

Kertzer, Jonathan, 1946–
Worrying the nation : imagining a national literature
in English Canada

(Theory/culture)
Includes bibliographical references and index.
ISBN 0-8020-4303-8

1. Canadian literature (English) – History and criticism.*
2. Nationalism in literature.   I. Title.   II. Series.

PS8101.N27K47 1998   C810.9'358   C98-931044-2
PR9185.5.N27K47 1998

This book has been published with the help of a grant from the Humanities
and Social Sciences Federation of Canada, using funds provided by the
Social Sciences and Humanities Research Council of Canada.

University of Toronto Press acknowledges the assistance to its publishing
program of the Canada Council for the Arts and the Ontario Arts Council.

For Adrienne, Joshua, and Nicholas

The atmosphere of education in which he lived was colonial, revolutionary, almost Cromwellian, as though he were steeped, from his greatest grandmother's birth, in the odor of political crime ... Politics, as a practice, whatever its professions, had always been the systematic organization of hatreds, and Massachusetts politics had been as harsh as the climate.

Henry Adams, *The Education of Henry Adams*

The meaning of planting this Great Tree is the Great Peace, and Good Tidings of Peace and Power, and the Nations of the earth shall see it and shall accept and follow the Root and shall arrive here at this Tree and when they arrive here you shall receive them and shall seat them in the midst of your Confederacy, and the meaning of placing an Eagle on the top of the Great Tall Tree is to watch the Roots ... This bundle of arrows signifies that all Lords and all the Warriors and all the Women of the Confederacy have become united as one person ... We have now completed our power so that we, the Five Nations Confederacy, shall in the future only have one body, one head and one heart.

Traditional History of the Confederacy of the Five Nations

I often think that in our search for a Canadian identity we fail to realize that we are not searching for definitions but for signs and omens.

Phyllis Webb, *Nothing but Brush Strokes*

Contents

Acknowledgments

An earlier version of chapter 2 appeared in *Canadian Literature* 130 (Autumn 1991): 70–89.

My thanks to the Aid to Scholarly Publications Program for their support. Thanks also to my editors at the University of Toronto Press – Gerald Hallowell, Barbara Tessman, and especially Emily Andrew.

WORRYING THE NATION

1. National + Literary + History

The need for theory and method is usually felt most acutely when, in a time of rapid changes, the object of theoretical inquiry no longer functions in its traditional context.

Robert Weimann, *Structure and Society in Literary History*

The object of theoretical inquiry in Canadian literary studies – Canada – no longer functions as it once did. English-Canadian literary history has been distinguished by its modest but persistent nationalism, by its mistrust of foreign influences, and above all by its casual appeal to historical conditions (roughing it in the bush, the garrison) and cultural forces (colonialism, regionalism, puritanism) as guarantees of coherence and value. Recently these approaches have been questioned from various quarters, thereby depriving the discipline of its formative principles. The orthodox line stressing thematic continuity in response to permanent environmental and cultural factors has virtually been abandoned in scholarly writing, if not in the classroom. John Metcalf and Robert Lecker both show, though for different reasons, how flimsy the 'Canadian tradition' is, how quickly it was canonized by editors and anthologists, and how easily it was abandoned. The Rise and Fall of the Great Canadian Tradition amuses Metcalf, who claims that our 'tradition' derives from the faulty judgment of a few academics lusting after tenure. But its alleged demise illustrates in condensed form a much wider problem, since literary history in general has become such a contentious topic. Giving literary history a national purpose exacerbates the problem, and the same scholarly concoctions that tickle Metcalf's fancy appear in other national literatures. American critics, too, now dispute their traditional themes and schemes: the frontier, American Adam, the New England mind, southern gothic. Where Leslie Fiedler once neatly divided American novels into northerns, southerns, easterns, and westerns, critics now find a 'deterritorialized' literature, unsure of its bearings.[1] Since losing one's bearings is de rigueur in Canadian literature – 'Where is here?' is the national riddle posed by Northrop Frye (*Bush Garden* 220) – we should be in a good position to survey the confusion. But how are we to proceed if we cannot agree who 'we' are? What sense of community produces English-Canadian literature, or can be produced by it?

Metcalf repudiates a parochial nationalism that would contaminate literature with well-intentioned but futile political aims: 'The idea that literature should serve what is essentially a *political* function, the defining of Canadian identity, is pervasive. It underlies most government thinking on the arts and is a concern of far too many critics. Intelligent critics and bureaucrats tend to wince when the idea is put baldly, so they disguise it with euphemisms. They talk of fiction and poetry as "introducing us to ourselves and to each other"; of Canada's literary "map"; of "filling in the white spaces" on the map. But they're still talking about using literature to promote national identity and unity' (28). In reply, Sam Solecki objects that Metcalf undermines the very basis of English-Canadian literature by pulling 'the theoretical rug out from under Canadian studies constituted as a separate branch of English studies' (22). 'That may not be a bad thing,' he continues half-heartedly, because he understands 'politics' in a different sense than does Metcalf. The latter means didactic writing or propaganda – what E.H. Dewart had praised in 1864 as 'the subtle but powerful cement of a patriotic literature' (ix). Understandably, Metcalf does not want literature to serve as ideological glue. Solecki is concerned not with the political use of literature, but with a more subtle problem: the political constitution of literary forms. Later in his essay Metcalf implicitly endorses the national view he seemed to reject, when he approves a warning made by John Sutherland: 'We could only use the word tradition if we believed that the poetry *was ... blended with the life of the country*' (42, Metcalf's emphasis). If Metcalf means that Canada is too immature to have nurtured a native tradition, then he is actually reaffirming the old romantic dream of fusing spirit, language, and place. He does not look beyond national literature but ahead to it.

At issue here is the explanatory power of nationality as it figures in literature, in critical accounts of that literature, and in literary history. To study literature 'insofar as it is *Canadian* literature, and ... a reflection of a national habit of mind' (Atwood, *Survival* 13) is to enter a theoretical thicket. For at least two centuries historians have carved up literatures according to national origin, because they believed that such categories correspond to something observable in a body of writing, even if the scope of that writing is debatable. They trust that there is such a thing as 'English-Canadian literature,' and that it is worthy of analysis because it is something more than just any work written by Canadians or about Canada. They trust that the labels Canadian, Québécois, or Mexican literature do more than suit the convenience of university syllabi, but mark a national discourse whose integrity, however tenuous, warrants study. These assumptions, which once seemed so secure and so fruitful, have now become uncertain.

This book studies the convergence of three formative terms: national, literary, and history. It examines the principles by which English-Canadian literature coordinated the three terms in order to establish itself as a field of literary accomplishment and critical study. It then asks: What happens to a national literature when the very idea of the nation has been set in doubt? In this chapter I begin by staking out the ground where my three terms meet and compete.

National

Joseph Roth's novel *The Radetzky March* (1932) presents a loyal bureaucrat bewildered by the dissolution of the Austro-Hungarian empire early in the twentieth century. 'To the District Commissioner [Herr von Trotta] the whole world consisted of Czechs, a people he considered to be recalcitrant, obstinate, and stupid, the originators of the concept "nations." There might be many peoples, but certainly no "nations". And over and above this, he received scarcely intelligible remissions and memoranda from the government concerning greater tolerance toward "national minorities," one of the phrases Herr von Trotta loathed most of all. "National minorities" were merely more extensive aggregations of "revolutionary individuals"' (222). Herr von Trotta, whose ancestors were Slovene and who governs part of what will soon become Czechoslovakia, feels loyal only to his Austrian emperor, Franz Joseph. His inability to conceive of a 'nation' in the modern sense of the word might place him, more properly, a century earlier, when enlightenment and revolution set Europe on a furious course that splintered its larger empires and alliances.[2] In the 1990s, the division of Czechoslovakia into Czech and Slovak republics demonstrates that nationalism is as obstinately divisive as ever. From Herr von Trotta's perplexity I draw three lessons.

The first lesson is that 'nation' is an old word used to describe a slippery idea. Political historians find the term only loosely definable, because no social unit and no elements composing it are essential to all national groups without exception (Birch 5–7, A.D. Smith, *Theories* 186). Variety is the norm. According to Peter Alter, a nation is 'a social group ... which, because of a variety of historically evolved relations of a linguistic, cultural, religious or political nature, has become conscious of its coherence, unity and particular interests' (17). Like most descriptions, this one seeks to balance objective conditions with subjective intent or sentiment: popular consciousness (the determination to constitute a community) is as important as shared qualities (language, religion, place, and so on). A nation is both a social reality and a state of mind (Xenos 134). It requires an 'intuitive sense of kinship,' where the intuition stems from a 'myth of common descent' (Connor 48)[3] as much as from historical fact. In order to maintain this balance of fact and feeling, however, commentators are obliged to define the nation in a circular manner: it is a group of people who feel they belong to the same nation.

Historians agree, however, that the category 'nation' is different from, though it overlaps with, the category 'state' (Tivey 2, 4). Most nations are not states; most states are not nations. 'A state is a legal and political organization, with the power to require obedience and loyalty from its citizens. A nation is a community of people, whose members are bound together by a sense of solidarity, a common culture, a national consciousness' (Seton-Watson 1). There are remarkably few countries – Walker Connor estimates the figure at about 10 per cent (53) – where nation and state coincide. Iceland is one example; Canada is not. Quebec is a nation, though not yet (and not necessarily) a state.[4] The modern ideal is the composite 'nation-state' in which cultural and political forms correspond effortlessly, although signs of strain are clear to Herr von Trotta. The nation-state is supposed to be natural and normal – words used recently by Lucien Bouchard to promote Quebec independence – when actually it is a precarious invention. It is supposed to be 'the focus of men's loyalties and the indispensable framework for all social, cultural and economic activities' (Kamenka 6), when actually it requires constant ideological tinkering. It is supposed to be the fruition of civil life, yet it is forever incomplete, a destiny to be fulfilled rather than an everyday state of affairs. Citizens must continually be reminded – for example, through the propaganda decried by Metcalf – of what they are supposed to know in their bones. In romantic theories, which tinge virtually all modern accounts of nationhood, historical analysis blends with mystical expectation: 'Nationalism is a vision of the future which restores to man his "essence," his basic pattern of living and being, which was once his undisputed birthright' (A.D. Smith, *Theories* 22). Here is the nation as promised land, or as a romance of identity lost and found.

Although nations are supposed to grow spontaneously from the soil, in practice they require a lot of work. Great creative effort is necessary to make national destiny seem like the inevitable reward of progress/modernization/sovereignty. Nations are supposed to spring from the 'folk,' when in fact 'nation building' has always been conducted by small, educated elites and inspired by political missionaries such as Mazzini in Italy or Mickiewicz in Poland (Seton-Watson ch. 3). They urge their compatriots to see what is supposed to be obvious: that they already are a nation and deserve to be a state. In countries like Canada, where the tension between cultural and political needs is acute, the incongruity of the modern nation-state is especially clear. Canadians mistrust the rhetoric of national glory, as E.J. Pratt shows when he depicts the botched last spike of the transcontinental railway. Such feeble patriotism is sometimes regretted, but it may actually be an advantage because it reveals the historical complexity obscured by nationalist rhetoric. It reveals that nations are invented, not born. 'The nation is not a "natural" or "biological" group – in the sense, for example, of the family. It has no "natural" rights in the sense that the individual can be said to have natural rights. The nation is not a definable and clearly recognizable entity; nor is it universal. It is confined to certain periods of history and to certain parts of the world. To-day [i.e., 1945] – in the most nation-conscious of all epochs – it would still probably be fair to say that a large numerical majority of the population of the world feel no allegiance to any nation' (Carr 39).

This quotation from E.H. Carr points to Herr von Trotta's second lesson: there are volatile inconsistencies within the very idea of nationhood. Cultural critics (notably Seton-Watson, Anderson, Bhabha, Chatterjee, Kamenka, Nairn, and Ahmad) have shown with increasing delight that nationalism is radically ambiguous. It presents itself as both universal and unique, natural and artificial, ancient and modern. It encourages diversity but insists on homogeneity. Its character is inward and local, yet it is produced by 'the machinery of world political economy' (Nairn 335). It is the battle-cry of minority liberation movements, yet also the banner of imperialism. Its goal is progress and modernization, yet it sanctifies a traditional past. It is a rational scheme fuelled by the non-rational (G. Smith 197, Connor 49), a popular upheaval that has to be imposed by government and intelligentsia (Mosse 46). As Carr complains, the nation is not a natural entity, yet its enthusiasts continually invoke nature to justify their policies by appealing to race, roots, blood, and soil. Nations are said to flower, mature, decay, and regenerate as if they were hardy political plants. As I will show in the next chapter, this robust political life seeks verification in literature, because it exhibits the same vital qualities.

The nation may not be a family, according to Carr, but metaphors of kinship and the hearth are irresistible. Nations serve as models of domestic peace, yet they encourage war, both civil and international. Because they are rooted in their own soil, their defining needs are always local, yet they inevitably conflict with other nations' needs. On the one hand, nationalism encourages heterogeneity through the proliferation of competing claims, which plague Herr von Trotta. Gone are the controlling unities that tied Europe together: Christianity, the Holy Roman Empire, and royal alliances and kinships. In their place lies the anarchy of the First World War, with which *The Radetzky March* ends. On the other hand, nationalism imposes the homogeneity of family resemblance. Countries are expected to share a domestic language, religion, culture, or race. Any variance from the norm becomes a threat to their integrity. Purity then becomes a prime value, and purity is not a natural state of affairs (nothing in nature is pure) but an ideological imperative, a way of thinking through exclusion. Hence the truism that the easiest way to love one's country is to hate one's neighbour. This is what Lord Acton objected to in his famous denunciation: 'The nation is ... an ideal unit founded on the race, in defiance of the modifying action of external causes, of tradition, and of existing rights. It overrules the rights and wishes of the inhabitants, absorbing their divergent interests in a fictitious unity; sacrifices their several inclinations and duties to the higher claim of nationality, and crushes all natural rights and all established liberties for the purpose of vindicating itself' (Kohn 124).

The third lesson, embracing all the others, is that modern nationalism engenders, or is engendered by, a new conception of history. Following enlightenment and romantic philosophies, the nation becomes the basic unit of historical activity. History means national, political history. Different countries live their own lives, which intersect in 'world history' – that is, inter-national history – as monitored by institutions like the League of Nations or the United Nations. A corollary of this argument has great literary importance. When nations are regarded as historical subjects, they take on the characteristics of people. They not only grant character to their citizens, but are themselves characters. Each nation can be treated as if it were a single person, so that national history becomes biographical, displaying the coherence and purpose of psychological growth. In Georg G. Iggers's account of German historicism, the relation between nation and person goes beyond analogy. Nations are not merely like people; individual experience is not just caught up in a collective life. Rather, the nation really has a personality of its own: 'Nations have the characteristics of persons: they have a spirit and they have a life span. They are not a collection of individuals, but are organisms ... [A]ll values come out of the spirit of nations' (35).

It is not far from treating a nation as a person to celebrating it as a national hero whose life has epic grandeur. Hayden White and Lionel Gossman argue that, although nineteenth-century historians aspired to turn history into a science, they actually cultivated the aesthetic aspects of their craft. They turned history into art. Their writing was artful, not just because they were lively stylists, but because of the way they envisaged history as a mode of understanding. According to White, 'Hegel had insisted that a specifically historical mode of being was linked to a specifically narrative mode of representation' (29). The link between history and narrative is instrumental. To think in historical terms is to summon the figures of narrative; conversely, to narrate the past is to invoke a vision of history. Historical attributes – causality, agency, law, social conflict, and authority – are treated as narrative categories (11–14). Conversely, narrative qualities – dramatic conflict, moral purpose, heroic action – are attributed to history (H. White 20–4, Gossman 260–1). And for the nationalistic writer, intent on realizing the dream of a nation-state, the historical narrative quickly turns visionary. History turns into myth. According to Gossman: 'After the French Revolution, the dominant ambition of historians was to make history – rather than fiction – the successor of epic as the repository of society's values and of its understanding of the world ... History, consequently, had to be cleared of the stigma attaching to the "merely" successive event, the isolated, individual episode. Historical discourse had to order individual events into episodes, individual episodes into stories, and individual stories into the single unifying and signifying history of humanity, of civilization, and of the modern bourgeois nation-states' (252–3). Even the most sedate, bourgeois state can see itself as the culmination of a splendid, mythological process.[5] A common historical romance portrays the nation as a sleeping giant that awakens, recalls its ancient glory, and resolves to fulfil its heroic promise. In this potent mixture of fact and fantasy, national history is both framed and validated by epochs that transcend history. It is inspired by a mythical pre-history (e.g., the Celtic Twilight) and fulfiled by a utopian post-history (e.g., the classless society, the peaceable kingdom). In extreme cases the utopian element turns messianic. Ardent nationalists cast Poland in the role of martyr, crucified by Russia, Prussia, and Austria and fated to redeem the world (A.D. Smith, *Theories* 20, 160). More modestly, Hegel showed that the grand sweep of world history culminated in Germany. Canadians have been less ambitious, but Sir Wilfrid Laurier did predict that the twentieth century would belong to Canada.

National + Literary

Literature, too, was reoriented in light of the patriotic missions of nineteenth-century nationalists. Given the ease with which ideological passion transforms history into myth, it is not surprising that politicians and historians sought the blessing of literature. If the nation is 'a theoretical scheme, a fictitious invention' (Alter 112), and if Canada is a multiple 'necessary fiction' (Blodgett, 'Is a History' 3), then who serves the national purpose better than our poets, singing of what is past and passing and to come?

> But the huge task announced
> Ten years before had now to start afresh –
> The moulding of men's minds was harder far
> Than moulding of the steel and prior to it.
> It was the battle of ideas and words
> And kindred images called by the same name,
> Like brothers who with temperamental blood
> Went to it with their fists.
>
> (E.J. Pratt, 'Towards the Last Spike' ll. 466–73)

E.J. Pratt's poetry is historical not just because of his theme (uniting Canada via the transcontinental railway), but because his vision of history is poetic and his vision of poetry is national. Through a battle of muscles, ideas, words, and images, Canada is moulded across the land and in the minds of citizens, who become authentic Canadians through this epic ordeal, and who find a national voice in Pratt's poetry. 'It is the magic of nationalism to turn chance into destiny,' Benedict Anderson advises (19), but even magic requires effort. Nation, history, narrative, and rhetoric confirm each other so forcefully that it is easy to forget how hard nineteenth-century writers worked to establish the connections.

Nationalism and literature have long been eager but fractious allies. If nation building is an triumph of imagination (as chapter 3 will show), so is nation deconstructing (chapter 4). I will return periodically to the restless alliance between national literature and the community whose life it sustains but also subverts. Literature makes the nation both possible and impossible, imaginable and intolerable. On the one hand, the nation owes its very 'life' to literature, and to all the arts of cultural persuasion, because they articulate a national life by telling its story and by supplying its motivating principle – justice. I will argue that the nation as social imaginary always relies on both a narrative of justice and the justice of narrative. On the other hand, literature exposes the national life as unjust, and even monstrous, because it has the paradoxical ability to criticize the ideology in which it is immersed and by which it is compromised. Why literature should enjoy the privilege of being at once inside (part of) and outside (critical of) the prevailing ideology is a question deserving a book of its own.[6] Here I would first note that faith in what I am calling 'artistic privilege' is so tenacious as to become an ideological imperative in its own right. Romanticism, modernism, postmodernism, feminism, and postcolonialism all accord a special status to art, though not necessarily for the same reasons. Every stylistic innovation from symbolism to aestheticism to surrealism to *l'écriture féminine* has invoked the powers of literary language to see into the heart of its own duplicitous making.

I would also note that any attempt to explain the provenance of artistic privilege will be compromised in turn; that is, it too will owe a debt to the ideology that it surveys. For example, romantic critics appeal to the keen insights of imagination that, according to Coleridge, summon the 'depth and energy' of all mental faculties simultaneously (179).[7] Marxist critics, recalling how Friedrich Engels praised Balzac's inspired ability to write bourgeois novels that unmask bourgeois hypocrisy, show how stylistic disparities such as irony, defamiliarization, or heteroglossia (Lukács, Shklovsky, Bakhtin) make class contradictions visible to the artistic eye. Post-structuralist critics show how the uncanny 'figurality of all signification' (Paul de Man's phrase in 'Shelley Disfigured' 62) makes literary texts privy to ideological tricks. The same privilege is accorded to national literatures by Lynette Hunter, who combines Marxist and post-structuralist explanations. She claims that even as a national literature celebrates the nation as the fruit of nature, it covertly exposes the rhetorical ploys by which 'nature' and 'nation' were constructed. It both conceals and reveals. 'The rhetoric of the nation-state structures its ethos simultaneously to build a norm as an artificial construction, and then to forget that it is artificial.' Yet literature also teaches us to remember what we forgot, because 'once you choose to focus on literary and language strategies, semiotics and rhetoric, you encourage a questioning of system, of what we take for granted as readers and writers – as well as human beings' (Hunter 16, 21). Nation and literature thus regulate each other insistently but inconsistently. According to Hunter's formulation, the nation politicizes literature so as to make its citizens forget politics, but literature responds by tempting them into a subversive remembering.

Earlier I noted John Metcalf's desire to cleanse literature of political taint, but his ideal of literary autonomy only arises in response to earlier theories by which language was seen as embedded in political culture. Romantic historicism regards language as the lifeblood of a nation, with literature as its pulse, and Metcalf does not really challenge this view when he diagnoses Canadian literature as anaemic. But if literature promotes social cohesion by imagining a nation, it also encourages social discontent. A common language inflected by a national voice is supposed to articulate the national life, but that very articulation can prove divisive, especially when the voice speaks in a colonial accent. Literature knits people together, but it also shows how the knitting was accomplished and at what cost. Language knits but also unravels. Any calculation of what a nation was (or imagines itself to have been), and what it hopes to become, will involve an appraisal of this dual function. Literature links people by rising above local differences. Dr Johnson advised that the poet 'must divest himself of the prejudices of his age or country; he must consider right and wrong in their abstracted and invariable state; he must disregard present laws and opinions, and rise to general and transcendental truths, which will always be the same' (*Rasselas* 528). In reaction, romantic critics argued that transcendental truths must be rooted in a national soil whose peculiarities nourish the true poet. Even general truths require a particular resonance. In order to reconcile the general and particular functions of national literature – functions that appear in the next chapter as 'Genius' and 'genius' – nationalist critics appealed to the new science of philology.

In an essay about the disarray of contemporary education, George Steiner laments that Western humanism has reached the end of a tradition once based on a noble ideal of nationality. Humanist studies were not directed towards crude patriotic ends, because nationality was a formative notion in virtually all historical, political, and literary thought, with literary philology taking the lead: 'As Herder, the Grimm brothers, and the whole lineage of German literary teachers and critics were frank to proclaim, the study of one's own literary past was a vital part in affirming national identity. To this point of view Taine and the historical positivists added the theory that one gets to know the unique racial genius of a people, of one's own people, by studying its literature. Everywhere the history of modern literary studies shows the mark of this nationalist ideal of the mid- and late-nineteenth century' (*Language* 79). Steiner insists that romantic infatuation with nationality was quite different from the fanatical violence of modern nationalism (82), and he regrets that a generous tradition was gradually perverted. Nineteenth-century philology studied language as the forum of a culture and the key to its history, both of which were essentially national in complexion. Philology (a classical term revived by Friedrich Wolf in 1777) aspired to be a theory of 'the speculative unity of knowledge,' comprising grammar, criticism, geography, political history, customs, mythology, literature, and art – all animated by the vitality of language (Graff 69).[8] Language and nationality provided a joint basis for all these disciplines, because nations developed in accordance with the character of their language (no bilingualism or multiculturalism here). Nationality thus provided a common ground for diverse cultural phenomena. Most important, it granted unity and identity to a people, since everything in a nation's life could be traced back to a ' "master idea" [Hippolyte Taine's phrase] defining the characteristic tendency of a national culture at a given moment' (Graff 70). Everything derived from a controlling genius. It is precisely this powerful idealism that offends critics today.

Throughout this book I will worry at the romantic basis of national literature, because it is a legacy that continues to enchant and plague us. I am following David Perkins's suggestion that literary history not only arose in the romantic period, but relied on romantic assumptions to formulate itself as a discipline. Indeed, the very notion of a 'romantic period' was one of its first accomplishments.[9] Its most important assumptions were: 'the importance attached to beginnings or origins, the assumption that a development is the subject of literary history, the understanding of development as continual rather than disjunctive, and the creation of suprapersonal entities as the subjects of this development' (Perkins 86). To this useful list might be added features that Peter Uwe Hohendahl finds in German literary history: an elegant sequence of great works framed by an early period of classical excellence and a future age of national fulfilment; political/ethical rhythms of rise and fall, integration and disintegration; and purposeful forces such as evolution, tradition, and synthesis. We will encounter many of these features in Canadian studies, but the suprapersonal subject that concerns me most is, of course, the nation. It became the hero of national literature, because '[w]ith the unfolding of an idea, principle, suprapersonal entity, or *Geist* as its subject, a literary history became teleological. It acquired a plot, could assume a

point of view, and might generate considerable narrative interest'
(Perkins 5). Individual literary works join in a larger adventure in
which the nation figures as hero. As befits a hero, it is armed for its
exploits by a loyal squire: the national literary critic. Romantic theories of nationality were good news for teachers and scholars, who
found themselves cast in the role of cultural custodian. If nowadays
the squire has deposed the master, so that criticism claims to be
just as creative as poetry,[10] we should recall the long, devoted
apprenticeship that critics had to serve.

As Gerald Graff shows, when scholars established American literature as an independent area of study, they called on the sanction
of German philology. At first the phrase 'American literature'
seemed like 'a laughable contradiction in terms' (211), because
writing by Americans was merely a colonial offshoot conveying first
a British and then a New England consciousness. To be an American literary critic was also laughable. Only after the patriotism of
the First World War was literature regarded as an authentic expression of American character and treated as a 'conceptual unity'
(217) in its own right.[11] Its office was to integrate and explicate
'American experience.' From that experience stem the various
forms of the 'American imagination,' which critics gradually codi-
fied as cultural myths. Their job became increasingly important, as
they combined these myths in a network of moral and thematic
dualisms such as innocence/experience, east/west, industrial/pas-
toral. The literary history that founded American studies is thus
itself a romance: a noble story about origins and the earning of
national identity. For several decades a comparable story has been
devised to justify English-Canadian literature as a field of study,
and the same is true of Quebec.[12] If romantic philology sounds too
idealistic for contemporary tastes, we should note how many of its
features persist in Canadian criticism: the relative isolation of each
country in a self-sustaining system of local traditions; the national
temper that shapes a people's development through their literature; the teleological model that charts the genesis and maturation
of a country; the reverence for national classics; the organic blending (or conversely, the unnatural alienation) of landscape with
individual and communal lives.

National + Literary + History

Philology blends history, politics, and art in a 'speculative unity' secured by the unifying power of language. Recent cultural theory proposes just the opposite: that language cannot be trusted to unify thought, because language is an agent of speculative dispersal. It exposes the radical incompatibility of all conceptual systems as well as the instability of their formative terms, so that 'national-literary-history' becomes a curious hybrid beast, like Dr Doolittle's Pushme Pullyou. Its three terms tug in different directions. The ways in which the three heads are encouraged to cooperate will define different kinds of history. Carl Klinck was well aware of this problem when he compiled the *Literary History of Canada*. He distinguished between a 'literary history,' which would be social, descriptive, and inclusive, and a 'history of Canadian literature,' which would be evaluative and exclusive (Djwa, 'Canadian Angles of Vision' 135–6). Because he favoured the former approach, he included eclectic studies of social significance, historical continuity, environmental impact, local colour, colonial influence, and artistic worth – without trying to negotiate their conflicting interests. The result was bound to be inconsistent and to dissatisfy purists in all camps.[13]

If national literary history is a hybrid discourse, then purity is both impossible and undesirable. The question is how to proceed in view of its conflictual nature, and I will have more to say about the 'contamination' produced when Klinck's two categories collide and collude. What he calls a history of literature is intrinsic: it is 'a narrative account of either literature as a whole or of specific modes (poetry, drama, fiction), genres (epic, comedy, pastoral), or forms (complaint, sonnet, ode), that covers either a broad sweep of historical time or confines itself to one of the chronological periods into which the cultural past has typically been divided' (Patterson 250). Strictly observed, such literary traditions appear self-contained, but in a broader view they fall within what Klinck calls literary (or cultural) histories: 'The goal of this extrinsic approach is to specify the forces that caused, governed, entailed, or were expressed by literary texts – what made them what they were rather than something else – and the routes by which these forces exerted their influence upon literature' (Patterson 250). An intrinsic history might trace the development of the sonnet from Petrarch to Milton Acorn. An extrinsic history might explain how uses of the sonnet express different social, ideological, or national conditions.

This analysis separates the 'inside' from the 'outside' of literature by distinguishing between aesthetic form and social function. As soon as we add our third – national – head to the beast, the neat opposition starts to break down, because the nation belongs to both literary and historical species, and forces them to interact. Inside and outside trade places with surprising ease and even appear to devour each other. On the one hand, the outside is brought within. National literature frequently incorporates history as setting or background, and more elaborately in historical novels, political satires, and national epics. If, as is sometimes argued, reality is 'somehow' transformed when it passes into fiction, then critics are obliged to account for the transformation more precisely than by appealing vaguely to the alchemy of art. On the other hand, the inside is brought out. If literature incorporates history, history in its turn incorporates literature. As I indicated earlier by citing White and Gossman, historical understanding takes narrative forms that use the nation as their meta-subject or hero. The nation's 'character' is analysed dramatically; its 'life' is explained biographically; its 'destiny' is plotted as myth, romance, or epic. Like sonnets about the sonnet, literary histories are strangely self-regarding beasts. They rely for their own composition and validation on the same literary forms that they take as their subject matter. Literary history aims to negotiate between its two components yet falls within both.

As I will show, national literary histories try to resolve this dilemma by using the nation as a mediating term between its historical and literary partners. Since the nation is both fact (historical reality) and fiction (imagined community), it promises to reconcile the competing demands of life and art by providing principles (sociability and justice) that apply to both. It supplies both historical and aesthetic values, and uses the values of one to authenticate the other. The great strength of this tradition is that it operates so smoothly as to seem effortless. The task of critics such as Weimann, White, and Gossman has been to make the tradition opaque by disclosing its conflicted assumptions.[14] Principles that the nation puts at the disposal of literary history include: organic growth, artistic and social integrity, authenticity, sociability, and justice.

Organic Growth

Nations are not natural, yet they appeal to nature to justify themselves and to build a literary home. If life and art are both organic, then they can grow together. For example, Francis Mulhern suggests that for F.R. Leavis 'the sovereign *topos* of Leavisian discourse was precisely the continuity of Englishness' ('English Reading' 253). Nationality was Leavis's primary principle, not just because he happened to be patriotic, but because it allowed him to integrate literary, social, and moral values so that each validated the others. The best English literature was the most skilful, the most serious, and the most English. In English Canada, the organic model was attractive because it excused social and literary faults as well as provided for their amelioration. In the earliest literary histories by Roy Palmer Baker (1920), J.D. Logan and D.G. French (1924), Archibald MacMechan (1924), and Lionel Stevenson (1926), Canada is a 'young' country whose literature is 'immature.' According to MacMechan, we are still a 'forest-feeling, railway-building, plowing, sowing, reaping, butter-and-cheese making people' (15) who have little time for the fine arts; but as our country grows, our art will improve in accordance with a scale of literary values matching our developing political sophistication. Consequently, one can trace a detailed parallel between the growth of the nation and a succession of literary styles and genres, each an improvement on the previous one. Anthologies often obey this principle. Records of first discovery (David Thompson) are followed by reflective travel literature (Anna Jameson), which are followed by exploratory narrative poems (Charles Sangster), and then by realistic stories of settlement (F.P. Grove). Matter and

manner grow together: 'It is, however, true that as a national literature develops it will focus increasingly on the problems of modern
urban life or judge concepts of authenticity by contemporary standards. The subject-matter of the novel moves from exoticism and
history to realism, protest, cultural assertion and then to the treatment of the psychology of individuals and personal problems'
(King 47). The sequence of literary forms is accompanied by a
series of styles, which are increasingly native in texture as the New
World abandons the Old World's idiom. It is positively reassuring
to find that Goldsmith's 'The Rising Village' sounds mechanical
and derivative, since these faults confirm that it is a product of a
rustic society.

The beauty of this theory is its intricate harmony. The problem
is that it forces everyone to sing the same tune. To maintain the
pattern of organic development, evidence must be selected and
assessed carefully to protect the alignment of social and aesthetic
values, which are liable to drift apart. Anomalous works are
excluded or judged inferior if they disrupt the pattern. Acceptable
works are assigned a suitable place in the chorus. Ideally writers
should improve in quality as the nation gains self-confidence and
self-government, but this is too much to expect. Canada is far too
disparate. The chronology is liable to get irregular, and it would be
helpful if Sir Charles G.D. Roberts had not lived quite so long. Similarly, realism is supposed to be an advance on romance, and it is
embarrassing when Grove's novels use authentic details to gain
romantic effects. A nice irony of Northrop Frye's influential work
is that even as he proclaimed the centrality of romance in his general theory (notably in *The Secular Scripture*), he was obliged to
favour realism in Canadian writing, a style that he otherwise dispar-
aged. Fortunately, beyond realism lay more sophisticated forms of
romance (*Divisions* 54).

Artistic and Social Integrity

The corollary of organic growth is organic unity, which is the virtue
and reward, but also the burden, of national literary histories.
They argue that artistic unity is conferred by the national life,

which in turn can be construed according to literary patterns. Through this elegant give and take, artistic and social integrity vouch for each other. When literature is viewed historically, individual works, as well as national literature as a whole, are all unified by permanent, native features such as terrain, climate, temperament, or national destiny. All cultural expressions are shaped by the same national character. Here we find those critical models that have successfully unified English-Canadian literature: the myth of the New Land; the cultural mosaic; Frye's garrison mentality; 'topocentrism,' which is Leon Surette's term for the way environment confers identity. Yet when history is viewed aesthetically, the nation is unified like a work of art continually being refashioned. No matter how disparate its regions or how fractious its politics, these fragments contribute to a national life that can be depicted as an idyll (Leacock), epic (Pratt), tragedy (Rudy Wiebe), comedy (Robertson Davies), or even postmodern carnival (Kroetsch). The same artistic/social integrity is imparted to literary histories. Carl Klinck was not worried by the conflicting styles used in the *Literary History of Canada* because, he later recalled, 'I thought unity would come out of the materials, out of Canada, so to speak, not necessarily from one author' (111). Canada itself would speak in its own voice. Klinck's optimism now is scorned as authoritarian by critics who favour heteroglossic critical styles, but out of the heteroglossia emerges another national composition – the nation as polyphony.[15]

Whether integrity is regarded as an inherent property of the nation, or as a formal property of writing about the nation, it becomes a burden when it exacts too high a price. All national literatures get caught up in a politics of inclusion and exclusion, whereby some writers are judged more central than others. Robertson Davies might have considered himself either blessed or cursed to be judged the purest of Canadian writers. Other writers and styles are judged extraneous or even dangerous if they threaten the integrity of the national project. For example, MacMechan (whose book bears the epigraph *ad maiorem patriae gloriam*) disapproved of the way Roberts's verse turned erotic and sentimental under American influence, and Sara Jeannette Duncan's fiction succumbed to the foreign example of Henry James (124, 138). J.G. Bourinot warned about the baleful effect of French realism in fiction (30). The further literary historians move from the centre (wherever it is placed), the more uneasy they feel. How are they to account for all the immigrants, emigrants and vagrants who populate Canadian letters: Malcolm Lowry, Brian Moore, John Metcalf, Louis Hémon? By what criteria should these writers be classed as Canadian? This problem used to seem like a joke at the expense of a 'young' nation trying to establish its credentials, in contrast to self-assured European countries, where there was no embarrassment about a good English name like Dante Gabriel Rossetti. But the joke is now at the expense of England, which has to find a place for writers like Salman Rushdie and Buchi Emecheta, who hardly fall into Leavis's great tradition. In this respect England has discovered a problem of cultural definition that has always been evident in Canada. As Timothy Brennan notes, because 'imperialism is, culturally speaking, a two-way flow' it gradually forces English critics to seek 'a new sense of what it means to be "English"' (47).[16] The same dilemma troubles France, which for all its cultural self-assurance and pride in welcoming political refugees now faces an influx of immigrants from North Africa who have provoked 'a crisis in national identity' (Kristeva 5, see also 36–40, 60).

Artistic and Social Authenticity

I have written as if there were only one line of English-Canadian literary history, but there have always been challenges to the nationalist ideology, first made in the name of regionalism, modernism, or cosmopolitanism, now made in the name of feminism, ethnicity, postmodernism, or post-colonialism.[17] Earlier literary historians, who were anxious that English Canada find its literary voice, listened for what is most authentic in that voice: the call of the wild, the colonial compromise, the ironic tone. By the mid-twentieth century, several critics were claiming that only a tentative/unending/fruitless quest for authenticity defines our literature. The questing itself grants authenticity, even when it is unsuccessful. Today's critics, always vigilant against essentialist thinking, characterize our literature by the way it studiously/playfully/sensuously renounces all claims to authenticity. Although these views differ drastically in their faith in authenticity, they all assume that a literary community, however combative, will produce 'our' literature, however conflicted. Even if the nation is splintered into competing solitudes, each group competes for power and recognition in a shared social setting, which takes it character from their competition. In varying degrees, then, even the most sceptical critics continue to presuppose a national forum in which aesthetic excellence, social responsibility, moral worth, and political maturity can be aligned, not effortlessly or permanently, but at least in some workable system. Not a perfect system, but one that 'works.'

How and for whose benefit does it work? Charting successive answers to this question is one way of writing a national literary history. For my purposes, this chart begins with romantic historicism, because it offers such a compelling model of artistic and social authenticity. The national model is endlessly self-validating, because each dimension (artistic, social, moral, political) derives its authenticity from the others. All cultural values become expressions of the national life, which grows under their direction. This idealist legacy is hard to resist, and I will speculate that it can never be utterly repudiated. If we repress it, it will return to haunt us in unexpected forms. Its fusion of aesthetic and social values is obvious in early literary histories of Canada, but it can be detected, suitably rephrased, in modern studies as well. The anthology prefaces by E.H. Dewart and W.D. Lighthall proudly declare that good poetry is not only beautiful, it is good for us, because it makes us good citizens. Lighthall indiscriminately praises moral strength, athletic prowess, colonial loyalty, and poetic beauty – a range of virtues that he sums up in the noble word 'virility' (xxi) and ascribes to the country as a whole.[18] To modern ears such enthusiasm sounds quaint, yet similar views persist in more acceptable terms and in unexpected places. The same resolve inspired E.K. Brown and A.J.M. Smith to attack the puritanism and colonialism that stultify much Confederation poetry. Although their tastes are more sophisticated, they too seek a fusion of aesthetic and social values.

They protest that puritanism and colonialism produce poetry that is not only bad as art, but inauthentic, because it is false to the spirit of the nation. Canada will find its true voice only when its writers mature morally, intellectually, and politically by ridding themselves of an oppressive burden. Smith found himself in Frye's dilemma. His own poetry is often touched by enchantment, yet he declared that the abject colonial spirit deludes itself with romance, whereas 'true nationalism rises out of the local realism of the pioneer' (A.J.M. Smith 34).

A generation later, Margaret Atwood and D.G. Jones followed the same line of argument, although at first glance they appear to reverse the perspective. When Atwood (*Survival*) advises Canadian writers to overcome the paralysis of victimization, and when Jones urges them to breach the garrison walls of puritanical rationality and to admit the vital powers of the wilderness, both critics imply that literature can be politically, personally, and aesthetically redemptive. Poetry will be authentic when it provides a vision of national authenticity. When Tom Wayman urges Canadian writers to 'articulate our lives' (2) accurately, in order to make us significant, worthy, and self-confident, he too asks literature to coordinate 'our national, artistic, personal existence' (5). When Dennis Lee ('Civil Elegies') depicts Canada as a nation of losers who lack an authentic 'civil space,' he shows that he has not abandoned the national ideal, only lamented its betrayal. So far we have been the victims of our history, as the flawed literature of the past testifies with perverse eloquence. Now the job of poet and critic is to diagnose our cultural malaise and advise us how to cure it. Matthew Arnold would approve.

Today when critics deconstruct the very notion of authenticity, they renounce not just literary nationalism, but the nation itself as a viable cultural form. What happens to 'our' literature when it is deprived of its conceptual and communal basis? I hope to show that the nexus of ideas concerning nationhood, nationality, and the nation-state is inescapable in cultural studies, especially in Canada. These ideas overlap, jostle, and compete. They enrage some and soothe others. Some critics have pronounced the nation *passé* or, worse, an insidious delusion masking the injustices of a political humanism that only pretends to be tolerant. The nation is offered as the natural forum of liberty and progress, when actually it encourages chauvinism and xenophobia. It claims to be universally benevolent, when actually it is tyrannical (Chatterjee 2–3, 15). Some writers condemned it categorically, as W.H. New remarks caustically: 'National adjectives, from this curiously fixed perspective, *must* be fascist in intent, *must* be authoritarian in desire, *must* require that authors and writings serve a single state design, *must* champion patriarchal unitary values, and *must* give precedence to conventional systems and holders of power and ignore all expressions of alternative possibility' ('The Very Idea' 2).

But even a cursory reading of its history reveals that the word 'nation' has a bewildering range of meanings, serving a variety of ideologies in different historical settings. To subsume these specificities within a single political motive (as does the reactionary Herr von Trotta) is to become ideologically domineering, and so to commit the very injustice that is being denounced. For this reason, Aijaz Ahmad objects that 'fashionable' post-structuralists, safe in their cosy academic jobs, are free to dismiss the nation as a misguided 'essentialism' (36); whereas post-colonial writers have no such luxury. For them, 'all relationships with imperialism pass through their own nation-states, and there is simply no way of breaking out of that imperial dominance without struggling for different kinds of national projects and for a revolutionary restructuring of one's own nation-state. So one struggles not against nations and states as such but for different articulations of class, nation and state ... [O]ne strives for a rationally argued understanding of social content and historic project for each particular nationalism' (11, see also 35–8).

In their many guises, nations have existed and continue to proliferate. They cannot be abolished by theoretical fiat. They are historically significant, even to those who denounce the nation's specious collectivity in favour of more authentic communities, even to those who reject the very idea of social authenticity. The former reconstitute the nation at a lower level (Quebec, First Nations); the latter maintain the nation, usually in idealized form, in a fretful, antithetical suspension.[19]

Sociability and Justice

I will argue that the nation is inescapable and continues to haunt us, because it informs all visions of sociability. No other issue is more urgent in current cultural thought, where people, ideas, and theories are all defined in terms of the communities that accord them power and legitimacy. In this view, meanings and values are produced collectively not individually. Even 'personal identity' is not singular but collective, the construction of gender, race, religion, textuality, and so on. If I define myself as a middle-class, middle-aged, white, Canadian male, I announce the communities (among many others) that willy-nilly make me what I am. Knowledge and judgment are always sociable, because they arise from the 'interpretive communities' and 'standpoint epistemologies'[20] through which meanings are shared. They compete with other value systems in a social/discursive field continually being reconfigured. But in that case, how is the larger configuration to be represented? The nation, which once proudly claimed title to this field, has now been displaced by what Frank Davey calls a 'transnational textuality' whose orientation is ethnic, feminist, racial, or sexual; whose rhetoric is post-structuralist; whose politics is post-colonial or anti-patriarchal. The unitary nation is a target for all such discourses whose philosophical aim is to confound essentialist thinking and whose political aim is to expose the coercion underlying the placid claims of humanist universality.

But as Davey notes further, even as they flout the old national boundaries, the antithetical discourses continue to rely on them in a 'combination of independence and complicitous intertwining' (*Canadian Literary Power* 76). National distinctions resurface within the counter-discourses that aim to displace the nation: American feminism encounters French and English feminisms; African-American feminism challenges white-American feminism; Canadian feminism distinguishes itself from American feminism.[21] When Fredric Jameson proposes that Third World texts oppose imperialist nationalism by devising 'national allegories' of their own (66), Aijaz Ahmad objects, not that the nation is an obsolete form of oppression, but that 'nationalism itself is not some unitary thing with some predetermined essence and value. There are hundreds of nationalisms in Asia and Africa today; some are oppressive, others are not' (102). As the editors of *Nationalisms and Sexualities* observe, 'politics' itself seems to require a national setting, as if only the rhetoric of nationality can confer legitimacy on communities seeking a political voice:

> That it is the nation rather than other forms of imagined collectivity that carries this immense political freight has meant, of course, that disenfranchised groups frequently have had to appeal to national values precisely to register their claims as political. Though black nationalism in the U.S. might often better be termed black culturalism, what helps to lend this movement its identity *as* a movement is its very recourse to the rhetoric of the nation. The same holds true for Queer Nation, the name recently adopted by gay and lesbian activists for their gender-transitive, militantly anti-homophobic organization. (Parker et al. 8)[22]

In a pluralist society like Canada, one of the most pressing problems today is how its communities are to declare themselves, how they might communicate profitably, and how they might share these profits. Communities, no matter how tightly knit, are never homogeneous and cannot seal themselves off from other groups: they cannot affirm their integrity without acknowledging inner tensions; they cannot preserve their differences except in concert or competition with other groups. When they compete for power, they must meet in order to conflict, negotiate, or cooperate.[23] The fiercer the competition, the greater is the need for a spacious collectivity, 'a social sphere to which all human beings have access,' as Davey calls it (*Canadian Literary Power* 194). Beyond the local constituency there is always a 'we,' however disputatious it may be. But how, Davey goes on to ask, is this broader sociability to be figured? 'At stake is both how a culture may be led to perceive its internal relations – as hierarchy, network, centre-margin, isolated regions, separate populations – and what constituency or alliance of constituencies will be perceived to have priority within the power structure of received perceptions' (239). A culture is an alliance (or misalliance) of constituencies whose shifting internal relations can be plotted and whose network sustains (or hinders) a system of justice. The nation in all its contradictoriness, and perhaps because of its contradictoriness, has been one of the chief means of proposing a sociability that can respect differences. Literature has always been a major testing ground of justice, not just because it takes human struggle as its subject, but because literary forms are themselves ruled by what I will call forms of justice and justness.

My treatment of sociability begins with the familiar structuralist distinction between language as a general system (*langue*) and speech as the specific use of that system by speakers and writers (*parole*). Language is sociable, not just because it allows people to communicate or dispute to their mutual (dis)advantage, but because language itself is always shared. No one has a private language, only a personal style, which is really a personal use of established conventions that in their turn are embedded in cultural history. This chain of priorities is expressed by the overworked phrase 'always already.' It means that however quirky one's speech, language is inescapably social in the sense of being common; it is always sociable in the sense of convoking a community. *Finnegans Wake* may seem utterly unique, but it draws on the languages of Europe and, through them, depicts an idiosyncratic fantasia of Western culture. Speech acts are sociable because language always precedes the speaker, who intervenes in discourses that are already underway and that determine the roles (subject positions) speakers may play. But what roles can they play, and what are the rules of engagement?

Liberal humanism contends that sociability is possible only if all citizens agree to respect a neutral forum where everyone can freely speak without fear of reprisal. There must be some common ground, a civil space where people holding different views can honestly air their differences. The nation should serve as such a forum, and Canadians have modestly offered themselves as models of tolerance and self-effacement. According to Malcolm Ross, Canada has excelled at being a community of communities, kept sociable by 'an anti-nationalistic nationalism to end all nationalisms' (123). In reply, feminist, anti-racist, and post-colonial critics decry the liberal consensus as ideological sleight-of-hand; it is a 'pragmatic contradiction, a particularism masquerading as the universal' (Taylor, *Philosophical* 237). They ask: Who controls the civil space, formulates its rules, and ensures its civility? How is it policed to control disruptive forces? Lorraine Weir maintains that Canadian critics have politely squelched opposition through 'sheer force of decorum and civility'; their 'rhetoric of sharing and mutuality has been used as a device of exclusion, casting beyond the pale the work of all those who choose other values, other styles' ('Normalizing' 183). Who defines and patrols the pale? People who hold widely different views seldom meet on an equal footing in public discourse, because real authority lies in prescribing the terms of the encounter, terms that are not negotiable. The party who sets the rules has already won a victory that was never in doubt, because more radical questions cannot be posed without breaking the rules and so acting uncivilly. And incivility is the one thing that cannot be tolerated in a civil forum. Justice demands that, after a certain point, even the best-intentioned citizen must not tolerate intolerance, or be civil to incivility.[24] In his acceptance speech at the Republican convention in August 1996, presidential candidate Bob Dole illustrated this civil paradox by declaring that any one who disagreed that the Republican Party was inclusive should be excluded from it and shown to the exit.

To be compelled by a sociability defined according to some one else's rules is to have lost in advance. Thus Frantz Fanon objected that what looks like a just debate about social 'values,' when viewed from the dignified vantage of power, becomes a 'narcissistic dialogue' (36) when viewed from a disadvantage. Referring specifically to the interaction of colony and metropolis, he warns that what may seem to be neutral and objective in their meeting is subtly, and even violently, biased against the colony: 'Objectivity, for the native, is always directed against him' (61). A narcissistic dialogue is really a monologue, fractured by its anxiety about how to maintain a dominant position – how to control the forum. The project posed by current theory, then, is not to magnanimously accept cultural differences but to reconceptualize their encounter. The solution will not be found in 'a commonplace, liberal plural-

ism that generously embraces diversity all the better to efface the
imbalances in power that adjudicate difference' (McClintock 8),
but in a radical critique of Western political discourse. We require
a new model of sociability or, as Henry A. Giroux says, we must
replace the liberal forum with 'a pluralized public space' (115):
'What is also needed is a social imaginary that configures a third
space, one that offers normative notions or forms of ethical
address that not only indicate, as Nancy Fraser has written, "what is
wrong with the power/knowledge regime and why we ought to
oppose it," but also points to a horizon of possibility in which the
terms for self-definition and social agency offer new sets of social
relations and a more compelling ethics of political and social
responsibility' (104).[25]

How the nation, which once served as the prime model of social
concord, might now function as a 'pluralized public space'
remains to be seen. However, Giroux's gaze beyond the horizon
(which hints at the utopian cast of recent criticism) also suggests
that sociability is impossible without a sustaining ethic of social
responsibility – that is, a vision of justice. My treatment of justice
begins with the ancient question about the relation between art
and life, not just in the sense that art mimics or expresses or per-
fects the lineaments of human conduct, but that both art and life
are motivated by principles of justice. What is the relation between
social and aesthetic justice, and how does the nation mediate
between them?

I will argue that national literatures owe their prestige to a
romantic historiography that treats justice as the very principle of
historical intelligibility. Hegel regards justice as the great rule of
adequacy in social order, historical advance, and artistic form. It is
the systematic equilibrium of human affairs, or more specifically
the restoring of stability to what has become an unbalanced system. History is a painful tale of 'mutual malice, treachery, ingrati-
tude,' but providentially it has the power to correct itself: 'This
equilibrium can, it is true, only be a living one by inequality arising
in it, and being brought back to equilibrium by Justice' (Hegel,
Phenomenology 277). Hayden White argues that, for Hegel, justice
animates history by giving it form and by correcting that form

when it grows distorted. To think historically is to assume a legality by which individuals are constituted as citizens, and through which conflicts within and between social groups can be assessed. To think historically is to deploy a legality that situates people collectively and charges their actions with practical and ethical significance: 'If, as Hegel suggests, historicality as a distinct mode of human existence is unthinkable without the presupposition of a system of law in relation to which a specifically legal subject could be constituted, then historical self-consciousness, the kind of consciousness capable of imagining the need to represent reality as a history, is conceivable only in terms of its interest in law, legality, and legitimacy, and so on' (13–14). Stated more simply, history is the story of justice, and people's lives are historically significant in so far as they play, or are assigned, a role in the story. In both narrative form and political content, historical writing always exhibits a desire for social and moral direction, or a frustration that it has not been achieved. History may be just or unjust, fair to some and unfair to others, but it is always a narrative of justice (for Hegel) or a problematic of justice (for his modern heirs). Even if history is regarded, as in some Kurosawa film, as a dreadful panorama of futility, then its scope, theme, and tone ensure that in/justice will be its motive. According to the same tradition, the nation is the most important historical setting. For Hegel the nation is the social forum in which the story of justice unfolds;[26] for Marxists, it is an ideological battleground where justice is thwarted; for postcolonial critics today, it is a tyranny promoting hierarchy and oppression, and therefore is in drastic need of correction.

Literature, too, relies on justice as a principle of intelligibility, adequacy, and redress, because it exhibits so intensely the many ways in which language produces and is produced by 'issues of rightness' (Taylor, *Philosophical* 84).[27] Again I begin by offering some preliminary observations.

When justice is not only done, but seen to be done, then the spectacle is partly aesthetic. Art not only depicts the right and wrong of human affairs, but is itself a rendering of justice – an aesthetic verdict. Justice motivates literature at all levels of analysis from the modest *mot juste*, which does perfect justice to its meaning, to the grand designs of literary genre, which conduct forms like tragedy and comedy to their fated conclusions. Comedies dispense comic justice when they reward their characters with laughter and marriage, or punish them with ridicule. Similarly, there are tragic, ironic, and romantic verdicts, each satisfying in its own way. Marriage may count as a reward or punishment, depending on the mode of presentation and reception. Indeed one might define genres in accordance with the kinds of justice they dispense and the kinds of satisfaction they grant. In each case justice is rendered both formally, in the sense that a work adequately (or inadequately) fulfils its defining conditions of style and genre; and rhetorically, in the sense that its readers, who form a sort of jury, are satisfied (or dissatisfied) with the verdict. If it fails to fulfil these conditions, it may be judged flawed – poorly constructed, inconsistent, pointless – or it may be re-categorized as another genre: an unsatisfactory tragedy may turn out to be a good parody. Feminist critics often use this strategy to reassess women's writing by appealing to different standards of definition and accomplishment. A clumsy autobiography turns out to be a subtle autography – the minor change of words signaling a major rethinking of feminist practice. A literary work can also be beautifully unsatisfying when it defies formal or rhetorical conventions, or when readers resist its appeal to be satisfied. As long as the defiance or resistance is effective, it produces its own satisfaction: irony, parody, multiplicity, *jouissance*. Oscar Wilde's verdict on Dickensian melodrama offers an example of delightful dissatisfaction: 'One must have a heart of stone to read the death of Little Nell without laughing' (Ellmann 441).

Please note, I am not offering a formula for generic purity, as if every work must fall neatly into a single category according to its definition of justice. Hybrid genres, postmodern *métissage*, and ambiguous narratives defying closure all flout conventional categories, but only by invoking the forms that they defy. Although such works refuse to honour traditional justice, either formally to their characters or rhetorically to their readers, justice is no less at issue when it is affronted. Otherwise there would be no affront. To read 'against the grain,' as recommended by feminist and ethnic critics, is to reject the verdict offered by a text, but this presumes that there *is* a grain to cut across; and usually such readers are motivated by a higher or more supple sense of adequacy (to women, to minorities, to differences). By the same token, these critics detect textual miscegenation when they sense competing notions of adequacy and fulfilment, or when they feel puzzled as to what sort of judgment is invited.

Poetic justice in its traditional sense is described by the eighteenth-century critic John Dennis in his condemnation of Joseph Addison's tragedy, *Cato*: ''Tis certainly the duty of every tragic poet, by an exact distribution of a poetical justice, to imitate the Divine dispensation and to inculcate a particular Providence ... If this is not done, there is no impartial distribution of poetical justice, no instructive lecture of a particular Providence, and no imitation of the Divine dispensation. And yet the author of this tragedy does not only run counter to this in the fate of his principle character, but everywhere throughout it makes virtue suffer and vice triumph' (Johnson, *Lives* 356). Dr Johnson, who cites this passage, replies that Dennis's objection is itself unjust, because it ignores how Addison has respected another literary duty, which might be called literary justness: 'Whatever pleasure there may be in seeing crimes punished and virtues rewarded, yet since wickedness often prospers in real life, the poet is certainly at liberty to give it prosperity on the stage. For if poetry has an imitation of reality, how are its laws broken by exhibiting the world in its true form? The stage may sometimes gratify our wishes, but, if it be truly the "*mirror of life*," it ought to show us sometimes what we are to expect' (356). Poetic justice and literary justness express two kinds of faith and two attendant duties. The first is fidelity to an ideal justice, which in this case is beyond question; the second is the fidelity of poetic artifice to the reality that it imitates. It is ironic that poetic justice, in Dennis's sublime sense of the phrase, should require poetic licence, or deviation from 'the world in its true form.' Literature is true to a higher form by being false to a lower.

The irony that justice and justness should be at odds, that fidelity to one might entail betrayal of the other, is the point of Oscar Wilde's quip in *The Importance of Being Earnest*: 'The good ended happily, and the bad unhappily. That is what Fiction means' (367). Wilde deftly slides from poetic justice to poetic licence to poetic licentiousness. Although his saucy wit suits modern tastes more than does Dennis's moral rectitude, the demand for poetic justice is as strong today as ever and sometimes is called 'political correctness.' It appears not only in Hollywood films, which mete out punishment with brutal fairness, but in both traditional and radical literary criticism. A traditionalist such as John Gardner refutes the 'jubilant nihilists' (55) of postmodernism by insisting that fiction still has a duty to provide models of moral excellence (18–19), while a radical such as bell hooks criticizes Jane Campion's film *The Piano* on similar grounds. She objects that Campion's fine feminist intentions are never realized on the screen because, although she employs feminist tropes, 'her work betrays feminist visions of female actualization, [by] celebrating and eroticizing male domination' (hooks 120–1). In effect, bell hooks agrees with Dennis that loyalty to a higher cause – in this case feminism and antiracism – is more important than fidelity to reality: 'Since this is not a documentary film that needs to remain faithful to the ethos of its historical setting, why is it that Campion does not resolve Ada's [the main character's] conflicts by providing us with an imaginary landscape where a woman can express passionate artistic commitment *and* find fulfilment in a passionate relationship?' (121). Why doesn't Campion use the liberty of her film to depict what should be, rather than what is?

The fact that *The Piano* is set in colonial New Zealand reminds us that all visions of (in)justice, whether historical or literary, require a suitable setting, since justice is not merely social in nature but informs the very texture of the social fabric. It makes society sociable. Justice defines how people live together by regulating the lives they share. The fact that New Zealand is both a historical site and an 'imaginary landscape' reminds us that the representation of any social setting, whether in history or literature, makes it simultaneously real and imagined. The nation is both a set of concrete relations, practices, laws, and institutions, and a social imaginary. It is 'a state of mind' (Kohn 9) or 'an imagined political community' (Anderson 15) as much as it is a geographical and social locale.

The nation has fascinated historians and poets precisely because it is at once the most insistent of historical realities and the richest of dreams. Or as Phyllis Webb says in one of the epigraphs to this book: 'I often think that in our search for a Canadian identity we fail to realize that we are not searching for definitions but for signs and omens' (109). In this study we are searching for both definitions and omens. Any national literary history – a tripartite genre whose name proclaims its hybridity – is concerned with the intertwining of social and aesthetic justice in so far as they meet, or fail to meet, in the nation. It relies on both the justness of historical narratives and the justice foreseen through poetry.

I have entitled this book *Worrying the Nation* in the modest hope of establishing worrying as a scholarly form comparable to the essay, confession, anatomy, and survey. Worrying might be called a dogged engagement with the problematic. To worry at a subject is to consider it persistently in different ways, in a spirit of diffident concern. It is not the most enlightening style of criticism because it tends to be gloomy, but what it lacks in consistency it makes up for in tenacity. My worries arose partly in response to the October 1995 Quebec referendum, which loomed and passed as I wrote most of the book, and partly in recognition that worrying characterizes much English-Canadian writing, which takes pleasure in strategic uncertainty ('Where is here?'), as it situates itself at the fateful place where three roads meet: national + literary + history. This space marks, to borrow Margaret Turner's words, a 'hybrid condition, positioned precisely between certainty and enigma' (65). The nation is inescapable, and cannot be banished by theoretical decree, but what also cannot be banished is its puzzling inconsistency. It promises to unify a people and/with/through their literature, but it simultaneously speaks of their irreducible plurality. It legitimates a discursive territory that feels like home, but it also provokes a 'category crisis,' that is, a 'failure of definitional distinction, a borderline that becomes permeable, that permits of border crossings from one (apparently distinct) category to another' (Garber 124). News reports that, just before the referendum, one-quarter of the Quebec electorate expected to keep sending members of Parliament to Ottawa even after independence suggests that the river between Ottawa and Hull marks a permeable borderline.

Chapter 5 will offer my chief worry at and about the nation as a literary-historical category, as a principle of formal and social analysis, as a discursive function, and as a forum for sociability and poetic justice. Chapter 2 prepares for this prolonged fretting by examining the legacy of romantic historicism as it applies, and fails to apply, to English Canada. The absence of Québécois and French-Canadian writing from this volume is another worry. Chapter 3 is concerned more specifically with nation building as a cultural enterprise beset by difficulties. For over a century English Canadians have yearned for a national literature that, through its power to unify and harmonize, would actually be false to the diversity of the national experience it was supposed to express. The resulting confusion can make the nation seem monstrous (chapter 4), but literature adores monsters, so demonizing the nation is one way of ensuring its longevity.

2. The National Ghost

Since we had always sky about,
when we had eagles they flew out
leaving no shadow bigger than a wren's
to trouble our most æromantic hens.
Too busy bridging loneliness to be alone
we hacked in ties what Emily etched in bone.
We French, we English, never lost our civil war,
endure it still, a bloodless civil bore;
no wounded lying about, no Whitman wanted.
It's only by our lack of ghosts we're haunted.

Earle Birney, 'Can. Lit.'

Birney's poetic barb ends with a familiar puzzle about the elusive Canadian character. Unlike the United States, Canada casts no heroic shadows because our bland, practical citizens lack the historical traumas and the responsive imagination to expose the dreams on which the nation was built. The creative introspection of a Dickinson or a Whitman would reveal our presiding ghost, which should serve – as Wordsworth advises in 'Tintern Abbey' – as 'The anchor of [our] purest thoughts, the nurse, / The guide, the guardian of [our] heart, and soul / Of all [our] moral being' (99). But our guardian spirit finds its home too vast and vacant to fill with images. We have no totemic eagle, only 'æromantic hens' – the ungainly phrase probably aimed at poetesses of the Canadian Authors' Association. One woman writer, Catharine Parr Traill, had already issued a similar warning: 'As to ghosts or spirits they appear totally banished from Canada. This is too matter-of-fact a country for such supernaturals to visit. Here there are no historical associations, no legendary tales of those that come before us. Fancy would starve for lack of marvellous food to keep her alive in the backwoods. We have neither fay nor fairy, ghost nor bogle, satyr nor wood-nymph; our very forests disdain to shelter dryad or hamadryad' (128).

Ironically, according to Birney's paradox we actually are haunted, but only by a palpable absence that marks our peculiar identity crisis. His warning that 'aeromantic' fancy cannot cope with Canada conceals his own romantic assumptions, as I have implied by citing Wordsworth. Wordsworth's reassuring tone might be more appropriate to the Wye valley than to the Mackenzie or St Lawrence, but his effort to touch a spiritual source in 'nature and the language of the sense' corresponds to Birney's search for a Canadian *genius loci*.

As W.H. New explains, Birney pursues the national spirit as it emerges from the wilderness and attains self-consciousness through art; but 'in a kind of cosmic joke' he finds 'nada' within 'Canada,' silence within our national speech. 'Silence and absence become curiously positive virtues,' New concludes (*Articulating* 260, 266). Birney's ghost-of-a-ghost is a curious virtue of English-Canadian writing whenever it strives to be national in character. My purpose is not to identify the ghost, but to show how it haunts all efforts to define, and even to renounce, 'our' literature. The ghost cannot be captured since it is a spectre of thought, banished by the same reflex that seeks it; but it cannot be exorcized either, even in an age of post-national theory. Entrapment and exorcism are complementary needs that arise whenever we investigate what precisely is national about a national literature. They correspond to all the motives of inclusion and exclusion to be discussed throughout this book.

If English-Canadian writers share a national discourse, what are its unifying principles? Unity is difficult to find in Canadian literature, yet we cannot help looking for it because it is a formative dilemma. By way of contrast consider 'The Englishness of the

English Novel,' an essay in which Q.D. Leavis has no trouble identifying 'the true English spirit.' It is pragmatic, sympathetic, Protestant, wary of absolutes, and responsive to 'the fullness of life' (311–15). She delights in all that is 'very English,' but what is remarkable is her own display of 'Englishness.' It appears in her national pride, in her mistrust of continental Europe, and in her confidence that she speaks from the very heart of her culture. The English novel is great because it both draws on and reinforces this centre. Consequently, the merits of particular novels reflect their relation to the central tradition: the best novels are also the most authentic. Canadians can supply a comparable list of national attributes. According to Richard M. Coe we claim to be civil, communitarian, cautious, and conservative. What is lacking in Canadian writing, for good or ill, is Leavis's confidence in a central focus that inspects the 'national life in all its minute particulars' (303).[1] She celebrates a splendid English tradition whose splendour is national in character. It is far more difficult to define a great Canadian tradition and to speak from its centre.

If there is no stable centre to English-Canadian culture, there are no clear borders either. Inclusion and exclusion are equally difficult. For this reason, the politics of devising a national canon has proven troublesome and sometimes farcical. Should we exclude Anna Jameson but include Josef Skvorecky, or vice versa? It is hard to say how much diversity a national literature can tolerate, but the difficulty is itself revealing because it highlights the ambiguity of any national literary history, which is obliged to set limits that are hard to police. In reaction, critics such as John Metcalf or John Moss (in 'Bushed in the Sacred Wood') reject the national question as a dead end and confine themselves to literary standards. But even if they could purify literature of political taint, they still must answer Leavis's claim that literary merit and social authenticity are reciprocal. They must be assessed together if literature is to speak for and about a people. Frank Watt sums up the chief aspiration of a national literature to unite spirit and place: 'Literature is then seen as a force which, quite apart from its motives, contributes to the articulation and clarification of Canadians' consciousness of themselves and of the physical, social and moral context in which they live their lives ... Canadian writers help to bring alive the shared history, limitations, fulfilments, virtues and depravities which make at least some Canadians feel related to each other and to their land' (236–7). We can detect Birney's ghost in Watt's assertion that literature articulates something that lies 'quite apart from' its immediate motives. Its ulterior purpose is to call forth a broad consciousness, which clarifies all aspects of our 'shared' life and can be elicited by sensitive reading. Note the distinction between the immediate matter of literature and its underlying moral ('virtues and depravities') character. This duality recurs in some form in all accounts of national literature. It is a duality of place and spirit, each shaping the other. Note too the need for sensitive reading – i.e., criticism – to read the subtext and release the ghost.

Spirit and place combine in the *genius loci*, a more common name for our ghost. It is a 'genius' in the Latin sense of guardian spirit, which was associated ambiguously, according to C.S. Lewis, with both the universal, generative God, and the specific *daimon* of any person. The former was the deity who presided over a given place, whether a sacred grove or an entire country, and who gave it a distinctive character. The latter was a spiritual double, who later came to represent the poetic self of a writer (169). Genius is both general ('Genius') and particular ('genius'), but in either case it is a fertile power. When modern critics try to pinpoint what joins spirit to place, they are apt to be less mystical but more vague. George Orwell explains the Englishness of the English by referring to the 'air,' 'flavour,' and '*mystique*' of the nation. 'Something' 'somehow' grants an 'emotional unity' by which the 'nation is bound together by an invisible chain' (64, 74, 77). Orwell is far from mystical when he confesses the impalpable nature of what he is trying to capture. He has a very practical sense of the deceptions involved in defining a national spirit, which may just as well be based on compelling illusions (71). Still, he trusts that the illusions are shared throughout Britain, that they unify the country and colour its character.

When Birney seeks a Canadian genius, he is closer to Orwell than to Leavis. He is less confident about the spiritual unity of his country, however, and registers his uncertainty in what might be called an anti-romantic romanticism. He wants to demystify the pretensions of 'æromantic' verse, but only because he seeks a more earthy and authentic mystery. The authenticity he seeks is clarified by René Wellek, who examined a comparable situation in American letters. The development of American criticism in the mid-twentieth century reveals 'an attitude of romantic historicism. It is ultimately derived from the body of ideas developed by [Johann Gottfried von] Herder and his successors, who looked for the organicity and continuity of literature as an expression of the national spirit, the folk ... Many recent critics are concerned with defining the nature of the American, the Americanism of American literature, often only dimly aware of how much is common to man, modern man, and common to Europe and America' (333). Wellek also notes that the quasi-mystical tendencies of Herder's philosophy were 'assimilated to the prevailing rationalist or pragmatist temper of the nation and certainly were rarely pushed to their irrationalist and often obscurantist extremes' (333). The same assimilation occurs in Canadian criticism, but first I turn to the legacy of romantic historicism.

The National Spirit

According to Herder, humanity is divided by fate and choice into distinct geographical/cultural units or *Völker* (nationalities). 'The history of the world for Herder is the history of these *Völker,* their formation as a consequence of the interpenetration of their physical environment and their being, their creation of a mythic cosmology, a music and a poetry, above all, a language. The union of their original nature, their genius, and the environment reaches a climax in a form-giving moment – it is not quite clear whether this is the discovery of religious or of linguistic identity. But nothing static results. The process of change is continuous as long as the people is [*sic*] alive' (Manuel xvii). Human identity is national in character, because its basis is cultural and collective rather than individual. Individuality is still important, but it too derives from the *Völker.* Each nation is unique, not just in the sense of being dif-

ferent, but of being comprehensible only in terms of its own inherent standards (Iggers 13, 38). Identity therefore derives from
place, genius, tradition, and language, and its highest expression is
in religion and the arts (Barnard 7ff.).[2] Birney's satire depends on
the comical mishap that Canada's 'form-giving moment' has failed
to yield a recognizable shape, but in a further irony, his rueful, self-
mockery expresses the Canadian temper he has failed to identify.
Although Herder emphasizes language as the key influence, Canadian critics stress place and genius as the physical and spiritual
factors appropriate to their nation. Viewed in Herder's terms,
Northrop Frye's riddle, 'Where is here?' takes on a deeper resonance. It refers not just to the disorientation of the pioneer, or to
cultural confusion about identity, but to an unsettling metaphysical plight.

This plight arises because Herder's philosophical idealism is so
stubbornly thwarted by Canadian experience. Herder treats mind
as the determining reality behind the phenomena of nature and
nation. The creative national moment produces a spiritual form, a
ghost. Material conditions are decisive, but only because they pre-
dispose the growth of mind. Herder speaks of the '*spirit of climate*,'
which 'does not force but incline: it gives the imperceptible disposition, which strikes us indeed in the general view of the life and
manners of indigenous nations' (Herder 20). Literature, at a further remove, is an epi-phenomenon, a network of symbols that give
tangible expression to an intangible spirit. Birney follows Herder
in regarding literature as the voice of a people, the highest expression of their history, society, and self. Even when he fails to hear
the voice, he treats that failure as a curious virtue of the Canadian
character. He renounces romantic idealism in favour of an ironic
idealism of his own.

Shifting from German to English romanticism, we find that Thomas Carlyle also treats literature as the 'genius' or 'national mind'
(227, 229) of a country: 'Thus the History of a nation's Poetry is the
essence of its History, political, scientific, religious. With all these
the complete Historian of a national Poetry will be familiar: the
national physiognomy, in its finest traits, and through its successive
stages of growth, will be clear to him; he will discern the grand spir-

itual Tendency of each period, what was the highest Aim and Enthusiasm of mankind in each, and how one epoch evolved in itself from the other. He has to record the highest Aim of a nation, in its successive directions and developments; for by this the poetry of the nation modulates itself; this *is* the Poetry of the nation' (225). National Poetry with its noble physiognomy is the ancestor of Birney's faceless ghost. For Carlyle, reality is spirit (essence) made forceful through will (Aim), which in turn shapes the physical world to spiritual ends. History is *Geistesgeschichte*, the perfecting of mind as it advances – according to Hegel – towards self-realization and freedom. This 'metaphysical optimism' encourages Carlyle's 'Enthusiasm' and Herder's faith that history is benevolent as long as a nation remains true to its native principles (Iggers 36, 16). For all three writers the course of history, although essentially a spiritual progress, depends materially on a sequence of cultures, all rooted in their own 'soil' (Hegel, *History* 80), which nourishes their 'National Genius' (63), which in turn expresses itself most nobly in poetry.[3] The same optimism appears as progressive self-realization in literary history. Literature is supposed to grow increasingly eloquent and authentic, as long as it remains loyal to native principles.

In Hegel we also find the idea, so seductive that it becomes irresistible, that 'each particular National genius is to be treated as only One Individual in the process of Universal History' (*History* 53). Since a country shares a national mind, it can be regarded as a single person: Britain becomes John Bull, the United States becomes Uncle Sam. This handy personification seems innocent, but it has far-reaching implications about the way history is constituted as a mode of understanding. Hayden White treats personification as one of several rhetorical figures by which history is linked to a narrative mode of representation. As I noted earlier, in romantic historicism historical causality, agency, social conflict, and legality are plotted as narratives; while narrative conflict, moral purpose, and action are attributed to history (H. White 11–14, 20–4). Personification conveniently assimilates the diversity of historical experience and civil discord into a single figure. Then it elevates that figure into a hero in quest of self-fulfilment. As personification turns into

apotheosis, history turns into myth: Uncle Sam pursues his Manifest Destiny. Canada is harder to personify, and accordingly is said
to be 'A Country without a Mythology' (in Douglas Le Pan's title).
But even these difficulties can be assimilated by the Hegelian
model. Canada and its literature are commonly characterized
through a 'lexicon of maturation' (Weir, 'Discourse' 24), by which
the country is pictured as an irresolute youth striving for maturity.[4]
History and literature can then be assessed biographically. For
example, the land is 'young' but eager to prove itself; or it suffers
from an identity crisis as it matures from colony to nation; or it
remains 'a highschool land / deadset in adolescence' (Birney,
'Canada: Case History: 1969 Version'). If Canadian history is not an
epic, it is at least a *Bildungsroman*.

Romantic historicism inspired nineteenth-century Canadians to
yearn for a national literature, but they had to adapt the theory to
a colonial society. Such adjustments became more taxing as the
country grew less rather than more homogeneous. Still, the ideal is
clear in Edward Hartley Dewart's introduction to *Selections from
Canadian Poets*: 'The literature of the world is the foot-prints of
human progress ... A national literature is an essential element in
the formation of national character. It is not merely the record of a
country's mental progress: it is the expression of its intellectual
life, the bond of national unity, and the guide of national energy.
It may be fairly questioned, whether the whole range of history
presents the spectacle of a people firmly united politically, without
the subtle but powerful cement of a patriotic literature' (ix). Once
again the nation is pictured as a single intellect, which shares in
the progress of humanity but leaves its footprints in its own soil. If
the idealism is less exuberant than Carlyle's, it is still sustained by
Dewart's enthusiasm for Confederation. Writing in 1864, he
stresses the unity of an emerging country which, he acknowledges
later in the same paragraph, already has a 'tendency to sectional-
ism and disintegration' (x). His insistence on unity is not merely
political; or rather, his politics derive from a view of history that
regards Canada as a single mind with its own 'national character'
and 'mental progress.' Although some of his terms may sound anti-
quated today, they are not so different from Watt's, quoted above.

It is remarkable how often Dewart's ideas recur in different guises whenever Canadian criticism becomes nationalistic, if not openly patriotic. One implication of my argument is that literature conceived in national terms will always be drawn to the romantic figures enunciated by Dewart.

His enthusiasm is checked, however, by a suspicion that the tenets of romantic historicism are ill-suited to the diversity of Canada, which threatens Herder's great principle: the spiritual unity of the *genius loci*. Dewart exhorts Canadians to overcome their differences in the name of national unity. Optimistically, he expects poetry to accomplish this end. Following Carlyle (as well as Coleridge) he calls poetry 'the essential unity of the mind ... the offspring of the whole mind, in the full exercise of all its faculties, and in its highest moods of sympathy, with the truths of the worlds of mind and matter' (xi). The nation's literature should be a grand projection of this perfectly integrated mind. Conversely, the nation should exhibit the flawless unity of a great poem. He offers various reason, which later become familiar in Canadian criticism, for the lack of national harmony: cultural differences, colonialism, utilitarian values, poor education, stupid critics. But the problem lies in the notion of unity inherited from Herder. The problem is not just that Canada is diverse, but that its particular kind of diversity elicits a different conception of unity – Confederation was one name for it – and hence a different conception of nationhood.

'Unity' means singularity, but not all kinds of unity are the same. Unity must be formulated in terms of the diversity that it unites – how it articulates and joins its parts. A different kind of diversity requires a different kind of unity. As an enlightened universalist, Herder begins by stressing the essential unity of all humanity (5), but he quickly distinguishes local expressions of humanity in the various *Völker*. 'Truth, value, and beauty are not one, but many. They are found only in history and manifest themselves only in the national spirit. True poetry and true art for Herder are thus always national and historical' (Iggers 37). Humanity is one; nevertheless each *Volk* displays a native unity determined by place, language, and tradition: 'For every nation is one people, having its own national form, as well as its own language' (Herder 7). Despite studious attention to the physical conditions of climate and geography, Herder really relies on spirit to secure the unique unity of a nation. A *Volk* shares not just a country, but a spirit of place and a spirit of climate. The 'national mind' is shared by all citizens; or in the loftier Hegelian view, it is a discrete fragment of the Universal Spirit of History. This idealist principle ensures that there will always be a ghost – a spiritual ideal conferring unity – to haunt a national literature.

Herder's theory raises problems for Canada, because it affirms both a transcendental and a local unity without negotiating between the two.[5] In the same way, C.S. Lewis noted an ambiguous conflation of universal Genius and local genius. The opposing needs of 'humanity' and 'nationality' need not be a problem, and Herder certainly never envisaged the ferocity that rival nationalisms would provoke.[6] But even colonial Canada challenged his optimism that discrete, cheerful homelands would develop under the aegis of their presiding consciousness. Birney's ghost-of-a-ghost expresses Canadians' wariness of national unity in its idealized and restrictive forms. To Herder, who disapproved of centralized government, colonialism, and 'cultural miscegenation' (Manuel xxi; see also Plamenatz 25), Canada would be an anomaly, a land without a ghost. Because its anomalous position has persisted since 1867, however, it casts doubt on the theory that it infringes. Canada has remained defiantly intact (so far) even though its climate and terrain are diverse, its regions are openly antagonistic, and its two main language groups compete with other ethnic traditions. 'But in Canada even history divides. The sharing of great events usually welds a nation together, but these in Canada have often as not been moments of acute inner conflict: the Riel rebellion and the two world wars (which brought about two conscription crises) were sources of division rather than unity ... In fact, the search for identity seems to be at odds in Canada with the search for national unity' (Taylor, *Reconciling* 25–6). Consequently, some historians argue that Canadians have had to devise a looser conception of national unity. They are united, not by a common spirit, but by their common differences. Paradoxically, they share 'particularist habits of mind' (Careless, 'Limited' 8).

I defer consideration of this paradox until later. Now I wish to examine the awkward legacy of romantic historicism in Canada.

The Canadian *Genius Loci*

The best Canadian literature must be 'autochthonous,' Charles Mair proclaimed in 1875; it 'must grasp with its roots, and be nourished by, the inner and domestic life of its people ... [It] must taste of the wood, and be the genuine product of the national imagination and invention' (Ballstadt 152). Unfortunately this earthy ideal has idealist sources that fit awkwardly into Canadian history and literature, with the result that we often find critical ambitions torn by conflicting impulses. Nationalists like Mair and Dewart found the local soil unsuited to their hopes for a transplanted-yet-native literature, because they had inherited from romantic historicism a legacy of glorious but unfulfiled promises. These promises will continue to haunt Canadian studies as long as they conceive of literature as the voice of a *genius loci*. The following topics are all expressions of a dilemma that has become so deeply entrenched as to serve as a tradition in its own right.

Nature / Nation

Romantic historicism bequeaths a legacy of images and metaphors that we can hardly resist, because they seem so natural, but that can be unreliable when applied to Canada. For example, I have already used the metaphor of 'transplanting' to describe the growth of Canadian literature. It is one of many figures derived from a vocabulary of soil, roots, fertility, and cultivation. Imagery of organic process and unity is, of course, pervasive in romantic theories.[7] Less familiar is their conflation of nature, nation, and narration (Bhabha 1–3, 295). More familiar is the corresponding triad supplied by Hippolyte Adolphe Taine in his *History of English Literature* (1864): race, milieu, and moment. In either case, literature is regarded as the story of a people who develop in accordance with a natural temper that impels a national destiny. This practical fusion of literary, political, and organic terms is compelling in the double sense that it imposes itself on us, so that we use it without question, and that it conveys comforting assumptions about the alliance of literature, spirit, and place.

Wilfred Eggleston is the critic who most fully exploits the figure of transplanting. In *The Frontier and Canadian Letters* (1957) he explains how difficult it was to uproot, transport, and transplant European culture in a new cultural soil (23ff., 28ff.).[8] What begins as a helpful analogy gradually works its way so thoroughly into the texture of his argument that the metaphors of planting and flowering take on the force of literal statement. When he seeks the 'working laws or principles' (18) of cultural transplantation, he moves beyond physical and cultural conditions, which he documents carefully, into a theory of historical progress. That theory proceeds by extending the gardening analogy, even though it was adopted only as a working hypothesis (23). A figure of speech has turned into a system of cultural growth. In Herder's theory, 'soil' denotes not just place, but the spirit of place. It is not surprising, therefore, to find Eggleston revealing his idealist premises in phrases like 'The climate of spiritual values is an intangible factor' (38) and 'a shift to such cultural, intellectual, social and spiritual values as may feed the spirit' (55).

Eventually Eggleston is betrayed by his own vocabulary. A 'strictly *native* literature' (2), he advises, must derive from the spirit of the frontier, not from the colonial spirit. But especially in the pioneer era when the frontier spirit is strongest, Canadian culture is positively anti-literary and anti-imaginative: 'The adverse influence of frontier life, in short, was capable not only of blocking the emergence of native artists, but also of killing off the literary ambitions of experienced writers among the immigrants' (73). At this point the argument becomes circular. 'Inspiration' cannot come from abroad; as the word implies, it must be breathed in from the local atmosphere. Unfortunately the *genius loci* remains breathless until Canada is transformed into 'an organic outgrowth of Western European culture' (30), in which case the genius is not local at all. A truly Canadian art is impossible. One solution to the dilemma is proposed in Le Pan's poem 'A Country without Mythology,' where the figure of Manitou, hidden in an apparently meaningless landscape, represents the unrecognized spirit of place waiting to be discovered by the invading Europeans. By shifting mythology, Le Pan cleverly reinstates the romantic genius in native dress.[9] This tactic is used at much greater length by D.G. Jones in *Butterfly on Rock* (1970). But Eggleston has explicitly refused this avenue: 'the spirit and philosophy of the new North American society was to be European, certainly not Indian, or anything else' (30). He wants a literature that is native but not too native.

Genius / Genesis

Romantic historicism bequeaths to national literatures the duty to rediscover and celebrate their origins, a duty that is bound to puzzle Canadians, whose origins are so diverse. Genius should be genetic – another term favoured by Herder – in the sense that it identifies a nation according to its moment of birth. Arguing against Eggleston's frontier thesis is 'The Case of the Missing Face,' an essay in which Hugh Kenner notes wryly that the 'surest way to the heart of a Canadian audience is to inform them that their souls are to be identified with rock, rapids, wilderness, and virgin (but exploitable) forest' (203). He condemned this 'half-conscious self-identification with the aboriginal wilderness-tamers' (204) as a hindrance to mature literature, and urged Canadians to 'cut the umbilical cord to the wilderness' (207). But the imagery of genetic originality, which he employs in mockery, actually reveals a national duty that Canadian writers cannot ignore.

Critics of various persuasions propose a pursuit of origins as the phantom goal of literature. Any theory concerned with tradition and modernity – that is, with literature conceived as a process of renewal and rebellion – will find expression in the endless quest for origins.[10] Any literary history that uses a founding moment – such as discovering a 'New World' – to begin its tale will also be enchanted by origins. In national literatures, however, origin means Herder's form-giving moment: the creative instant when spirit and place first join. If a writer can touch the native spirit when it broods over the virgin soil, then the two competing aspects of genius described by C.S. Lewis will harmonize: the writer's individual talent will speak for the national Genius. Accordingly, Canadian writers often feel, or are encouraged by their critics to feel, that they have a duty to rediscover the land as if for the first time. They must all become Jonahs, in Frye's striking image, who give themselves to the Canadian leviathan. Or they must be imaginative pioneers, as Rosemary Sullivan advises: 'one way of looking at Canadian literature is to see it as an ongoing dialogue with the wilderness, an obsessive repetitive effort to relive (and perhaps reframe) that moment of original encounter' (39). Margaret Atwood invokes Susanna Moodie and turns her into the spirit of the land she once detested. Margaret Laurence appeals to Catharine Parr Traill, George Bowering to George Vancouver. Jack Hodgins reinvents Vancouver Island. Barry Cameron notes (111–2) that attempts to define a Canadian tradition usually take the form of hunting for a source, which will create 'Canada' as a cultural presence and authorize a legitimate line of descent. Numerous poets have followed Archibald Lampman into the woods, not only because they were heeding Wordsworth's advice, but because they reinterpreted Wordsworth's guardian spirit as the *genius loci*.

Cultural studies such as Atwood's *Survival* (1972), Moss's *Patterns of Isolation* (1974), and McGregor's *The Wacousta Syndrome* (1985) are committed to the same belief. When Atwood proposes for the sake of argument to treat all literary works 'as though they were written by Canada' (*Survival* 12), her off-hand remark conceals a grand assumption sustained by the same rhetorical ploy that turned the United States into Uncle Sam. She asserts rather than proves the psychological unity of her subject. Canada is to be treated as a single patient whose neuroses take the form of literature. Arguing on this basis, she can then track to its colonial and Calvinist sources the *genius loci* or, as she calls it, 'the Canadian psyche' (73). Similarly, when Gaile McGregor studies the Canadian 'langscape,' she devises a composite word to probe the point of fusion between land and language, place and spirit. To describe the Canadian qualities of this encounter, she too returns to Frye's garrison and Richardson's *Wacousta,* where she detects the 'conceptual underpinnings of the Canadian imagination' (412). The same borderline confrontation, she suggests, must be repeated by subsequent writers as they obsessively re-enact the primal discovery of the land. Granted, McGregor is no idealist; she analyses the encounter in psychological and ideological terms. But directing these terms in all their manifestations is a Canadian frame of mind genetically shaped by frontier and colony.

Merit / Authenticity

For Q.D. Leavis, the best English novels eloquently express the Englishness of England. Individual talent, aesthetic skill, and national character harmonize perfectly: 'For the ideas in *our* best novels arise naturally from a sensitive open-minded exploration of the fully human world and from a sustained creative effort in which the important parts of the novelist's experience of life are drawn on' (Leavis 313). She never worries that cultural and creative values might drift apart, so that poor novels might perversely be more authentic than good ones. Canadian critics hope for the same balance of aesthetic and social qualities, but they discover the precariousness of that pairing. Frye begins his conclusion to the *Literary History of Canada* by praising the volume for treating weaker writers who nevertheless are truly Canadian. The greatest literature 'pulls us away from the Canadian context towards the centre of literary experience itself' (*Bush Garden* 214); it draws towards a universal validity without national flavour. Canadians lack such classics, but in the meantime our literature, precisely because it is inferior, gives us a clearer view of the 'Canadian context.' For Leavis, merit and authenticity reinforce each other; for Frye, they tug in different directions.

The fault is not so much with the writers as with a theory that they fail to endorse. A more detailed example of the conflict occurs in Dick Harrison's *Unnamed Country* (1977). Beginning with the orthodox assumption that place and spirit are intimately (authenticity) and eloquently (merit) allied, Harrison examines dozens of western novels in order to identify the prairie mentality. At first he prefers accurate writing: 'From a *purely literary standpoint,* the work of Begg, Hayes and MacLean is no more accomplished than that of Mackie, Ballantyne, or "Zero," but it shows a certain promise which was not fulfilled in the writing that followed. The early "realists'" documentary impulse might have provided a base from which an *authentically western regional literature* could have risen' (66, my emphasis). The first group are not better writers but are more genuine, and realism is sure to be a virtue when authenticity is the standard of judgment. Elsewhere, however, Harrison shifts ground when his evidence threatens to lead to the wrong conclusion. Of the many early novels examined, he judges only a few to be valuable, even though they are not typical. Most novels are romantic, optimistic, and sentimental, whereas the few important ones are pessimistic, tragic, and (more or less) realistic. Because the evidence does not seem to bear out his theory, Harrison must shift the basis of his judgment. To defend the authors whom he prefers (Grove, Ross), he shifts his critical ground from authenticity to literary merit, and the tension between the two standards is, to my mind, not resolved.

The problem is all too familiar. We often study authors whom we do not consider particularly 'good,' but who are 'important' in historical or cultural terms.[11] Canons and standards of excellence are now hotly disputed, and the current unease with objective standards should alert us to the difficulty of aligning the true (authenticity) with the beautiful (merit), especially when we limit ourselves to Canadian truth and beauty. John Metcalf again comes to mind as someone who would sweep away all inferior writers. More diplomatically, John Moss distinguishes between the rival demands of aesthetic excellence and thematic validity, and calls for a return to the former: 'It is time now that Canadian literary criticism serve the literature itself, time to stop considering literature a map of our collective consciousness; a mirror of our personality; a floodlight illuminating the national sensibility. It is time to consider Canadian literature as literature and not another thing' ('Bushed' 175–6). The trouble is that as long as the literature in question is specifically Canadian and 'not another thing,' then we cannot make so clear a distinction. Moss's final phrase (echoing T.S. Eliot), which calls for a formal purity of aesthetic response, ignores the critique of formalism conducted over the last thirty years. His assurance that '[n]ationality must be recognized as having more to do with nationalism than with art' (176) also misjudges the tenacity of romantic historicism, with its (apparently) effortless fusion of nature, nation, and narration. Later I will argue that it is neither possible nor desirable to isolate these three terms, even when they tug in different directions. Nationality cannot be ignored, even if it has served purposes that are now judged unworthy.

National / Native

Displays of English-Canadian nationalism often seem forced in contrast to St Jean Baptiste Day parades in Quebec. Frye explains the contrast by saying that in Canada, unity is national in scope, whereas identity remains stubbornly local and regional (*Bush Garden* ii). His explanation would please Herder, who might insist further that so fragmented a country will never achieve a native literature, because it lacks the spiritual unity of a true *Volk*. Nevertheless the national ghost continues to haunt Canadian writing, perhaps because, as Jacques Derrida claims, all notions of unity are ultimately theological in nature. In all philosophies, materialist as well as idealist, unity is a spectral projection of the mind as it wanders through language but covers its traces.[12] Because the nation is not just an actual place, but an ideal of social and spiritual cohesion, the *genius loci* is bound to reappear whenever writers get nationalistic or stress the unity of their country.

To illustrate this point, I turn to the sober writing of history, which should be free of ghosts yet also proves to be haunted. In his survey of Canadian historiography, Carl Berger detects an oscillation between idealist and materialist theories, and notes that at times of intense nationalism, idealist views reappear, often in a romantic tone. On the one hand are historians such as Frank Underhill and Harold Innis who insist on the 'material realities' of staples, markets, technology, and political institutions (98) because they mistrust the way constitutional historians rely on patriotic but impalpable matters of sentiment and moral union (96). On the other hand, we detect phantoms in Arthur Lower's 'pantheistic feeling for the mystery of the forest' (115) and in his fascination with Canadian unity and the 'national soul' (125).[13] We detect them again in the assumption made by the Massey Commission in 1951 'that there were important spiritual resources in the nation that inspired its people and prompted their actions, and that national unity, while resting on material foundations, belonged ultimately to the realm of ideas' (179).

A better example for our purposes is provided by W.L. Morton. He argues that geography and settlement have given Canada 'a distinct, a unique, a northern destiny' (4), which pervades all aspects of Canadian culture from manners to politics to literature. Like Herder, he insists on physical conditions, especially the ruggedness of our 'perpetual' frontier (72), but he accounts for the unifying force of environment by appealing to spiritual qualities: 'The line which marks off the frontier from the farmstead, the wilderness from the baseland, the hinterland from the metropolis, runs through every Canadian psyche' (93). Every Canadian may be haunted by the North, but as Stan Dragland observes wryly, for most of us this is only an imagined place, glimpsed in books and all the more haunting for being imaginary.[14] Like Stephen Leacock, we cautiously 'embrace ... the North from a distance': 'Most of us, living in a settled strip along the southern margin of the country, don't let our distance from the North prevent us from claiming it as our own, sometimes to the dismay of those, white as well as Native, who do live there' (Dragland, *Floating Voice* 230). We embrace our northern destiny by keeping it at a safe distance. This irony explains why Morton, like Eggleston, is forced to reverse his perspective when he has to reckon with the native culture that he seeks to promote. He argues that the same hinterland conditions that forge our national identity also have made the country utterly dependent on foreign metropolitan centres. Subservience is pervasive and has shaped all aspects of Canadian life: 'The whole culture of the northern and maritime frontier, to succeed as well as survive, required from outside a high religion, a great literature, and the best available science and technology to overcome its inherent limitations. These very limitations of climate and of material and human resources made the frontier dependent on a metropolitan culture for those essentials. The alternatives were extinction and complete adaptation to the lowest level of survival in northern conditions' (Morton 94). According to this hierarchy, all the 'high,' 'great,' and 'best' cultural features, which previously were indigenous, now are transplanted. For Morton, as for Eggleston, the 'lowest level' of native (i.e., Indian) culture is unacceptable. Both authors are describing a historical process rather than a static condition, a progressive shift in authority and autonomy from Europe to Canada. But the shift is in the very cultural values that, they earlier claimed, should spring naturally from the local soil with its frontier spirit. They raise the national ghost only to shy away from its native features.

History / Myth / History

The *genius loci* is not just the spirit of place, but the spiritual history (*Geistesgeschichte*) of that place. Because the national genius blends the ideal with the actual, it readily expresses how myth informs history, how history rises into myth, and how myth in turn lapses into history. It used to be common for English Canadians to lament that somehow they had no history or myth. Birney's poem, 'Can. Lit.,' expresses both the dilemma and the romanticism that provokes the discontent. Such complaints have dwindled but not disappeared, even in the present, post-national age.[15] I would argue, on the contrary, that our vexed desire for a national literature has made us obsessed with history and myth, which we produce in abundance because they offer two major discourses for interpreting national identity. They provide two ways of identifying – or failing to identify – the Canadian ghost. The two styles dominating literary criticism until recently have been historical and mythological. As Barry Cameron's chapter in the revised *Literary History of Canada* reveals, most of the studies published before Frye are literary and cultural histories (E.K. Brown, A.G. Bailey, Roy Daniells, Eggleston); following Frye, we find a varied mixture of history and mythology (Atwood, W.H. New, D.G. Jones, John Moss's earlier work).

Canadian critics are tossed between history and myth, and where they land depends on whether they regard the *genius loci* as immanent or transcendent, that is, within or beyond the patterns of history. I noted in the previous section how historical studies drift towards idealism and even myth. Donald Creighton's 'Laurentian thesis' is a prime example. According to Berger, Creighton had a 'literary conception of history' (213), which made his work 'a monument to the belief that history was akin to drama, that it moved in accordance with the deeper truths contained in the very forms of literature and music – that history, in short, imitated art' (237). The converse is true as well: in literature, myth often lapses into history. Works like *Tay John* and *The Donnelly Trilogy* trace the fall from a heroic age to a debased age of mundane reality. Instead of apotheosis, we find *Götterdämmerung*. The arguments, shuttling back and forth between history and myth, recall René Wellek's observation that the mystical and irrationalist tendencies of Herder's philosophy were assimilated to the rationalist temper of America. A similar caution has caused Canadian critics to treat myth in the cool, orderly way that Frye does; or to keep it at a narrative distance, as in Rudy Wiebe's treatment of Natives and Métis; or to turn myth into parody, as in Robert Kroetsch's novels. The Canadian *genius loci* is usually treated as immanent rather than transcendent, embedded in history yet pushing gingerly towards myth.

Kroestch has said in conversation: 'I have considerable disdain or distrust for history. History is a form of narrative that is coercive. I don't trust the narrative of history because it begins from meaning instead of discovering meanings along the way. I think myth dares to discover its way toward meanings' (Neuman 133). Other remarks show, however, that he cannot leave history alone. In one mood at least, he would like to advance beyond nationalism and its persistent idealism. This resolve leads him to Michel Foucault's notion of 'genealogy,' which opposes history by acting as a dissenting, anti-metaphysical mode of inquiry. But as Foucault admits in the essay that Kroetsch cites, 'The genealogist needs history to dispel the chimeras of the origin' (Foucault, *Language* 144). Genealogy cannot supersede history; it conducts a running battle with it. Similarly, Kroetsch disdains the supreme promise of history – the identity and destiny of a nation as rooted in its origin – but he remains dazzled by it. In 'Beyond Nationalism' (*Lovely Treachery*

64–72) he tries to exorcize the phantom of history, but even as he does so, he re-animates it by generalizing freely about the peculiar qualities of Canadian imagination. He rejects nationalism but preserves the national genius. In *The Crow Journals,* where he records his plan to write the mythic history of a prairie town, he again reveals his fascination with origins and genesis (69), and with the 'genius of place, of that new old place, [that] must be located in the literature itself, not in the absent gods' (17). The new old place is located at the narrative juncture of history and myth. Kroetsch has an aggravated case of the Canadian malaise. He mistrusts the ghost, which corresponds to what he calls 'meaning': it is the promise of a unified, spiritual presence. Yet he remains enchanted with it, and even includes an equivocal spook in *What the Crow Said.* The oscillation between history and myth, falling and flying, becomes a structural principle in the novel.[16]

Exorcism

Following the publication of Margaret Atwood's *Survival* in 1972, the condemnation of thematic criticism by Frank Davey, Barry Cameron and Michael Dixon, Russell Brown, and W.F. Garrett-Petts marked an important shift from the historical and mythological models that had dominated Canadian writing.[17] These critics took issue not so much with specific themes as with what Francesco Loriggio calls 'an ideology of theme,' whose function is cohesive and whose vision is federalist (59, 63).[18] In this chapter I have kept my view retrospective in order to assess the rich rewards promised, though never quite delivered, by this ideology. It promises the identity and destiny of a nation as rooted in its origin. Romantic historicism treats national literature as a benediction: part blessing, part prayer, it is the eloquence through which a people aspires to immortality. It is clear, however, that these splendid rewards have not been shared equally by all Canadian citizens, and were earned at a price that literary historians are no longer willing to pay. They condemn the nationalist ideology on various grounds – for being ethnocentric, imperialist, sexist, racist – but especially for its essentialism. It evaluates literature in so far as it expresses a national essence. Current criticism challenges conventional notions of both essence and place, and since the *genius loci* is the essence of place, it is particularly vulnerable to the postmodern critique whereby literature is set in a no man's land rather than a native soil. The implications are unsettling for any national literature, because the national ghost is given no place to settle. Spirit can hardly unite poetically with place, when not only spirit (idealism, unity, genius) is rejected as a domineering illusion, but place (the ground of being, thinking and speaking) is reconfigured as 'placelessness.' Place is not geography or geology, but 'an unstable metaphorical construct' (Huggan 56, 122).[19] The question therefore arises: Is it possible to exorcize the Canadian ghost?

I will worry at this question periodically, but now I want to note the oddity of exorcizing a spirit too elusive to identify: 'It's only by our lack of ghosts we're haunted.' In *A Tale of Two Countries* (1984), for example, Stanley Fogel condemns the Canadian fixation on national identity, because it has kept our writing claustrophobic and naive. While postmodern Americans cheerfully debunk national myths, conservative Canadians still pursue the phantom of identity, which all the best critics have discredited. 'National identities are inflated constructs, products of advertising and politics' (30), not of literature, whose duty, on the contrary, is to explode such delusions. Americans have identified their ghost and grown tired of its false glamour, while Canadians have not. Nevertheless, Fogel has no qualms in praising American critics who have 'defined and redefined the contemporary American sensibility as it is manifested in American fiction' (8). He readily traces this national sensibility to its origin by summarizing the familiar history of the 'American dream': 'With both beneficent and deleterious consequences, the myth has taken hold of and shaped the American character' (10). Therefore he has not dispelled the illusion of an American genius, only rejected some of its manifestations as facile, while elsewhere the wily American temper continues to animate the work of Coover, Pynchon, and Gass. He has displaced the ghost and rendered it more sophisticated, not exorcized it.

A more subtle displacement occurs in Barbara Godard's survey of criticism written since the 1970s. She notes with disapproval that when critics such as Davey, Cameron, and Eli Mandel purged their analyses of paraphrase and Canadian content, they drifted towards phenomenological and historical positions. In view of the preceding discussion, this drift should not be surprising, since it leads back towards the safe ground of myth and history. Godard in effect complains that these critics were not radical enough. Still, the remarkable grip that history has on Canadian critics is confirmed by Linda Hutcheon's *The Canadian Postmodern* (1988). It presents as the pre-eminent Canadian literary form 'historiographic metafiction,' which is 'intensely, self-reflexively art, but is also grounded in historical, social, and political realities' (13). This anti-formal mode is more problematic than earlier models of writing, but it retains their appetite for history and their tendency to read history as myth and myth as history. Like Fogel, Hutcheon finds a more sophisticated home for the ghost, but one that is still 'grounded' in the national soil. Godard takes a step further by treating Canadian writing as a discourse of 'the Other' rather than of national genius:

> Canadian literature is a deterritorialized literature. At the centre of its concerns is the Other – women, natives and immigrants – to produce a hybrid, 'littérature mineure,' an a-signifying language, in which cultural difference is the difference encoded within language itself ... The hybridization and dissemination occurring within the Canadian literary discourse as the writing of these minorities is included are themselves emblematic of the place of Canadian literature within world literature, as the rise of the repressed, dislocating and undermining the logic of the literary systems of the Anglo-American world, produces a limit to writing. ('Structuralism' 44)

'*Littérature mineure*' is Gilles Deleuze and Félix Guattari's term for a 'deterritorialized' discourse that shadows and disrupts mainstream culture. It is the marginal literature that a minority writes in a major language.[20] Yet with this counter-definition, we return to our point of departure. Compare Godard's description with Lionel Gossman's account of romantic historiography, which relies on the same symbolic figures:

> In Romantic historiography, nature, the Orient, woman, the people, and the hidden past itself are almost always metaphors of each other and of the oppressed and the repressed in general – figurations of the Other of reason and bourgeois order. At the limit, the historian could claim to be reestablishing communication with a very ancien régime indeed – a remote realm prior to all separations, distinctions, and prohibitions, prior to law itself, an original condition of fusion in which, in Michelet's words, 'beasts still had the power of speech and man was still wedded to his sister nature.' (Gossman 259)

Godard treats literature as an ongoing, hybrid dislocation, not as 'an original condition of fusion'; yet her terms and the oppositional form in which they are offered (a-signifying, lawless, repressed) are strikingly similar to those of Gossman. She too uses the nation to envisage a conceptual limit, which can be approached but never breached. The Other is a mirror image of the Genius, not its essence but its absence, not its significance but its 'a-significance,' not its central focus but its 'dissemination.' It is the Canadian way of erasing history and myth. Just the same, Godard is still concerned with literature that is characteristically Canadian, and so is drawn to speculate about that character. Hegel suggested that a nation resembles a single person; Dewart pictured Canada as a Victorian gentleman. When Godard favours women, Natives, and immigrants, she deliberately works against traditional stereotypes, but, even in so doing, she gives 'emblematic' features to something that defies definition. Ironically, the national argument has reversed itself. In romantic historicism, where social and aesthetic values collaborate, the nation was unified like a poem, preferably an epic. Now the nation is dispersed and eccentric, again like a poem, preferably postmodern.

I suspect that any 'Canadian literary discourse,' no matter how antithetically defined, will retain the trace of a ghost, which cannot be exorcized because it is a local version of a provocative feature of all literature. Recalling C.S. Lewis's distinction between 'genius' as individual ability, and 'Genius' as a universal power, Geoffrey Hartman describes an endless contest between the two, a contest intensified by the resurgence of the *genius loci* in romantic poetry. Genius and genius require yet contradict each other, and their intimate rivalry will appear whenever writing is defined as national in character. On the one hand, the regional genius is comforting and protective. It roots a writer in his or her own soil; it confers identity by serving as the voice of local history and national destiny; it fosters a native, 'natural,' and vernacular art (317–19). On the other hand, the *genius loci* always retains something of its unruly, demonic origins. It becomes transgressive, as it breaks out into a 'higher destiny' of inspiration and prophecy (313). It then promotes anxiety about the talent of the individual poet and the worth of his or her country (373). If the *genius loci* provides a base for identity, it also disperses identity.[21] In Wordsworth's introspective treatment of the figure, Hartman finds a hesitancy that sounds surprisingly like Birney's attitude: 'Wordsworth creates a new and distinctly Hesperidean mode – deeply reflective, journeying constantly to the sources of consciousness. There are no ghosts, no giant forms, no genii in the mature Wordsworth. He is haunted by a "Presence which is not to be put by," but it is a ghost without a ghost's shape, not a specter but an intensely local and numinous self-awareness' (330).

For Hartman, the conflict of genius with Genius represents a permanent identity crisis, not only within national literatures but within literature itself (329). It expresses the desire for a consummation of meaning, figured as a holy marriage of spirit and place; but it shows that the union is always threatened by a demonic agent that is never far away (333). This conflict is exacerbated by any attempt to formulate a national literature, even after we have renounced its idealist legacy in favour of international solidarity or transnational correspondence. Today, the menacing destiny that troubled romantic poets reappears as the radical instability of postmodern textuality and intertextuality. Anxiety about one's country now appears as doubt about the ground of any identity, as it is tossed in the waywardness of discourse. Instead of the romantic 'Portrait of the Poet as Landscape' we now find the postmodern 'Portrait of the Poet as Nobody' – A.M. Klein's earlier title for the poem. Whether we choose to read his poem as an elegy about the betrayal of the *genius loci* or as a postmodern parody about the disappearance of the author, the ghost lurks within the poem, unseen yet waiting to re-emerge.

3. Nation Building

A nation-state is commonly defined as a polity of homogeneous people who share the same culture and the same language, and who are governed by some of their own number, who serve their interests. If we ask when such a state of affairs came into being, we should say, at no time. There is no people in the world that shares such homogeneity, where there are no regional or cultural differences, where all speak the same language or share the same linguistic usages and where the rulers do not differ in rank or wealth or education from the ruled. Actual nation-states rather approximate to an ideal type than mirror it, and do so in very different degrees.

Cornelia Navari, 'The Origins of the Nation-State'

Which came first, the nation or the state?

Common sense might suggest that people sharing a nationality would resolve in the course of their political development to create a nation-state, which would give formal standing to their community. The state would emerge of its own accord from a shared background like a flower unfurling its petals, and then be cultivated by appropriate institutions, which would direct subsequent national growth. As Cornelia Navari explains, however, this political blossoming never occurs quite so naturally, because the homogeneous nation-state approximates to a ideal found not in history, but in literary myth. True, there are instances when the nation precedes the state, but even then the relation between cultural community and political institution can be uneasy. On the other hand, in modern and post-colonial histories the state usually is created first, and a sustaining sense of nationhood must be forged afterward. Hugh Seton-Watson contrasts the old, continuous nations of Europe (English, French, Castilian, Portuguese, Dutch, Danish, Russian) with newer nations that developed in the wake of the Enlightenment (German, Italian, Greek), and with modern nations that developed in the wake of colonialism. In the first category, a strong national consciousness did not necessarily produce nation-states (Catalan, Basque). In the second two categories, the state usually came first and a nationalist ideology had to be fostered by educated elites who instructed the 'folk' from whom they allegedly drew inspiration.[1] As the Italian nationalist d'Azeglio declared, 'We have made Italy: now we must make Italians' (quoted in Hobsbawm, 'Mass-Producing' 267).

The business of fostering a national consciousness is usually called 'nation building,' and its purview is both retrospective and prospective: 'Apart from a few exceptions, the nation is a goal rather than an actuality. Put simply, nations are not creatures of "God's hand," as post-Herder prophets of nationalism often claimed; instead they are synthetic – they have to be created in a complicated educational process ... The aim of nation-building is to integrate and harmonize socially, regionally or even politically and institutionally divided sections of a people' (Alter 21). According to the romantic-nationalist project outlined in the previous chapter, the phrase 'nation building' is oxymoronic, since nations, which should issue from nature, are not supposed to be 'built' at all. They are supposed to grow organically without contrivance. Consequently, nation builders are obliged to efface their own artifice by teaching what Lynette Hunter calls 'the nervous instruction of remembering to forget' (16). We are taught to forget precisely those political instructions and constructions that make the nation-state appear to flower so spontaneously. The instruction is nervous, however, because nation building is beset by all the anxieties that I noted earlier. The nation is simultaneously natural and artificial, traditional and progressive, popular and elitist, diverse and homogeneous, rational and irrational. How to satisfy these contradictory needs?

When nation-states are built through political resolve, they establish themselves like nouveau-riche families who adopt a coat of arms in order to appear ancient, but always have to remember to mind their manners. Nationalism disguises novelty as antiquity by resorting to what Eric Hobsbawm calls 'invented traditions' – all the ceremonies, symbols, folk songs, costumes, sports, statues and flags that honour a country's past but often are of recent vintage.[2] '[E]ven historical continuity had to be invented' (Introduction 7), he reports, as in the Tudor myth of Shakespeare's history plays, which imposes a moral pattern on civil chaos. Historical continuity is legitimized by exactly the sort of nationalist ideology that Canadians have found too restrictive. Hobsbawm stresses the integrating power of the nation, which forcefully unifies aspects of society that previously had been either distinct or only loosely associated. Culture, politics, civil society, religion, family life, and recreation are all mustered under the nationalist banner in 'all-embracing pseudo-communities' (10). People may share little more than the resolve that they be the same. Ironically, even as bourgeois society extols individuality, it promotes a sense of (pseudo)community by imposing stricter conformity than did earlier social forms. In the United States, for instance, Hobsbawm notes a curious anxiety arising from a disjunction between its ideal of individual liberty and its longing for national unity: 'The concept of Americanism as an act of *choice* – the decision to learn English, to apply for citizenship – and a choice of specific beliefs, acts and modes of behaviour implied the corresponding concept of "un-Americanism." In countries defining nationality existentially there could be unpatriotic Englishmen or Frenchmen, but their status as Englishmen and Frenchmen could not be in doubt, unless they could also be defined as strangers' (280).[3]

This argument conflates several assumptions, since not all Americans make the same kinds of national choice, and it is dangerous to enforce a consensus. Immigrants to the United States choose a new political and cultural nationality, although in effect they already made their decision by immigrating. In varying degrees, they retain old national ties by considering themselves ethnic Americans (Irish American, Chinese American). Tensions arise only when allegiance to their new land conflicts with older loyalties. For example, German Americans (including those of German ancestry such as General Eisenhower) agreed to fight against Germany in the Second World War.[4] People born in the United States do not have to make the same deliberate choice, unless they reverse the immigrants' path by returning to their ancestral home. A third kind of choice applies to Native (indigenous) Americans, who may embrace or reject white American culture, as Thomas King illustrates so cleverly in *Green Grass, Running Water*. But Hobsbawm assumes, I think, that the United States keeps alive a tradition of national choice, partly by constantly receiving new immigrants (although not all are welcome) and partly by inventing traditions that dramatize national allegiance. When social pressures stress a citizen's duty to choose the United States in a continual reaffirmation of faith, it becomes difficult to say no, as draft resisters discovered during the Vietnam War.

Contrast the Canadian anxiety expressed in Margaret Atwood's famous Afterword to *The Journals of Susanna Moodie* (1970): 'We are all immigrants to this place even if we were born here: the country is too big for anyone to inhabit completely, and in the parts unknown to us we move in fear, exiles and invaders. This country is something that must be chosen – it is so easy to leave – and if we do choose it we are still choosing a violent duality' (62). A different kind of choice is offered here, one that makes it easier to say no than to say yes. I do not offer this quotation to represent *the* English-Canadian attitude, since I have already cast doubt on characterizing the nation so reductively. I offer it to illustrate how difficult it is, given an attitude like this, to choose one's nationality or to be confident about one's decision. Similarly, in 'Civil Elegies' Dennis Lee pictures Canadians as continually 'saying no to history' (56). Although he hopes to redirect this instinct for refusal towards a constructive end, he also sees the ordeal of negation as a salutary one, because it reveals his home to be necessary but unstable, or necessarily unstable. How is one to build a nation on a violent duality, a savage field, or on two (or more) solitudes? Is it necessary to invent traditions in the conventional sense at all?

In 1961, Mort Sahl, come to Toronto to entertain, was confronted by

a nationalist zealot. 'Do you realize,' he charged, 'that this country
hasn't even got a flag?'
  'That's a start,' Sahl replied. (Richler 150)

In order to consider what it means to choose Canada and to
build a nation here, I turn to three poems about nation building.
All three are in search of national legitimacy. All three cultivate
visions of sociability suited to a 'new' world – a sociability that they
express as both communal justice and aesthetic justness. Both
nation and poem should be harmonious. But in different ways, all
present the nation building project as anxious and flawed, as if the
dualities are too violent to be resolved, as if violence is too
ingrained in Canadian history to be subdued.

Oliver Goldsmith, 'The Rising Village' (1825, 1834)

According to Jürgen Habermas, the consolidation of the bourgeoisie in the late seventeenth century produced a new notion of the
'public sphere' as a busy, sociable space into which (male) individuals could enter freely, and from which they could retreat into
their own domestic refuges. The public sphere is framed by a network of opposed categories such as domesticity and business,
intimacy and traffic, personal belief and public opinion, private
initiative and public regulation. These categories distinguish publicity from privacy, but also make them interdependent; they infiltrate each other (Habermas, *Structural* 141). The family, especially,
is 'humanity's genuine site' (52), but it is a divided site: 'The line
between private and public sphere extended right through the
home. The privatized individuals stepped out of the intimacy of
their living rooms into the public sphere of the *salon*, but the one
was strictly complementary to the other ... The privatized individuals who gathered here [in the *salon* and other social settings] to
form a public were not reducible to "society"; they only entered
into it, so to speak out of a private life that had assumed institutional form in the enclosed space of the patriarchal conjugal family' (45–6). Habermas dwells on the paradox that early bourgeois
society devised an increasingly privatized vision of publicity,

whereby the free market permits a congregation of autonomous individuals who refuse to relinquish their autonomy when they enter public space (79ff.). Although he does not proceed to discuss nationalism, we can see how the nation later came to function as the strongest affirmation of publicity, yet also the furthest expansion of the domestic. Because the nation is regarded as one great family, its public scope is accorded private intensity: 'The sphere of the public arose in the broader strata of the bourgeoisie as an expansion and at the same time completion of the intimate sphere of the conjugal family' (50). The private refuge has to be protected from incursions from the public sphere (a man's home is his castle), yet the nation displays domestic virtues. The nation figures as a larger model of sociability, yet remains a cosy setting. This is the model proposed by Oliver Goldsmith in 'The Rising Village.'

When one member of the family leaves home and sails across the Atlantic to Canada, what effect does his errancy have on the public sphere? Expressions of sociability require a social typology linking symbolic places of assembly such as forum, town square, assembly hall, parliament – and, more recently, Internet. Studies of eighteenth-century England stress the role of coffee house, library, and club room in consolidating the power of bourgeois and professional classes. These gregarious locales provide both a physical and a discursive space in which ideas can be exchanged.[5] They permit visions of publicity because they are themselves richly symbolic sites: 'Discursive space is never completely independent of social place and the formation of new kinds of speech can be traced through the emergence of new public sites of discourse and the transformation of old ones. Each "site of assembly" constitutes a nucleus of material and cultural conditions which regulate what may and may not be said, who may speak, how people may communicate and what importance must be given to what is said' (Stallybrass and White 80). 'The Rising Village' can be read as a poetic attempt to build a public sphere in the wilderness, far from the comfort of coffee houses and libraries. Goldsmith's task is to build a nation: first, by clearing the site of past associations (banishing the Natives); second, by configuring the 'empty' territory as public space (raising the village and its 'sites of assembly,' such as tavern, house, and school); and third, by protecting the public sphere from an internal malaise, which he presents as moral corruption.

'The Rising Village' is customarily regarded, however, as torn between its intent and its method. It praises the New World in the style of the Old. It envisages a new society, but only in colonial terms. It uses the sophisticated, symmetrical forms of heroic verse to portray a rustic society. For the most part I agree with this assessment, but with a cautionary shift in emphasis. Goldsmith sets out to raise a nation by rousing cultural and moral powers whose legitimacy he trusts completely. Although he acknowledges difficulties (wilderness, winter, Natives) and vices (moral laxity, incompetence), he never sees these problems as insuperable. On the contrary, his pioneers are strengthened by their efforts to overcome obstacles, and their strength makes them all the better suited to a rugged land. Nevertheless, he provides a vision of sociability that proves difficult to sustain in his new nation. Or in my own terms, justice and justness, principle and practice, remain at odds.

My first caution is that the rhetorical and thematic tensions that now are judged faults may well have seemed like virtues to Goldsmith. He imposes dualities on his poem with a regularity that seems positively obsessive, but only to a modern eye that relishes obsessions. As well as couplets, caesuras, parallel forms and balanced contrasts, he offers a network of polarities: old/new, mature/young, civilized/wild, waste/busy, near/far, competent/incompetent. Where modern critics tease out the disjunctions and contraventions in these pairings, Goldsmith expects conjunction and accommodation.[6] Where Smaro Kamboureli finds 'a borrowed discourse that neutralizes the problems and concepts inherent in the Canadian context' (*On the Edge* 18), Goldsmith trusts principles of political, moral, and aesthetic order that are neutral only in the sense of being finely poised.[7] The peaceful village and the new nation should display the lineaments of a well-crafted poem, which in turn correspond to the moral complexion of a well-balanced, Christian gentleman. As D.M.R. Bentley notes, the poem confidently assumes a congruence of 'structured form, civilized landscape, and providential design' (94). Such confidence is sustained by 'heaven-born faith' (l. 175) in 'a Great First Cause' (l. 184),[8] and while Goldsmith's prayers may sound like conventional piety, they correctly identify the poem's highest source of legitimacy: an ideal justice that he never questions, any more than John Dennis (who supplied my earlier definition of poetic justice) would question divine providence.

My second caution is that the modern denigration of 'The Rising Village' can presuppose, or at least invite, a 'native' Canadian idiom arising from a 'natural' fit between the New World and an 'authentic' new style. According to this view, Goldsmith describes the New World in the idiom of the Old; therefore the New World must find is own national/natural idiom, which poets will devise after Confederation. In this respect Desmond Pacey was exactly wrong when he praised Goldsmith for recognizing 'the poetic possibilities of the Canadian social scene' (*Ten* 12). Authentic poetic possibilities are just what he missed. This is a familiar argument in American literary histories, which correlate their literary and historical duties by means of an ideologically charged style. Established English styles are judged inappropriate to American subjects and sensibilities, whereas a native American style allows the nation to sing its own song in its own voice. Whitman is the prime exhibit in American literature. F.R. Scott offers a Canadian example in 'Laurentian Shield,' where the land is 'Inarticulate, arctic' until human and natural languages correspond:

> This waiting is wanting.
> It will choose its language
> When it has chosen its technic,
> A tongue to shape the vowels of its productivity. (Scott 58)

Scott traces an elaborate rhetorical interaction between natural resources, political civility, linguistic sophistication, and sociability. In part this interaction is accredited by the same English tradition that was supposed to be abandoned when the poet entered the chilly speechlessness of Canada. Like Birney, Scott is an anti-romantic romantic. Specifically, he draws on the romantic *topos* of the language of nature, according to which nature's words are translated into the language of the senses, and then echoed by poetic speech as uttered by the national voice. Wordsworth's 'Immortality Ode' offers a familiar example:

> I hear, I hear, with joy I hear!
> – But there's a Tree, of many, one,
> A single Field which I have looked upon,
> Both of them speak of something that is gone:
>   The Pansy at my feet
>   Doth the same tale repeat (Wordsworth 153–4)

Wordsworth's view is nostalgic as he imagines a lost home, whereas Scott's view is hopeful as he imagines a new home acquiring its own voice. But Goldsmith can hardly be expected to share either view, since his sensibility is pre-romantic. In other words, modern critics tend to condemn 'The Rising Village' for failing to devise a style that was never available to it.

Nevertheless, Goldsmith does attempt to lay the foundations of his new nation. As he announced in prefaces and autobiography, his task is to provide a sociable vision that will redeem the social failures lamented by his great-uncle, the British poet Oliver Goldsmith who wrote 'The Deserted Village.' Where it is retrospective and elegiac – 'Remembrance wakes with all her busy train, / Swells at my breast, and turns the past to pain' ('Deserted Village,' ll. 83–4) – the Canadian poem will be prospective and hopeful. But what kind of prospect does it offer?

'The Rising Village' begins with an invocation to brother and uncle that treats companionship and partnership as paradigmatic social bonds: 'Thou dear companion of my early years, / Partner of all my boyish hopes and fears' (ll. 1–2). This intimate sharing is the basis of all the social relations that follow: in the pioneer family, in neighbourhood, village, and nation. The relationship of Canada to Britain is also filial: 'May all thy sons, like hers, be brave and free' (l. 549). The first public institution described is the tavern, because it is a safe, companionable place: 'When, thus in peace are met a happy few, / Sweet are the social pleasures that ensue' (ll. 157–8). (Contrast Hawthorne's *The Scarlet Letter*, where the first social institution is a prison.) At this early point, however, hints of social and moral failure intrude. Goldsmith's ethos of companionship is suited to 'a happy few,' but will have trouble reckoning with a larger population beyond the village. Moreover, the tavern is also the setting where companions turns nasty, when the host is impertinent and friends are too curious and gossipy. These sound like minor faults, but they mark a lapse when social bonds become excessively strained, and they mark an important shift in Goldsmith's argument. His tone is not whimsical or indulgent, and I share Gerald Lynch's view that Goldsmith is a fairly stern moralist, if not a puritan.

Lynch and Ronald E. Tranquilla see moral laxity as the vice that periodically threatens Goldsmith's vision of social peace, and both trace rhythmical cycles of effort and relaxation through the poem. I find the same role played by *excess*: too much of anything is dangerous. Both Goldsmith and his uncle celebrate what the latter calls 'rural virtues' ('Deserted Village' l. 400), which are humble, moderate, decent, chaste: 'For him light labour spread her wholesome store, / Just gave what life required, but gave no more' ('Deserted Village' ll. 59–60). To have more than enough is to invite trouble. Excessive behaviour is destructive and is associated, especially by Uncle Oliver, with luxury and trade. The Canadian Oliver uses the word 'busy' ambiguously to suggest honest industry (the 'busy mill, l. 461), excessive curiosity (the busybody in the tavern who 'seeks to know all business but his own,' l. 152), the 'busy crowds' (l. 39) of the city, and expanding commerce. Lynch claims that Goldsmith welcomes the new 'mercantilist ethos' (xv), and it is true that commerce eventually 'expands her free and swelling sail' (l. 520). But the pedlar turned merchant is praised only as long as he humbly deals in 'useful things' (l. 215), in contrast to the incompetent doctor and teacher. Goldsmith's busy villagers are doomed by both failure and success. Too little effort and they succumb to the harsh climate. Too much effort and they curse themselves with demoralizing prosperity.

'The Rising Village' is therefore caught in the familiar moral dilemma that appears in far greater detail in Max Weber's *The Protestant Ethic and the Rise of Capitalism*. Goldsmith praises 'patient firmness and industrious toil' (l. 103) because they are worthy virtues, but their practical effect is to produce wealth and ease, which are corrupting. Because excess – that is to say, profit – is the goal of capitalism, honest labour is eventually rewarded with disaster. The greater the honesty and the harder the labour, the more likely the disaster.[9] Commenting on a comparable theory of colonial development, Bentley notes that 'the commercial stage of a society's development brings with it, not merely such advantages as civility, convenience, patriotism, and the arts, but also a variety of evils, most notably luxury and vice, that can lead to the ruination of individuals within a society (especially women) and, if not checked, to the decadence of an entire society or nation' (144–5). This perverse truth appears in the cautionary tale of Albert and Flora. The poem's prospect of disaster, even at the moment of triumph, explains why Albert's caddish misconduct is so unmotivated, although one would hardly expect psychological complexity in this little melodrama. Betraying the marriage bond is the ultimate betrayal of sociability, since the family is 'humanity's genuine site,' in Habermas's phrase. According to the allegory, the more lovely Flora/Nova Scotia is, the more likely Albert/the English settler is to betray her, since his corruption is not a response to her failings, but to her success. When the new nation becomes too busy and too prosperous, it will be caught in the same dilemma.

I agree with W.J. Keith ('*The Rising Village* Again' 10–11) that the poem never makes clear exactly how much Goldsmith appreciated the trap he had built for his villagers, who are condemned by their success.[10] The ideal agricultural life, based in small towns and sustained by humble toil, is doomed by the excessive mercantilism proclaimed at the end. The ideal of sociability based on companionship is also doomed, partly because it can only prevail in small communities, and partly because it depends on the organic coherence of kinship and agricultural labour. When Goldsmith traces the seasonal cycle in his final survey of the scene, he celebrates the cyclical pattern of pastoral life. This reassuring rhythm of continuity and renewal is quite different than the expansive economic pattern on which the mercantilist ethos depends. Social relations, and the very conception of sociability, will be quite different when

Nova Scotia emerges from the eighteenth century and joins the Canadian nation. Ironically (as Keith also notes) the banished Natives are closer to Goldsmith's tribal ideal than are his villagers.

At this point I am in danger of committing the same fault I warned against: of criticizing the poem retrospectively for not being ahead of itself. To this charge I plead guilty. It is impossible to divest oneself of modern attitudes so as to read the poem purely 'in its own terms' (as Tranquilla proposes),[11] since even defining such terms requires an interpretive effort that reflects our current understanding. We cannot reconstruct the pastness of the past without distinguishing it from the presentness of the present, that is, without making historical judgments in which we find ourselves implicated. Such judgments cannot be made from some neutral ground, only from our own place within history. Similarly, we cannot read the poem purely in formal terms as a timeless idyll or pastoral, because history and nationhood are woven into its argument. 'The Rising Village' is rising precisely because it looks towards the future, towards a new nation that the Canadian reader now inhabits. It is impossible to read it without being aware of subsequent historical complications, from the initial resistance in the Maritimes to Confederation, to the current crisis in the fisheries. When Goldsmith praises the honest merchant, even the most austere reader might glimpse the proleptic shadow of K.C. Irving. Such ideas can be held in abeyance, of course, and I am not recommending that they be indulged. I am suggesting that any attempt to appreciate 'The Rising Village' will depend on a competition of literary, social, and historical values, some of them emanating from the poem, some of them from our own reading. In later writing, the idea of the nation will be used to reconcile these competing values, but Goldsmith cannot do so, because he cannot see beyond the fellowship of the village as social paradigm. He conceives of the new nation as a child of Britain, but he does not reckon the cost of growing up. Bentley aptly remarks that poets of the 'baseland' – those who find comfort in social unity and legal authority – often 'remember forward into their Canadian environment the achievements of the European tradition' (105), even when that tradition is already out of date. 'The Rising Village' is an exercise in remembering forward. Uncle Oliver presented a similar social vision more successfully because he recognized that it had already vanished and could only be evoked by a pensive, poetic historian. Goldsmith projects his social vision into a future for which it is unsuited even in the moral terms that he himself supplies. Nova Scotia will not be ruled by humble, chaste capitalists. In this sense his intent and his method are still at odds: he offers a model of sociability that cannot endure in the nation that he foresees.

E.J. Pratt, *Towards the Last Spike* (1952)

In *Towards the Last Spike,* a rising village becomes an expanding nation. The poem is so enthusiastic about building a nation by imposing 'civil discipline' (l. 1131) on both inchoate nature and a divided populace that some readers have grown wary of its enthusiasm. While earlier critics praised its intent but cast doubt on its execution,[12] recent critics, who regard chaos as liberating and unifying powers as patronizing, mistrust its 'anachronistic ideology' (Kamboureli, *On the Edge* 29). Several commentators point out the 'all-pervading air of ambiguity' (A.J.M. Smith 111) in Pratt's style,[13] but few have found an acceptable function for it in *Towards the Last Spike,* where it threatens to undermine the heroic enterprise that he details so avidly: 'a nation's rise, / Hail of identity, a world expanding' (ll. 28–9). How seriously should we take the botched attempt to drive in the last spike?

I argued that Goldsmith depicted the rising Canadian nation in accordance with two rhythms, one organic and cyclical, the other mercantile and progressive. He either did not recognize or was not troubled by the incompatibility of these two rhythms. Pratt not only acknowledges the incongruity but turns it into a source of wonder and pride.

> As grim an enemy as rock was time.
> The little men from five-to-six feet high,
> From three-to-four score years in lease of breath,
> Were flung in double-front against them both
> In years a billion strong; so long was it

Since brachiapods [*sic*] in mollusc habitats
Were clamping shells on weed in ocean mud.
Now only yesterday (ll. 1324–31)

As in 'The Truant,' Pratt suggests it is absurd yet glorious for puny men to attempt so monumental a task. The organic rhythm is slowed down until it becomes the primordial 'leisured time' (73) and 'geologic space' (56) of the reptilian Laurentian Shield. By contrast, historical time jumps quickly from 'only yesterday' to an eagerly anticipated tomorrow. The monster is ageless, whereas people rush at the hectic pace of historical advance, scientific progress, and national growth.

Now time was rushing labour – inches grew
To feet, to yards; the drills – the single jacks,
The double jacks – drove in and down (ll. 1359–61)

The progressive impulse, which will complete the railway and build Canada, quickly takes on a life of its own. Robert G. Collins observes that '[n]ot fate or destiny – both of which are personal – but inevitability and necessity – which deal with objective elements – are associated with the completion of the railway' (138). A compulsive, historical energy becomes the driving force of the poem, an energy that may reside in heroic individuals like Macdonald and Van Horne, but that is greater than they are. If it were not greater, it would be no match for the monstrous continent.

The poem's historical urgency corresponds to the ethical and intellectual powers that have long been remarked in Pratt's work. These constructive powers clash with destructive forces variously identified as cosmic, natural, instinctive, primitive, and atavistic. Sandra Djwa suggests that under the influence of Jan Smuts's 'holistic' philosophy, Pratt's later work grew more optimistic in its view of evolutionary conflict. Instead of waging an implacable struggle for survival, rival forces are subsumed within 'a friendly universe' (Djwa, *Pratt* 124), where moral and practical progress is possible and even natural. If humanity advances in concert with, rather than in defiance of, nature, then ethical concerns cease to be outlandish. Pratt's truant had refused to join the cosmic ballet – where ballet was a deliberately inappropriate image of mechanical order – but his defiance should no longer be necessary. Similarly, Canadian confederation becomes a natural development as well as a historical improvement; it is 'the political form of the general process of holism which Smuts sees as animating all nature' (Djwa, *Pratt* 123). *Towards the Last Spike* celebrates the victory of human order over cosmic accident, of history over geology. More correctly one should say that geology (scientific understanding) is itself a victory over mere rock (incomprehensible matter), while national history is a victory over fragmentary circumstance. In James Reaney's words: 'All of the world's life, then, advances a sort of railroad of increased complication, intelligence and ability to communicate over a continent of brute simplicity, ignorance and silence' (74).

Given this view, one would expect *Towards the Last Spike* to be a fine example of the romantic nationalism described in chapter 2. It is a national epic celebrating a myth of origins, complete with heroes, damsels, and founding fathers. But Canada never quite matches the traditional model, and the poem refuses to satisfy the reader's romantic expectations. The brutish continent should be a worthy opponent that eventually fits into the friendly universe but, as is his custom, Pratt stresses the uncanny alienness of a land that is supposed to be home to a new nation. Paradoxically, the land is personified (jealous, surprised, itchy, female) yet inanimate – 'too old for death, too old for life' (l. 884). The same paradox appears in *The Titanic* and *The Roosevelt and the Antinoe*; for example, in the latter the sea is shown 'Contesting with its iron-alien mood, / Its pagan face, its own primordial way' (ll. 615–16). Given this characterization, the Laurentian reptile can never join the human ballet of nation building. Because it represents 'survival without function' (l. 910), that is, passive, purposeless being, the monster can never participate in history, which must be active and purposeful. The workers, who are agents of history, seem 'human and unnatural' (l. 972) in their opposition to the land, and the fruit of their labours will be unnatural as well. As we have seen, the logic of romantic historicism links nation and nature as intimately as possible (Anderson 131–2). But Canada is created despite nature, and even, as Sir

John's first soliloquy shows, despite the natural lie of the land, which leads south rather than west. If in one view the railroad is a heroic achievement, in another view, which the poem also acknowledges, it is ridiculously fragile. Canada is tacked by steel threads to the back of an alien monster. The same ambiguity finds expression in another romantic metaphor – the language of nature. *Towards the Last Spike* is enchanted by words, but it makes no provision for the nation to hear or to be instructed by the language of nature. From the monster's viewpoint, Canada is outlandish.

> [The men] did not crawl – nor were they born with wings.
> They stood upright and walked, shouted and sang;
> They needed air – that much was true – their mouths
> Were open but the tongue was alien.
> The sounds were not the voice of winds and waters,
> Nor that of any beasts upon the earth. (ll. 930–5)

Whatever the glory in building the railroad, the monstrous land is so alien, the mountains are so oceanic that they can never engage in human history, whose busy temporality exists in an entirely different dimension. The continuing disjunction between nature and history is reaffirmed in the closing lines, where the lizard returns to sleep as the nation celebrates. 'The Rising Village' also ends with a transcendent perspective that makes all human efforts seem paltry: 'And bliss and peace encircle all thy shore, / Till empires rise and sink on earth, no more' (ll. 559–60). But Goldsmith alludes to a divine calendar that will mark the fulfilment of human time at the end of days. Pratt ends with indifference, as he does in the closing lines of *The Titanic*. If, in his heroic argument, the land-as-monster stands outside history, then it effectively ceases to be of historical significance. I do not mean that the physical battle against nature is insignificant. I mean that to figure in the poem at all, the land must evoke as its counterpart, not history but myth. Opposing the monster is not just Sir John, but a wizard (l. 1158), not just Van Horne, but Paul Bunyan (l. 1009). History must be transfigured into a grand, masculine adventure of fighting the monster and wooing the Lady of British Columbia.

Transfiguration, transmutation, elevation, and even digestion recur in the poem's rhetoric to express the transforming powers that enable Pratt to make an imaginative leap into romance.

> To smite the rock and bring forth living water,
> Take lead or tin and transmute both to silver,
> Copper to gold, betray a piece of glass
> To diamonds, fabulize a continent,
> Were wonders once believed, scrapped and revived (ll. 627–31)

The age of heroes is revived. Oatmeal becomes a breakfast of champions. All human abilities are augmented: mentally through determination and genius; linguistically through similes, catalogues, and hyperbole; practically through the technology of telescope, microscope, telegraph, and dynamite, which grant

> ... speed
> And power, and means to treat myopia
> To show an axe-blade infinitely sharp
> Splitting things infinitely small, or else
> Provide the telescopic sight to roam
> Through curved dominions never found in fables. (ll. 1–6)

Pratt's poetic dominion exists only in fables, where facts are transformed into fantasies. He is, of course, famous for his love of facts and his thorough research.[14] David Pitt shows how carefully he investigated the history of the railroad, the geology of the route, and even, Pratt joked, the inspiring effects of alcohol (Pitt 419–25, Gingell 147–8). In his essay 'The Relation of Source Material to Poetry' (1945), Pratt insisted on the poetic importance of factual accuracy, since 'the knowledge of the subject is related to the aesthetic value of the result' (Gingell 19). *Towards the Last Spike* is rich in facts, yet for all its technological sophistication, the railway is built in defiance of facts, which are obstacles to Sir John's national vision. The sobering facts belong to Edward Blake, who marshals them to argue against the foolhardy venture – 'The logic left no loopholes in the facts' (l. 338) – whereas Sir John is a political realist who must appeal beyond facts to the 'substance of things unseen' (l. 863). Similarly, Van Horne is a man of the earth (geologist, naturalist) who performs wonders: 'Miracles / Became his thoughts' (ll. 1229–30). The railroad is conceived in wonder and built through alchemy (l. 628) and wizardry (l. 1158).

Thoughts become miraculous through what Pratt calls 'the trespass of our thoughts' (l. 11). This evocative phrase, which describes the daring of modern astronomy, has little religious resonance here (in contrast to *Brébeuf*). When Van Horne recites the 'Athanasian damnatory clauses' (l. 1485), Pratt merely intensifies the rhetoric of debate, rather than adding a sacred dimension to the conflict. He is just as content to call on 'the gods' (l. 994) and 'imps' (l. 1445), astrology and alchemy. The trespass of thought refers instead to the audacity of the human mind as it enlarges its scope. It is the venture of thought impelled by a 'driving will' (l. 1233), comparable to the 'daring' (l. 192) of Arctic explorers and the 'daring' (l. 785) of Van Horne's all-Canadian route. *Towards the Last Spike* celebrates intellectual, imaginative, and physical daring by exaggerating their powers until they achieve the impossible.

The trespass of thought is a venerable literary theme that takes various forms. Its tragic form appears in the story of Doctor Faustus, the learned man who wants to learn absolutely everything, but in so doing transgresses the natural and moral bounds of humanity. His tragic *hubris* is echoed in Pratt's *Titanic*. Modern psychological and existential trespasses appear as inner voyage and heart of darkness, where Conrad's Kurtz tries to kick himself free of the earth. Several of Pratt's shorter poems study such residual, primitive instincts. A recent philosophical account of trespass appears in Michel Foucault's essays on transgression, where he contemplates the impossible glory of confronting things-in-themselves, pure energy, or elemental consciousness.[15] A benign form of trespass, more in keeping with romance, appears in the story of Ulysses as extended by Dante and embellished by Tennyson. They tell how the intrepid voyager sails beyond infirmity, and even beyond mortality, until he reaches the mountain of purgatory. His powers of thought and action are also heightened until they become magical, but in this case the magic is redemptive rather than destructive.

Towards the Last Spike recalls this last category, although the magic is tempered by irony and oatmeal. Pratt acknowledges that hardship and death are the price of daring to build the railroad, but the price is worth paying since the reward – a new nation – far exceeds the cost. Mourning bells acknowledge the sacrifice of Blackfoot (l. 1137), Chinese coolies (l. 1139), and Métis (l. 1417), but their specific, historical suffering is immediately subsumed within an abstract mortality – signalled by 'that universal toll' (l. 1141) – and then drowned out by the engine bells of progress: 'Tomorrow, and the engine bells again!' (l. 1147). The poem's argument, too, is obliged to make sacrifices if it is to 'fabulize a continent.' Critics differ as to whether this price is worth paying. The poem must brush aside competing visions of justice (the Riel Rebellion) and relegate political embarrassments to titles ('The Pacific Scandal'). It must skip over hints that the epic battle cannot be simply between 'nature' and 'humanity,' because humanity is itself divided by rival interests and needs. Thus in his rejoinder, 'All the Spikes but the Last,' F.R. Scott admonishes Ned for ignoring the thousands of coolies, but Pratt, who knew history well enough, cannot afford to entertain their view, because it would disrupt his own. 'I have tried to show that contrariety of interests' (Gingell 149) in the Riel Rebellion, he claimed, but he cannot let them get too contrary, or they will contaminate the poem with a different vision of nationhood. In effect, they would turn it into a different kind of poem. This is one kind of transformation that Pratt cannot afford. He therefore lets Edward Blake speak for the opposition, but an opposition that is ideologically no different than Sir John's, only less daring.

Towards the Last Spike exhibits great confidence in civilization and progress, in the myth-making powers of thought, and in the legitimacy of the national dream. In view of so much confidence, it is surprising to read in David Pitt's biography that when Pratt began the poem in 1950, he was dismayed by the nuclear tests just conducted by the United States. In fact he was so troubled that he expressed his feelings in a series of poems that Pitt calls 'the H-bomb group' (417): 'Myth and Fact,' 'The Good Earth,' and 'Cycles.' All the doubts that will be suppressed in *Towards the Last Spike* prevail in these poems about misusing human intelligence to blight the earth and make it monstrous. Here the magic is sinister and uncontrollable, a genie released from its bottle ('Myth and Fact'). The monsters are man-made rather than natural. Science, which deromanticizes life (Pitt 418), is at best a mixed blessing and more likely a curse. 'The Good Earth' even links atomic physics to Faust. In these poems a religious yearning haunts the trespass of thought, which cannot police itself but requires an infusion of 'plasma from Gethsemane' ('Cycles,' l. 36).

Towards the Last Spike begins by asserting the essential continuity of humanity, despite the increasing tempo and precision of modern life: 'It was the same world then as now' (l. 1). By contrast, the H-bomb poems (and earlier ones) insist on drastic differences disrupting the course of human history, which does not merely repeat the same patterns but exhibits an evolution that makes the modern world dangerously different from the past. Where *Towards the Last Spike* speaks of sameness and continuity – qualities that will be transferred to the new community of Canada – the other poems question the controlling principles that give *Towards the Last Spike* its confident vision of nationhood. These are principles of conceptual and social unity, justice, and legitimacy. Here they are articulated through the daring 'trespass' of nation building, a trespass without sin. It may be, as Pitt suggests, that Pratt seized so enthusiastically on the theme of the railroad because it offered compensation for distressing current events. He turned to poetry, he wrote to Earle Birney, 'to get the pressure of hydrogen off my chest ... the only release (if one may call it such) was through verse' (Pitt 416). Whatever his motives, the idea of compensation is an important aspect of both railroad and nation building.

In the traditional view, life is messy, art is neat. Life is chaotic and unfair, but art surveys the mess and glimpses a compensating principle of poetic justice within the disorder. The verdict of literature – a judgment for compensatory damages, so to speak – can figure in various ways: as nostalgia, as wish fulfilment, as a stubborn reaffirmation of ideals, as heroic refusal, as a just reward or unmerited grace. In *Towards the Last Spike* the railroad is a 'venture' (l. 992) in several senses of the word. It is an intellectual and technological challenge, a political risk, an imaginative leap, a business investment. The pattern of risk and reward suggests an underlying current of justice, as Robert Collins argues: 'Pratt is no social revolutionary in his ode to power. On the contrary, the unfolding of human destiny is based on a proper functioning of the order of things, a Platonic concept of justice that depends on the fulfilment of all parts according to their nature ... Capital here is a positive good ... [I]t is the farsightedness of wealthy individuals who create the line, eventually' (145). Justice is one system of compensation, and, as Collins shows, there is one view of justice that makes it indistinguishable from a wise investment. When Pratt describes 'The Lake of Money' (68), he includes venture capital in the epic operation. However, the poem's magical transformations hint at something further. Justice gives you what you deserve. Romance gives you more than you deserve, especially when it combines daring (self-assertion) with sacrifice (self-denial). If there is a religious promise lurking in this poem about profane accomplishments, I think it resides in the ideal of sacrifice. This ideal figures more prominently in earlier works, notably in the martyrdom of Brébeuf. As Sandra Djwa observes, self-sacrifice is the highest ethical virtue for Pratt, because it heroically contradicts the brute law of self-preservation (*Pratt* 6–7, 18). In a sense, sacrifice runs counter to the natural order because it envisages a different kind of order. Sacrifices are not just. Indeed they are clearly unjust when the innocent are killed (lamb, child, scapegoat). But the result of this injustice is redemption, which far exceeds the fair compensation of justice. To sacrifice means to make holy, that is, to raise to a higher level of value.[16] This transcendent, unmerited reward is clearest in a Christian context (the 'plasma of Gethsemane'), where salvation is far more than sinful mankind deserves.

In *Towards the Last Spike* the value of sacrifice, like the nature of trespass, is secularized. It appears as an enormous expense of time, energy, hope, ingenuity, and money: 'his, the greater task; / His, to commit a nation to the risk' (ll. 1171–2). It appears as the lives risked and lost during construction. The bounty that exceeds even this great expense is Canada – that is, an ideal Canada whose harmonious future (the 'continental chorus' [l. 1600]) is assured in the closing section. Canada is worth more than the cost of building it, partly because it was built through daring and sacrifice, and partly because it permits a prosperous national life extending far into the future.

> For on the morrow
> The last blow on the spike would stir the mould
> Under the drumming of the prairie wheels,
> And make the whistles from the steam out-crow
> The Fraser. (ll. 1612–16)

Canada is not holy; it is no New Jerusalem. It is more like a sovereign idea that blesses its citizens, dignifies their history, and unifies the poem.

Canada also supplies Pratt with a vision of sociability, because the nation is a perfected communal form within which individuals can define themselves. The corollary of this process is an ethic of responsibility, loyalty, and ultimately self-sacrifice. Because the community confers identity, individuals ought to devote themselves to it. 'What are the gods' in Pratt's poetic world, asks Frank Davey, 'but organization, efficiency, regimentation, discipline, and order?' These are the virtues of 'men uniting in a common cause and gaining strength and inspiration from their own communality' (*Surviving* 17, 25). To portray this communality, Pratt draws on three main tropes. The first is work, understood as arduous toil, of course, but also as a joint investment of physical and mental energy. Everyone who works on the railroad is drawn into a magnificent, common effort. All engage in what Pratt called elsewhere 'an Operation with a capital O' (Gingell 27) – that is, an idealized model of human ingenuity and accomplishment. Pratt's preference for collective heroes is well-known, and in *Towards the Last Spike* he concentrates on 'gangs.'

> As individuals
> The men lost their identity; as groups,
> As gangs, the massed, divided, subdivided,
> Like numerals only (ll. 832–5)

The loss of individuality here does not express industrial alienation, but rather the way people are utterly united through shared
work. They may differ about how best to accomplish their task, but
not about the worth of the task itself, to which all are equally committed. While people may disagree about which route to follow or
what tools to use, the business of working together legitimates
their task. In other words, because they construct Canada together,
they are all Canadian at the end. The same effect is gained by the
second trope: the family. Pratt continually refers to kinship, court-
ship, brothers, and especially marriage, to suggest that the nation
will be one large family. British Columbia is a bride. The railroad
lines are 'baptized with charters' (l. 387). Sir John has 'fathered /
The Union' (ll. 1206–7). Blasting through the mountains is even
compared to 'a hundred clean Caesarian cuts' (l. 1531), so the
birth of a nation is not far off. A third trope, language, suggests
that all Canadians eventually come to speak in the same way.
Although they do not literally speak the same language, they draw
on the same set of images to articulate their nation. They share a
national discourse. More on this point below.

We are still left with the problem of interpreting that bungled
last spike as a clue to Pratt's vision of Canadian sociability. *Towards
the Last Spike* ends, not with 'they lived happily ever after,' but with
'they were united in prosperity for a long time to come.' That
happy future had already arrived when Pratt wrote the poem; it
may seem behind us today. I have already suggested that to read literature historically is to situate it in fictive time (in this case, mid-
nineteenth century), in the time of writing (mid-twentieth century), and the time of reading (late twentieth century). Or as Pratt
restates this feat of temporal legerdemain: 'The past flushed in the
present and tomorrow / Would dawn upon today' (ll. 19–20). To
read historically a text that takes history as its subject is to make
competing demands of both the text and ourselves, with the result
that no interpretation can avoid a conflict of perspectives and
judgments. Indeed, it is our effort to interpret fairly – to establish
our own sense of justice – that produces a conflict in understanding. This difficulty affects *Towards the Last Spike* in a curiously personal way. If we are Canadian readers, we recognize ourselves as

the fruit of that daring sacrifice. But are we worth it? We may well feel uncomfortable in celebrating a railroad that is now in decline, or a nation whose unity has never been secure. We cannot avoid finding irony in Pratt's exaltation of science precisely when he was most fearful of its amoral energy. Nevertheless, we should not feel superior to the poem. Perhaps Oliver Goldsmith was politically naive, as critics have suggested, but Pratt was a highly sophisticated poet who wrote with an 'all-pervading air of ambiguity' (A.J.M. Smith 111).

Consider, for instance, his skilful use of blank verse to create a national discourse. His verse creates various effects – narrative, dramatic, meditative, lyrical, ironic – but it is especially successful in cultivating an authoritative, reassuring tone that speaks as the voice of history. Through this voice, Pratt keeps Canada at arm's length, where it can be surveyed and admired from sea to sea. To maintain the spectacle, he must maintain his and our distance from it, as he acknowledges in one description of the mountains:

Terror and beauty like twin signal flags
Flew on the peaks for men to keep their distance.
...
They needed miles to render up their beauty,
As if the gods in high aesthetic moments,
Resenting the profanity of touch,
Chiselled this sculpture for the eye alone. (ll. 986–7, 993–6)

Readers of the poem adopt a comparable position of aesthetic detachment. Ironically, Canadian readers must be detached from their nation – that is, from events shaping their own lives – if they are to appreciate its aesthetic glory. Too close a view of people or events (such as the Riel Rebellion) would profane the sublime moment. Accordingly, characters are generalized, events traced only in outline, and the cunning passages of history are transformed through rhetorical flourishes into a play of images, which can be enjoyed for their virtuosity: a tug of war, an orchestra tuning up, a parade of smells or colours. Davey objects that the oatmeal passage offers 'metaphoric whimsy in the guise of historical understanding' (*Surviving* 39). This judgment, while unkindly expressed, is accurate in its view that Pratt's fondness for language invites more attention than the events being described. The reader may or may not accept the invitation, but the strategy is not a fault in the poem, since it achieves exactly the desired effect. I presume that Métis readers might be less willing than Scots to subdue their personal interests for the sake of art. They might prefer 'the profanity of touch' to the detached, aesthetic gaze. But some degree of quiescence is necessary for all Canadian readers, who are put in the curious position of celebrating their nation by keeping their distance from it. Perhaps this is a requirement of all patriotism, which cannot afford to be too inquisitive.

Magdalene Redekop makes a similar point about *Brébeuf* when she finds its Christian story shadowed by 'a subtext, a story of people destroyed, a story which cannot find expression in this poem but one to which the poem has sensitized us' (57). Sensitivity to rival histories is bound to be stronger in *Brébeuf*, where the Huron and Iroquois have a prominent role, than in *Towards the Last Spike*, where the antagonist is a sleepy, prehistoric monster. However, Redekop's next comment applies equally well to the later poem: 'Our response to that unspoken story, however, is fraught not only with a sense of history but also with awareness of our own participation in the writing of history' (57). We recognize that all histories are partial, and that our own practice of reading the poem implicates us in the process. Pratt makes the writing of history an explicit theme in *Towards the Last Spike*. Virtually all critics, following Frye, have commented on the prominent role of language and conflicting styles to articulate a vision of Canada. The nation is created in, as, and through words:

> It was the battle of ideas and words
> And kindred images called by the same name,
> Like brothers who with temperamental blood
> Went to it with their fists. (ll. 470–3)

Pratt uses Edward Blake's windy oratory to make the opposition seem less convincing. Sir John's romantic metaphors not only help

him win the great debate (Pitt 426), but permit him to set the
terms in which the nation will be understood:

> The words
> British, the West instead of South, the Nation,
> The all-Canadian route – these terms were singing
> Fresher than ever while the grating tones
> Under the stress of argument had faded
> Within the shroud of their monotony. (ll. 448–53)

Nevertheless, the poem cannot avoid hinting through historical
facts and rhetorical effects that other styles might be less persuasive
yet are valid in their own terms. In the earlier passage, the imagery
of kinship confines the conflict to a single family ('brothers'), thus
obscuring the possibility that other families (Native, Métis) might
have a say in the matter. To be victorious, Sir John must defeat an
opposition, and so Redekop's caution applies here as well: 'We are
always aware of one group of readers whose desires and expectations are not reflected in the poem' (51). The company of such
readers (which Stanley Fish calls an 'interpretive community') is
likely to grow in numbers as time passes and critical tastes change.

In the preceding paragraph, I found only a rhetorical hint to
evoke a contrary point of view. Pratt's style suggests more explicitly,
however, that he is well aware of conflicting demands made of his
readers. He offers 'Romance and realism, double dose' (l. 193),
although I have argued mainly on behalf of romance. If reality is
transmuted into myth, at other times 'myth resolves into fact,' as
W.H. New shows (*Articulating* 36). Many passages deflate the
poem's epic pretensions: through comic diction (Sir John has
'arrowy chipmunk eyes' [l. 258]); through mock-epic parodies (the
paean to oatmeal, Blake's 'Ministry of Smells' [l. 308], the absurd
apotheosis of Van Horne); and even through a few bathetic
touches ('For Moses, Marco Polo, Paracelsus, / Fell in the retort
and came out *Smith*' [l. 633–4]). Evidently Pratt found one
omelette metaphor too mundane and excised it at his publisher's
request (Pitt 435). Other examples could be cited, but they would
only defer my final question: If fact is transmuted into myth (apo-

theosis) and myth resolved into fact (*Götterdämmerung*), how are the two modes finally related? New examines the collision of 'visionary imagination and expediency' (34) and finally decides on a just balance of the two: 'Yet Pratt reaches not towards golden Eden but towards the inhabitable Canada, rugged and imperfect, a myth of men rather than of gods' (41). According to this judgment, mythic realism unites its two modes in a supreme fiction of Canada, populated not by gods but (to borrow Wallace Stevens's vocabulary) by 'major men' who are stalwart citizens.

While I agree with New's analysis, I sense that *Towards the Last Spike* is not content with a fair balance or with mere justice. It aspires to a loftier reward. Against Stevens, I would cite T.S. Eliot's lament in *Murder in the Cathedral*: 'Mankind cannot endure too much reality.' In my view, romance proves too powerful to be subdued and realism too dangerous to be indulged. When challenged, romance quickly takes the upper hand, so that we conclude not with mythic realism, but with a romance of technology, politics, hardship, and facts. If Pratt periodically brings his poem down to earth, it is only so that he can find material for another trespass. The botched last spike distracts attention, but not for long.

Dennis Lee, 'Civil Elegies' (1972)

Habermas argues that public and private spheres 'infiltrate' each other in bourgeois ideology, but the filtering between the two shifted dramatically with the rise of capitalism. The earlier vision of cosy, domestic sociability – and of the nation as an extended family, which I applied to Goldsmith – was eroded by the success of the bourgeois revolution, which made the state increasingly powerful and intrusive. Society could no longer be regarded as a voluntary congregation of free individuals because the distinction between publicity and privacy became increasingly strained, as did their sustaining principles of freedom and justice:

> Only this dialectic of a progressive 'societalization' of the state simultaneously with an increasing 'state-ification' of society gradually

destroyed the basis of the bourgeois public sphere – the separation of state and society. Between the two and out of the two, as it were, a repoliticized social sphere emerged to which the distinction between 'public' and 'private' could not be usefully applied. It also led to the disintegration of the specific portion of the private realm within which private people assembled to constitute a public and to regulate those aspects of their commerce with each other that were of general concern, namely, the public sphere in its liberal form. (*Structural* 142)

The social ideal by which free individuals judiciously regulate their general concerns became problematic because the disintegration of the private realm impaired faith in fruitful privacy (the sense that citizens can creatively direct their own lives) and increased alienation and political helplessness. These conditions torment Dennis Lee's 'Civil Elegies,' which can be read as a poetic attempt to re-secure an individuality that can participate in a sociability that will maintain the nation. When Lee enters public space, in Nathan Phillips Square in Toronto, he finds himself strangely vulnerable yet invisible, as if he were one of the civic ghosts haunting his own poem. 'Civil Elegies' might be subtitled 'The Sinking Village' in accordance with the falling, debasing cadence through which it descends into the land, the self, and the void within each:

> For
> many are called but none are chosen now, we are the evidence
> for downward momentum (41)[17]

The lower it sinks, the more 'Civil Elegies' sounds like a forlorn reply to Goldsmith and Pratt, in which Lee worries that all their toil and trespass have produced an alienated colony, lost in a stupor, haunted only by the absence of ghosts.

These bitter spectres swoop down on the public square, where they inspire a poetic meditation inappropriately called elegiac.[18] An elegy mourns for a worthy person or contemplates death, but Lee laments an unworthy nation that has never lived. Even the biblical parody of Matthew 22:14 ('For many are called, but few are chosen') mocks a fall from grace not into damnation, but into lethargy. Because English Canadians are homeless in their own home, Lee broods on absence, humiliation, and pollution.

> In a bad time, people, from an outpost of empire I write
> bewildered, though on about living. It is to set down a nation's
> failure of nerve; I mean complicity, which is signified by the
> gaseous stain above us. (47)

The bumbling syntax of the first sentence expresses the speaker's bewilderment. The final clause illustrates how he explicitly allegorizes the cityscape, so that its features testify against him and his country. In effect, a retributive justice operates through the symbolic setting. Because Canadians have been oblivious to their failures – obliviousness being itself a failing – everything in the city signals their cowardly incivility. If they could read the writing on the wall, they would find themselves proclaimed 'a nation of / losers and quislings' (44):

> For we are a conquered nation: sea to sea we bartered
> everything that counts, till we have
> nothing to lose but our forebears' will to lose. (56)

If a retributive principle motivates 'Civil Elegies,' what exactly is its nature? In order to answer this question, we have to identify the forces that have perverted the nation and the counter-forces that, Lee hopes, will set it right. By 'motivate,' I mean a shaping power that permits him to distinguish a beginning, middle, and end in his vision of Canadian sociability. An inciting force, which he calls a 'guilty genesis' (48), marks the beginning. Some vital principle, however torpid, keeps Canada alive: he feels it in the thrum of the city (39) and 'the miscellaneous clobber of day to day' (53). And he seeks a redemptive end through which

> we might come to our own
> and live, with our claimed selves, at home in the difficult world. (51)

Goldsmith calls on providence and Britannia for guidance. Despite some reservations, Pratt trusts in evolutionary and human powers. For Lee, what is the justice that both impels and imperils nation, poet, and poem?

To pose the question in this way is to assume that there is, or should be, an interlacing of nation, citizen, poet, and poem. That is, my approach to 'Civil Elegies' is already cast in nationalist-romantic terms. Lee actually claimed to be anti-romantic (Twigg 247), although I suspect he might more accurately be called a lapsed romantic – where lapsing is another dying fall. Whatever label we choose,[19] the legacy of romantic nationalism appears as a source of both inspiration and anguish in his poem. He struggles to orient himself spiritually and socially by undergoing an ordeal of panic and emptiness. He taxes the reader to do the same. To orient oneself, however, requires some trustworthy 'measure' (38), whether it is called national fate, justice, or authenticity. I want to examine how Lee measures these measures – how he encounters and assesses them – and how he treats the confusion that results when they fail.

Canadians cannot read the writing on the wall, but Lee can. The persona that he labelled the poem's 'civil consciousness' (Munton 156) interprets the Toronto scene like an anxious Isaiah, warning the city of its iniquity (contrast Isaiah 1:4–9) and prophesying a 'civil habitation' (36) yet to be built. Where Isaiah is sure of his standards, however, Lee lacks any measure by which to pass judgment. This double insecurity (in the world, and in himself within that world) is registered by the poetic voice in its relation to place. Both are debased. Lee revised the poem partly because he was dissatisfied with its 'heavy, high-pitched public voice,' which he wished to make more supple and bemused. As he remarked in conversation, finding the right tone was essential, because voice 'manifests your ways of being human, it embodies how you are in the world and how things make themselves real to you' (Stedingh 46).[20] Being-in-the-world – Heidegger's *Dasein* – is the subject of 'Civil Elegies.' The earnest, self-doubting voice that modulates from reproach to scorn to anguish to hope suggests that Lee's being-in-the-world is tenuous, just as Canada is tenuous as a dwelling-place. In a true nation, word, voice, and place should all verify each other. Because they do not, Lee is obliged to use inauthentic language to report on an inauthentic place. He must find 'words for our space-lessness,' as he says in his eloquent essay about colonial silence ('Cadence' 163).

He is an unlikely prophet, however, because he lacks both traditional religious faith (John Dennis's standard for poetic justice), which he declares untenable in the modern world, and faith in the modern religion of technological mastery, which he condemns as vicious. Consequently, he feels spiritually bereft, cut off from past and future. '[W]e cannot / malinger among the bygone acts of grace' (41), he warns, even though he is engaged in a prolonged poetic malingering as he loiters in the square and deciphers its signs of disaster. Goldsmith and Pratt also sought authenticity, which they expressed as a new land asserting itself even as it maintained its link with Britain. By looking backward and forward, they envisioned a maturing national life secured by historical and moral continuity. Loyalty to one's roots and commitment to a worthy social purpose is also important to Lee's quest for national well-being. But he can find no secure faith within himself and no secure political principle within his country to justify either loyalty or resolve. Instead everything is inauthentic, and is variously expressed as deprivation, asphyxiation, aimlessness, entanglement, and vacuity – conditions all displayed by the cityscape. If a retributive principle can be discerned amid the debris, Lee seems intent on obscuring it.

Given this dilemma, 'Civil Elegies' might seem to be an exercise in nation deconstructing rather than nation building, except that the nation as a valid political form is not questioned. Canada has failed to achieve that form, but the ideal itself remains intact. Whereas Pratt claimed a national space extending 'from sea to sea,' Lee confines himself to Nathan Phillips Square and environs.[21] But this 'civil space' is a synecdoche for the entire nation, as the poem's subtitle ('Pro patria') indicates. His vision of sociability is national in scope, as he demonstrates by looking (briefly) north to the Canadian Shield – Pratt's mythological lizard – and beyond to 'whatever terrain informs our lives' (35). He, too, foresees a unity encompassing all Canadians and giving them a sense of fearful but authentic self-possession:

> To be our own men! in dread to live
> the land, our own harsh country, beloved, the prairie, the foothills –
> > (35)

Meanwhile, Canada is adrift in 'civil nonbeing' ('Cadence' 168), a ghostly state that projects as its opposite an authentic nationhood – home: the domestic sociability that Habermas consigns to nostalgia. In the true home from which Lee feels barred, national unity survives social disruption because it is legitimated by a resilient civil life. In its grander moments, the national life is a record of noble ventures and daring trespasses: the conquest of a New World, the taming of a continent. Lee presents no such record, but he implies it by the passion with which he mourns its absence:

> to furnish, out of the traffic and smog and the shambles of dead
> > precursors,
> a civil habitation that is
> human, and our own. (36)

'To furnish' is an evocative verb to suggest the inhabiting and fulfiling of a rich national life. Unfortunately, Canadians have been wimps rather than heroes, as we see in the routing of William Lyon Mackenzie's timorous rebels by equally timorous loyalists:

> the loyalists, scared skinny by the sound of their own gunfire,
> gawked and bolted south to the fort like rabbits,
> the rebels for their part bolting north to the pub: the first
> spontaneous mutual retreat in the history of warfare. (34)

The fiasco is so silly as to become a parody of history, as if English Canadians had clownishly reversed Marx's saying that history repeats itself, first as tragedy, then as farce (320). Here, farce comes first, followed by indifference. But again, Lee evokes by force of contrast what might have been if Canadian history had not been cursed by a series of self-inflicted injuries. First came the exhausting toil of settlement, then colonial subservience, and finally the tyranny of technological modernity, which annuls any sense of place or particularity. Looking backward and forward reveals only what might have been. Behind lies a shameful legacy:

> And what can anyone do in this country, baffled and
> making our penance for ancestors, what did they leave us? Indian-
>   swindlers,
> stewards of unclaimed earth and rootless (34)

Ahead lies the blandness of modernity, which will swallow up any Canadian distinctiveness:

> And what can we do here now, for at last we have no notion
> Of what we might have come to be in America, alternative, and how
>   make public
> a presence which is not sold out utterly to the modern? (34)

Lee is thus a nationalist without a nation. When he is less despondent, he finds humour and even comfort in this existential conundrum.[22] He agrees with writers such as Herschel Hardin and A.B. McKillop (whom we will encounter later) that, at their best, English Canadians have learned to live stubbornly with their cultural contradictions. For Lee, stubbornness becomes positively heroic in a poet such as Al Purdy, who registers the Canadian paradox so sharply: 'In *that baffled enduring*, he lives the paradox of this half of the continent. For we have been in North America but not whole-heartedly of it; and somehow we have also been of North America, but not whole-heartedly in it; and as we have lived those contradictions – consistently, though in confusion – our primal necessity has been to survive' (Lee, 'Running' 16). The words 'our primal necessity' show that, for all his scepticism, Lee still yearns for a formative, national fate. When he tries to articulate that fate, however, he is faced with another puzzle: the Canadian destiny is to live 'consistently, though in confusion.' This nicely ambiguous phrase illuminates 'Civil Elegies,' which displays either consistent confusion or confused consistency in both its vision of nationhood and its poetic practice. Lee rigorously argues himself into a muddle, or more precisely into a void, at which point the void becomes either the effacement of all nationhood or a possible source of redemption.

In order to see how he treats this dilemma, I will explore the consistency of his poetic argument. It presents Canada as a confusing place, partly because the country is a historical anomaly, partly because the poem's style is so disruptive, and partly because Lee feels that poetry relies on 'alogical ... hunches' rather than logical proofs (quoted in Munton 147). If this last condition is true,[23] then a tussle with the alogical (the void, the ghost-of-a-ghost) is also part of the poem's argument.

Lee yearns for a true nation, but as I noted in chapter 1, there are volatile inconsistencies within the very idea of nationhood, which claims to be both specific and general, natural and artificial, rational and instinctive. Gordon Smith finds the nation-state inherently problematic because its two terms 'bring together quite conflicting sources of legitimacy. On the one hand, the affinities – cultural and ethnic – that make up the bonds of the nation are essentially non-rational sanctions. On the other hand, the modern state – whatever the nature of particular regimes – embodies the principle of "legal rationality." It is a peculiar mixture' (197). The same peculiarity afflicts George Grant's account of Canadian nationalism. He regards nationalism as heterogeneous and quirky, in contrast to the impersonal homogeneity of liberal modernism, which he presents as a tidal wave abolishing all national differences in the name of freedom and efficiency: 'Liberalism is the ideological means whereby indigenous cultures are homogenized' (*Lament* 80; see also *Lament* 5, 16; *Technology* 19, 33). To love and cultivate what is distinctive in one's nation is a great virtue for Grant, whereas modernism is not concerned with virtue ('the good'), only with technological expertise. Consequently, English Canada, French Canada and all other local pieties are doomed by the very ideology they think will allow them to take their place in the modern world.

The duty of nations to protect cultural differences can be traced back to romantic historicism, which depicts national uniqueness as the *genius loci*. This spirit appears sporadically in 'Civil Elegies' as an avenging fury, a missing god, and an intimation of lost unity:

> I saw that we are to live in the calamitous division of the world
> with singleness of eye and there is
> nothing I would not give to be made whole. (52)

'Wholeness' refers to personal and social integrity, which require each other, since one cannot be a complete person in an incomplete society, and vice versa. When Grant inspects the nation, however, he no longer insists on heterogeneity, but on centrality and wholeness. Nations may differ from each other, but within themselves they are expected to be homogeneous, sharing the same background and purposes: 'A society only articulates itself as a nation through some common intention among its people' (*Lament* 68). The alienation of a dispossessed people arises when they lose contact with what Grant simply calls 'one's own' – 'this particular body, this family, these friends, this woman, this part of the world, this set of traditions, this country, this civilisation' (*Technology* 73).[24] And this nation. Lee echoes the phrase when he hopes 'that we might come to our own' (51). Yet Grant also recognizes that Canada is dual, because it is a union of two (but only two) smaller nations: English Protestant and French Catholic. Indeed, he insists that the validity of Canada-as-a-nation derives from its essential duality: 'The keystone of a Canadian nation is the French fact' (*Lament* 20). Grant does not pay much attention to this complication – if Canada is dual, why not treble or quadruple? – and he certainly does not wish to fragment Canada into ever smaller regional and ethnic groups. This is probably because he is preoccupied with the rising tide of Americanism, which will obliterate all local differences in any case. Still, his view of nationalism is too restrictive to accommodate the calamitous division of Canadian cultural life, a division that he not only acknowledges, but sees as constituting Canada's national character.

A similar inconsistency appears in 'Civil Elegies,' but inconsistency in poetic arguments need not be judged a fault, especially in a poem that argues oxymoronically that Canada is a bewildered place. There are at least three ways of justifying poetic inconsistency, and they produce three different readings of 'Civil Elegies.' In formalist analysis (such as New Criticism), inconsistency often figures as part of a poem's drama – for example, when it portrays a puzzled persona who worries through conflicting ideas or moods. Lee's elegy 'The Death of Harold Ladoo' illustrates this technique: the speaker's attitude changes as he seeks an honest way to understand and mourn for his lost friend. Following this sequence, the reader is progressively perplexed and enlightened by the poem's incongruities, which intensify its psychological struggle. However, the spectacle of that struggle – the poetic drama – remains formally consistent. A similar interpretive strategy is used by social critics (Hardin, McKillop, Malcolm Ross) who regard Canada as an inherently volatile nation, continually threatening to fall apart; but it remains intact because even volatility can participate in a framework of stable cultural attitudes. These attitudes define 'the Canadian contradiction,' which is another example of consistent confusion. In effect, Canada is being 'read' like a modernist poem. I said that, for Goldsmith, the rising nation should display the consistency of a well-crafted poem, which corresponds to the moral balance of a Christian gentleman. Extending this argument, we might say that, in another reading, Canada displays the turbulence of an avant-garde poem, which corresponds to the neurosis of modernity.

'Civil Elegies' can be read as a consistently confused, modernist poem.[25] Lee-the-author offers a coherent sequence of attitudes by which Lee-the-prophet struggles towards a tentative affirmation of his native land. T.G. Middlebro' analyses the structural principles that organize this spectacle and that testify to the decisive hand of the artist, which does not waver even when his protagonist is befuddled. In keeping with the poem's two epigraphs, one political, the other mystical, the elegies alternate between public and private inquiries, between social and religious valuations. The sequence hits a low point in Elegies 5 and 6, and then after a meditation on love (Elegy 7) re-ascends towards 'muted positive assertions' (207). Other alternating patterns are based on the oppositions void/

home, sick/healthy, past/present, observation/meditation, and so on. The poem does not resolve these terms as handily as 'The Rising Village' treats a comparable set of dualities. Still, 'Civil Elegies' is not baffled by inconsistencies, because it subsumes their rhythmical alternation within a spiritual quest corresponding to Canadian destiny. Private and public domains remain neatly aligned, in keeping with the principle that individuality depends on citizenship. The conclusion, which is uncertain but not inconsistent, is neatly summarized by Dennis Duffy: 'Because the poet does not try to tie up a series of conflicts within a conciliatory knot, the reader must rest content with the contemplative acceptance of division and renunciation as a way of coming to grips with our situation now' (124). 'The poet' may be uncertain, but he is still in command and does justice to his unruly material.

I am not content with this treatment of 'Civil Elegies,' and I presume that Lee would not be satisfied either, because he has a different conception of who or what is in command. He looks to more mysterious powers, which he serves rather than commands. In his essay 'Polyphony: Enacting a Meditation,' he offers a subtle account of poetic consistency based, not on the continuous experience of persona or nation, but on the poem's larger, rhythmical structure. He claims that poetry is unified by an intricate fusion of meditating consciousness, the contents of consciousness, and the voice in which the first two are enacted (87). The 'originating unity' of the poem is the dynamic orchestration of all three functions, which he calls 'the kinesis of polyphony itself – the concrete trajectory of voice which the meditation enacts' (88). His fondness for the verb 'enact' shows that he too regards a poem dramatically, but the drama is ontological and linguistic in nature rather than psychological. It is a drama of being and saying performed, so to speak, by life and by language rather than by any individual speaker. A poem's authenticity does not reflect the sincerity of the writer but the integrity of the poetic performance. This performance is a 'meditative quest' (88) that traces 'a fundamental gesture in the kinetic vocabulary of what-is' (94). Instead of the modernist's consistent confusion, we have the postmodernist's confused (polyphonic, kinetic) consistency (the fundamental gesture).

Sean Kane reads 'Civil Elegies' in this second manner by distinguishing two poetic voices, one public and social, the other private and religious. As they debate their relative positions, each shows up the deficiencies of the other, but also reveals its own faults. The other-worldly voice is flawed by 'a self-conscious, hurt-seeking idolatry of nothingness'; the worldly voice is flawed by 'the heroic melodrama of the individualistic last stand' (140). The voices rhythmically 'enact' rather than state their positions, until their conflict is dissolved by a 'proper wisdom' (140) that does not rely on oppositional logic or manipulative relationships. Kane does not pretend that Lee is masterminding this complex drama. After all, the mind-that-masters is the source of the problem. It is the mind of exploitive modernity. It, too, must dissolve into a luminous attentiveness that hears 'the intimations of a more authentic speech – though one that remains unspeakable in its polyphony' (141). This speech sounds mysteriously through the poem's cadences, and Kane describes them as if they were secretly in charge and the poet were merely their servant:[26] '[Cadence] cannot express itself honestly in words, since all words now have been invested with the language of control. It cannot speak in silence. But Cadence might provide the impetus and the ground of an enactment which reveals the fragile words and gestures of being human in a space without authentic being or belonging' (142). What the poem does (enacts) in defiance of logic, rather than what its author or persona says, is the source of proper wisdom.

The two interpretations summarized here subsume the poem's apparent confusion within a poetic justness that has it own consistency. For Kane (following Heidegger), this larger propriety can only be intuited by readers who are willing to undergo the same verbal, moral, and philosophical penance as does the Voice in 'Civil Elegies.' They, too, must venture into the 'alogical' by abandoning themselves to the poem's rhythmical enchantment. Still, Kane suspends his logical powers only so far. He does not doubt his own ability to analyse the interwoven voice patterns in the poem. He continues to trust in intellectual history, by which he traces a fall from intuitive wholeness into modern disarray. He accepts Heidegger's doctrine of being, which provides the secure 'measure' that Lee seeks in 'Civil Elegies.' But what if confusion extends to all such measures? In that case there is no stable framework within which inconsistency can be set, because that framework, whether logical, psychological, ontological, or social, is itself undermined by the poem's relentless 'rhetoricity.' In this case, as Paul de Man advises: 'Rhetoric is a *text* in that it allows for two incompatible, mutually self-destructive points of view, and therefore puts an insurmountable obstacle in the way of any reading or understanding' (*Allegories* 131). If we read 'Civil Elegies' (and Canada) as the product of incompatible, mutually self-destructive points of view, then we place an insurmountable obstacle in the way of any firm sense of nationhood.

In this third, deconstructive interpretation, inconsistency contaminates all aspects of theme and style, delivery and reception, so that resolving contradictions at one level merely displaces them to another. For example, 'Civil Elegies' continually argues through oxymorons, which by their very nature give ambiguous signals: 'living unlived lives,' 'a passionate civil man,' 'ordinary glory' (33), 'bitter, cherished land' (35), 'real absence' (37), 'living stillness' (39) 'inhuman / yet our *own*' (40), 'greedy / innocence' (42), 'abundant psalm of letting be' (43), 'exile at home' (45), 'willing defeat' (51), 'vacant...occupied' (56). My point is not that these phrases are meaningless, but that they convey too many meanings. How can we navigate through their conflicting and conflated claims in order to decide what the text affirms, or even entertains as the most likely possibility? What authority can we trust? As readers we require either a confident rhetorical presence, such as a character or an authoritative voice, or an embedded interpretive theme such as the Dark Night of the Soul, by which the poem directs its own progress.

I have already suggested that the first strategy is lacking. Lee revised the poem to make its voice more untrustworthy, so that even when he makes (more or less) clear assertions, we cannot be sure how to receive them. In his quest for certain knowledge, he associates certainty with reality (43): he wants to live fully in the presence of the real. But he discovers instead that reality and illusion are interwoven:

What is real is fitful, and always the beautiful footholds
crumble the moment I set my mind aside, though the world does
     recur. (46)

He therefore turns from the fitful world to its opposite, hoping
that the void will be a source of 'regenerative absence' (55). But it
too is beset by inconsistencies. He advocates detachment, because
it is a selfless denuding of the lethal ego (46); yet it is also
supremely selfish, since it puts personal griping before the much
greater agony of history's victims, for example in Vietnam (47). 'Of
high detachment there are many counterfeits' (54), he warns
when faced with a maddening proliferation of voids, some authentic and some factitious. It takes a connoisseur of chaos to distinguish one nothing from another. There is the void of unlived lives,
of history, of spiritual negation, of vapid indifference, of existential
being. There is the void of empire and of complicity with it. There
is 'the lore of emptiness' (53) and the emptiness of learning.
There is the void purgatorial and the void punitive, the void aesthetic and the void delusory. Understandably, Lee had trouble in
finding an idiom to express vacuity, as is illustrated by this excessively cute example, which he excised in revision:

But how do you go to a void? Do you bark your shins on it?
Can you sit on Nonbeing? What about Nothingness?
How many toes does it have? Does it eat corn flakes? (quoted by Robert
     Grant 99)

Stan Dragland gives a useful survey of the species of void proposed
in 'Civil Elegies' and divides them into two 'movements – towards
regenerative void and away from void as abomination' ('On *Civil
Elegies*' 179). He judges that these contrary currents eventually
achieve an 'uneasy tension' in Elegy 9 – a reading that recalls
Kane's treatment of the poem's two voices. I find this analysis consoling but counterproductive. Dragland's ability to maintain moral
distinctions contradicts Lee's claim that to 'honour the void'
('Civil Elegies' 42) means to humbly accept the loss of all measures
and faculties. If we can distinguish kinds of void, then we remain

untouched by it. We fail to honour Lee's paradoxical conclusion that 'void is not a place, nor negation of a place' (56).

If readers cannot trust Lee-the-prophet to interpret his own dark prophecies, they might turn to a master theme. Those familiar with seventeenth-century poetry of meditation and the Dark Night of the Soul, and even those familiar with the Canadian double hook,[27] will not be surprised to learn that the way up is the way down. That is, they will recognize a mystical pattern by which sinking into a spiritual void is part of a painful, redemptive exercise. This conventional pattern might then provide a stable form to control the oxymoronic fury of Lee's meditation. 'Civil Elegies' explicitly recalls this tradition through its Christian imagery and through its portrait of Hector de Saint-Denis Garneau as 'a man made / empty for love of God' (53). However, detecting the pattern and ensuring its efficacy are quite different things. Just as heroic history gives way to farce, so religious faith gives way to idolatry. 'John of the Cross, patron of void' (53) is invoked, but only as a patron for Garneau, not for Lee or for Canada. Whenever Lee is tempted by a transcendent solution to worldly problems, he chastises himself:

> But it is two thousand years since Christ's carcass rose in glory,
> And now the shiny ascent is not for us (41)

This passage illustrates how Lee mocks his own nostalgia for religious solace by summoning a style that diverts him from heaven back to earth. The word 'carcass' is a calculated insult to the religious diction that keeps creeping into the poem. Later he uses the same strategy:

> But we are not allowed to enter God's heaven, where it is all a
> drowsy beatitude, nor is God, the real above our heads but
> must grow up on earth. (56)

Unfortunately, returning to the very earth that Canadians have exploited and betrayed merely complicates the problem by looping into a vicious circle. We 'must grow up on earth,' but the earth in Canada is not our home, and in our voicelessness we again turn to heaven for a consoling word. When Lee struggles to express his own faith, he falls again into oxymoron:

> but I am one who came to
> idolatry, as in a season of God,
> taking my right to be from nothingness. (55)

This passage is ambiguous. It might suggest that religious idolatry is still religious ('a season of God'), just as despair is a lapse within religion, not from religion. It might suggest that faith in the void is idolatrous, since the right to be comes from God, not from nothing. Or it might declare an atheistic, existential faith – in the beginning there was nothing – in which case there are no rights at all.

To pursue the saintly and sickly Garneau is to reject absolutely everything. When T.S. Eliot follows the dark path in 'Ash Wednesday,' he finds the hardest test is not abjuring sin, but relinquishing love, virtue, and the beauties of the world. They too must be lost if the void is to be truly empty. '[H]ow should a man stop caring?' (43), Lee wonders. He finds his answer in Elegy 5, when he realizes that he cannot stop loving children or being incensed when they are slaughtered. The world is still too much with him, and he refuses to abandon it for the sake of his own misery. Although he admires Garneau, he realizes that the path of negation does not fulfil his own needs as poet or citizen. In fact, when he was writing 'Civil Elegies' he also embarked on his career as a writer of children's poetry. I offer this biographical fact not to prove that he really does care for children, but to suggest that, unlike Eliot and Garneau, Lee's devotion to poetry is more inspired by nursery rhyme, play, and childhood wonder than by ascetic denial.[28] This means that the Dark Night of the Soul cannot be used as a measure to settle the poem's oxymoronic logic. The poem can hardly endorse a pattern of experience and meaning that it discovers to be inappropriate. Moreover, Lee's decision remains ambiguous:

> And I will not enter void till I come to myself
> nor silence the world till I learn its lovely syllables (54)

Since the void is an essential part of himself, it is hard to see how he can 'come to' himself by ignoring the void within him. Since the void is also within language – and for the colonial writer especially, 'the *words* of home are silent' (Lee, 'Cadence' 163) – it is hard to see how he can become an authentic poet by ignoring the silence of his world.

The more he tries to clarify his situation, the more obscure it gets, because the means of clarification are themselves disruptive. Here is another self-inflicted injury that Lee makes part of his argument. George Grant taught that modernity distorts civilized instincts so successfully that we can define 'civilized' only in the jaundiced terms supplied by modernity. It prevents us from conceiving of a nation except as one undifferentiated, greedy competitor among others. The liberal ideology of free, objective evaluation engulfs us so completely that we cannot formulate a legitimate criticism of it, because we lack an alternative theoretical ground from which to launch that criticism. 'Modern liberalism has been a superb legitimizing instrument for the technological society, because at one and the same time it has been able to criticise out of the popular mind the general ideal of human excellence and yet put no barrier in the way of that particular idea of excellence which in fact determines the actions of the most powerful in our society ... The tight circle then in which we live is this: our present forms of existence have sapped the ability to think about standards of excellence and yet at the same time have imposed on us a standard in terms of which the human good is monolithically asserted' (*Technology* 129, 131). 'Excellence' is Grant's measure of personal and communal authenticity, but it is virtually unthinkable to the modern mind. His response to this vicious circle is to make the problem as visible as possible by writing a lamentation, whose anguish and irony express his fierce desire for a truer mode of life. In short, he turns to literary expression (notably in *Lament for a Nation*) because he trusts in what I have called the privilege of art to survey the ideology in which it is lodged. Poetry is not only more philosophical than history, as Aristotle advised; it is more philosophical than philosophy.

Since Lee is a poet, we might expect him to venture further

along this trespass of thought. His aim is far more transgressive than Pratt's, because Pratt merely wants to amplify human faculties, whereas Lee takes up Grant's challenge to reformulate modern rationality. He shows what is at stake in his essay 'Reading *Savage Fields*,' where he dares to step outside of liberal ideology into the 'alternative matrix of coherence' (163) that he proposed in *Savage Fields*. He wants to 're-conceive the character of rational coherence – to imagine a different *logos*' ('Reading' 161) in which contradiction and simultaneity would be the rule. With this daring intellectual mutiny, he makes the harshest challenge to the nation to be encountered in this book. He joins a host of critics of very different political stripes who agree in condemning a single conceptual paradigm for the woes of modernity. It is remarkable that radical conservatives, religious conservatives, Marxists, feminists, deconstructionists and post-colonialists agree that all Western thought (with honourable exceptions) follows the same epistemic model, sometimes called metaphysics, or Cartesian analysis, or dialectical thinking, or bourgeois rationalism, or phallologocentrism, or 'the epistemology of European modernity-in-imperium' (Tiffin and Lawson 7). My point is not to deride this condemnation, although I mistrust its reductiveness, but to trace its effects on the nation, which it treats as the poisonous fruit of Western thinking. In his critique of the authoritarian nation, Partha Chatterjee presents a post-colonial protest that clarifies Lee's position as a colonial Canadian: 'From such a perspective, the problem of nationalist thought becomes the particular manifestation of a much more general problem, namely, the problem of the bourgeois-rationalist conception of knowledge, established in the post-Enlightenment period of European intellectual history, as the moral and epistemic foundation for a supposedly universal framework of thought which perpetuates, in a real and not merely a metaphorical sense, a colonial domination' (11). Nationalism is the battle-cry of colonial liberation, but the conception of the nation on which it is based is a monster that will only perpetuate its domination in other forms. 'Nationalist thought has not emerged as the antagonist of universal Reason in the arena of world history,' Chatterjee warns. 'To attain this position, it will need to supersede itself' (168). Liberation requires a counter-discourse that does not fall within 'the ambit of bourgeois-rationalist thought, whether conservative or liberal' (11).

Lee also fears the rational domination of colonial space, but his response, unlike Chatterjee's, is to undertake a quasi-religious penance.[29] He will oppose the voracious national will by relinquishing his own will, until he envisions a new *logos*. He makes three assumptions about this 'alternative matrix of coherence.' First, for all its savagery it will be more ethical than the despotism of Cartesian thought. The hostility of savage fields is a robust, Nietzschean vitality that will liberate us from Descartes's analytical autopsy: 'The villain of the piece is the Cartesian *Cogito,* the consciousness that created the division of subject and object, value and fact which is the ground of liberal thinking. The modern dilemma begins here' (Blodgett, 'Authenticity' 110). Second, the new *logos* is actually very old: it corresponds to 'alogical' poetic thinking, whose prophetic power has long been celebrated by vatic and orphic traditions.[30] Third, poetic thinking reveals and responds to ontological truth. It gives an intimation of pure being, not by reasoning it out discursively, but by resonating with the primary rhythm of being. Lee rhapsodically explains this third point in 'Polyphony':

> To be tuned by cadence is to vibrate with the calamitous resonance of being. And that is what is mimed in the polyphonic voice of [poetic] meditation ... Cadence invites the poem to be, by being.
>
> The poem reaches out to participate in those gestures of being-at-all. (98–9)

Viewed in this light, the falling cadence of 'Civil Elegies' expresses a delving into the vital flux of things.

Art is offered as the ultimate means of insight in 'Civil Elegies,' but it too is embroiled in inconsistencies that vitiate Lee's vision of nationhood. The privilege of art appears specifically in the architecture of Toronto's City Hall, in Henry Moore's sculpture, and in the work of Garneau and Tom Thomson. All testify to what Lee and his nation lack. Viljo Revell's graceful building expresses civil space – what Lee calls 'world' in *Savage Fields*. Moore's massive sculpture expresses primordial space – what he calls 'earth' in *Savage Fields*. Through their art, Garneau and Thomson mediate between the two domains and foresee a 'homecoming' (38) whereby earth and world might coexist. But in true Canadian fashion, their success destroys them. They are beautiful losers whose insights into nature and culture cause them to drown rather than to rise. As Lee's invasive imagery shows, at the very moment of trespass they are penetrated by land (53) and water (41), as if they had indeed stepped out of modernity, only to discover that there was no other place for them to live.

> and you watched the ferns come shouldering up through your body, the
> > brutal ferns in spring it was all
> detachment you hoped, it was
> exquisite penetration, it was
> fear of life, the mark of Canada. (53–4)

In view of their martyrdom, Lee is right when he declines to follow their lead, but he still has to find a viable place of his own.

Precisely how earth and world, Canada and Canadians, are to coexist is a dilemma, since Lee insists in *Savage Fields* that earth and world are utterly distinct and cannot be reconciled, even though they mutually invade and dominate each other (6–8). Observing this situation, Leah Bradshaw contends that Lee gropes for a mystical solution to the logical and moral dilemma raised by his alternative model of understanding: 'What he is suggesting is that we reach out beyond ourselves as world-creatures and embrace the pre-conceptual source of our being: earth. Lee seems to envisage an almost mystical act of forgiveness on the part of earth. Justice requires that we, as world, extend ourselves beyond our experience of phenomena, of what appears, in order to experience the whole within which we are merely one part' (141). Lee haughtily dismissed this view in his reply to Bradshaw ('Reading' 174), but whatever his intent in *Savage Fields,* his argument in 'Civil Elegies' suggests that she may be right. In the poem, his self-recrimination becomes so involuted that he ties a Gordian knot that can be cut only by transcendental surgery.

What is the effect of using a human artefact like Moore's sculpture to represent primordial space? It is an odd choice, perhaps deliberately so. Because of its shape, the piece is commonly called, though not actually named, 'The Archer,' but it is non-representational. It is not a human form, and in the poem it expresses the alien otherness of the Canadian Shield: 'the Archer declares / that space is primal, raw, beyond control and drives toward a / living stillness, its own' (39). As the poem's public persona inspects the raw form, he finds himself pulsing to its cadence, but he makes an unexpected judgment:

> And when it came I knew that stark heraldic form is not
> great art, for it is real, great art is less than its necessity.
> But it held, when the monumental space of the square
> went slack, it moved in sterner space. (39)

The poetic voice speaks confidently here, yet it should not dissuade the reader from asking: why is the Archer *not* great art, if it pierces so authentically to the substratum of Canadian being? Apparently it is too 'real,' too successful in conveying its 'necessity,' which is mere space, pure form. Apparently great art should resist its own rhythmic pull into primal stillness and should defiantly assert human worth in the face of the non-being that underlies all being. In this view, great art is a necessary lie, a resolute fiction. Its greatness lies in refusing to be merely 'real,' and in insisting on some compensating value beyond reality. On the other hand, I have already noted that Lee associates certainty with reality (49) – in which case art must be resolutely uncertain. Furthermore, the Archer is said to be 'heraldic,' and heraldry is a stylized rendering of nature (e.g., a lion rampant) used to dignify human lineage. If the sculpture is heraldic and 'muscled' like an archer, then it is humanized after all – in which case it is 'less than its necessity' and qualifies as great art.

Do I fret too much about inconsistency? Lee might reply: 'If that violates logic, or bends the speaker's nervous system into dismayingly uncomfortable postures, so much the worse for logic and his nervous system' (quoted in Munton 167). If 'Civil Elegies' aims to induce a disorienting ordeal, there is no point in quibbling that it is confusing. My purpose, however, is to chart its inconsistencies until the effort becomes futile, in order to see what poetic futility can achieve. In this case, I note that while my reading of the lines seems justified, it confounds the poem's own argument as well as Lee's philosophical musings elsewhere. Lee seems to accept Heidegger's lesson in 'The Origins of the Work of Art' that art is intimately allied with the truth of being. This intimacy is forged by cadence, which is the rhythm of art resonating with the energy of being. For Lee, the romantic *topos* of the language of nature turns into a primal pulsation that infuses poetic language: 'Cadence impinges as a kind of magnetic din, a silent raucous multiform atmospheric tumult you move around in, very clean though; and *always* – when you perceive it, when you don't. I could write hymns to it, almost' (Lee, 'Polyphony' 90). All poetry is a 'hymn of the fullness of being' (Lee, *Not Abstract* 2) in the sense that it hails or woos or salutes (all Heidegger's terms) authentic being. Thanks to this concurrence of human and cosmic energies, beauty is truth. In this respect, Heidegger is a true romantic: 'Truth is the truth of Being. Beauty does not occur alongside and apart from this truth. When truth sets itself into the word, it appears. Appearance – as this being of truth in the work and as work – is beauty. Thus the beautiful belongs to the advent of truth, truth's taking of its place. It does not exist merely relative to pleasure and purely as its object. The beautiful does lie in form, but only because the *forma* once took its light from Being as the isness of what is' (Heidegger 81). Yet, the counter-argument that I have disclosed suggests Nietzsche's more sceptical view that art is a gorgeous and necessary lie shielding us from truths too dreadful to face. Beauty is the mask of truth, and an imaginary solution to real problems.

> The essential feature in art is its power of perfecting existence, its production of perfection and plenitude; art is essentially affirmation, the blessing, and the deification of existence ...
>
> It is absolutely unworthy of a philosopher to say that 'the good and the beautiful are one'; if he should add 'and also the true,' he deserves to be thrashed. Truth is ugly.

> Art is with us in order that we may not perish through the truth.
> (Nietzsche 264)

Lee told Alan Twigg that he rejected the Nietzchean view that art is 'a compensation for having lost belief in a meaningful cosmos *and* in a higher realm of value' (Twigg 245). Whatever his feelings during this conversation (conducted several years after he wrote 'Civil Elegies'), he incorporates Nietzsche's view as a heretical possibility in his poem, where it joins a series of idolatries. Most interesting for my purposes is the way the two views converge on, or diverge from, Moore's sculpture. It acts as a sort of visible oxymoron. Stan Dragland interprets the Archer much as I do,[31] and then makes a perceptive observation: 'The Archer seems not to have been created by Henry Moore, but by the earth itself, like the Laurentian Shield; it has therefore somehow directly tapped energies almost always outside man's jurisdiction' ('On *Civil Elegies*' 181). Here is a Faustian transgression that makes even 'great art' seem like a feeble delusion. How much greater to confront being and absence directly than to construct a flimsy heraldic fiction! But the price of so great a trespass is too high, as Dragland's final word, 'jurisdiction,' indicates. Lee himself interpreted the passage I have been examining: 'So the Archer *judges* the square by recalling us to our deeper vocation in Canada, of coming to terms with the most primordial processes of earth – with which we really have to live (or fail to live), in that we inhabit a country in which the Shield occupies so much space' (quoted in Munton 156, my emphasis). Like the biblical writing on the wall, the Archer reprimands Canadians by recalling how they might 'come to terms' with the earth. One such term appears in the word 'judges.' Scrupulous judgment is necessary if we are to remedy our plight and find justice for our nation.

> But massy and knotted and still the Archer continues its space,
>   which violates our lives, and reminds us, and has no mercy upon us.
>   ('Civil Elegies' 41)

Lack of mercy is not a sign of indifference but of stern justice (which is also a divine attribute). It is the obverse of the mystical act of forgiveness foreseen by Bradshaw, a forgiveness that Canada has not yet earned. Justice is a measure that she correctly sees as motivating Lee's writing, and when it too is about to be swallowed up by the void, he draws back. As we have seen, he refuses to enter the void because he is unwilling to relinquish justice for children. He also refuses to relinquish justice by admitting that it, too, might be just another heraldic delusion. He refuses to accept what his own meditation has dared to think: that art offers only a dream of justice, a noble lie that ultimately is futile. T.S. Eliot reaches the same self-disqualifying point in *Four Quartets,* when he accepts that 'The poetry does not matter' (*Poetry* 198).[32] By contrast, Lee continues to insist that art does matter, that it is not impotent because it renders its own justice. Its 'necessity' is poetic justice.

I therefore agree with Bradshaw's judgment, although I apply it to 'Civil Elegies' rather than *Savage Fields.* Despite his protestations to the contrary, Lee uses the Archer to reach out to (Bradshaw), or tap into (Dragland) earth – primordial Canada. The Archer sternly embraces the pre-conceptual source of being, but without sacrificing its own standing as a human and humanizing artifice. In a special sense, the sculpture both is and is not an archer. Because it is mere matter made articulate by imagination, it straddles the savage fields and obeys two contradictory 'necessities.' Granted, for Lee everything straddles world and earth, because everything (which he calls 'planet') exists simultaneously within both orders. But art is blessed by its powerful aesthetic duplicity. It is both real and unreal (fictive), superbly necessary (as aesthetic form), and 'less than its necessity.' It judges us mercilessly, yet is an avenue to forgiveness. It condemns us by recalling our failures, but reassures us by prophesying a redemptive state. Through this paradox it transcends the limitations of ordinary discourse to participate passionately in being, meaning, and saying.

I have finally answered the question I posed at the beginning of this section: what retributive principle motivates 'Civil Elegies'? Poetic justice – a redemptive vision of what should be – is the ruling principle. But its rule is not peaceful. It is unsettled by the poem's own heretical suspicion that poetry does not count and affords no real justice. And it is unsettled by history, which also cannot provide the justice that Lee seeks.

Earlier I noted one reading of the poem according to which it successfully subsumes its many confusions within a spiritual quest corresponding to Canadian destiny. Now it seems that the personal quest and the national destiny remain at odds. George Grant taught that 'some form of political loyalty is part of the good life' (*Lament* 4), but Lee has found no avenue for political loyalty and no basis for citizenship. After his ordeal, when he turns back to secular history, he returns to a field of activity that he has made almost as alien as the Canadian Shield. Out of his intricate confusion, he envisages a goal (social and personal authenticity) that cannot be achieved by the practical means of understanding and action available to him. He yearns for an authentic nation so fervently that it takes on a mystical complexion and, as such, transcends history entirely. The problem is that Lee provides no possibility for the *historical* realization of this goal, because he presents history as both inherently tainted (a 'guilty genesis' 48), and as corrupted further by technological modernity. Consequently, he can envision no instances of national excellence that do not rely on conquest and betrayal. America, Britain (48), Germany (47), and even ancient Rome (49) are cited, as if to confirm Walter Benjamin's famous dictum: 'There is no document of civilization which is not at the same time a document of barbarism' (Benjamin 256). If history is written in napalm, why should Canada even try to become 'normal'?

> I am one for whom the world is constantly proving too much –
> nor this nor that, but the continental drift to barbarian
> normalcy frightens me ('Civil Elegies' 49)

The tone and allusiveness of this passage are suggestive. The first line recalls a phrase from Elegy 2 ('I know / the world is not enough' [37]), and is probably meant to echo Wordsworth's sonnet: 'The world is too much with us; late and soon, / Getting and spending, we last waste our powers' (Wordsworth 186). This romantic echo and the ironically prominent Americanism, 'normalcy,' suggest that Lee will find no remedy for his problems in 'the world,' that is, in the normal course of history. Nevertheless, he does not renounce the world. On the contrary, in conversation he rejected romanticism precisely because of its self-indulgent escapism: 'It's an aesthete's solution, a formalist solution, which glorifies the value-imputing imagination of the artist, but at the expense of confirming the devaluation of the real world even further' (Twigg 245). In 'Civil Elegies' he wishes to revalue 'the real world' by establishing a measure that will make honest evaluation possible. At the end he resolves to sink into the Canadian soil, rather than reach up to heaven or retreat into an aesthetic nirvana. Nevertheless, his rhetoric suggests that he still conceives of the 'real world' in metaphysical terms. He concludes with a prayer to the earth intended to allay the despair expressed in an earlier supplication to an absent God (Elegy 2). In the first prayer, 'The poets spoke of earth and heaven' (38). In the second, he speaks only of earth: 'Green of the earth and civil grey' (57). But he speaks in a vocabulary so charged with religious fervour ('Like God like the soul ... like eternity') that, for all his denials, he keeps heaven in view. Only it can provide the valid measure that he seeks. If so, he might welcome another remark in Benjamin's essay: 'To be sure, only a redeemed mankind receives the fullness of its past – which is to say, only for a redeemed mankind has its past become citable in all its moments. Each moment it has lived becomes a *citation à l'ordre du jour* – and that day is Judgment Day' (254). When historiography claims to master its subject fully, it assumes a vantage point beyond history and even beyond narrative (the writing of history). Lee never claims to master history, but he does yearn for a redemptive justice by which, in Bradshaw's words, we might reach beyond ourselves as world-creatures (historical beings) in order to experience the whole within which we are merely one part. We reach beyond history.

Here is the same 'transcendental displacement of human desires' that Jerome McGann attributes to romantic poetry, when it strives 'to effect a unmediated (that is, an aesthetic) contact with noumenal levels of reality' (26, 115). One objection to my interpretation of Lee as a relapsed romantic is that, far from reaching for the stars, he explicitly scorns escapist and other-worldly abstractions. He is no idealist. In 'Polyphony' he insists that the experience of cadence is direct and visceral. In *Not Abstract Harmonies But* he sticks to the grit of reality when he rejects the idealist's cry (echoing Baudelaire) – 'Anywhere! one of us, earlier, cried so long as it is out of this world!' (1). In *The Gods* he hails the 'lethal otherness come clean / in each familiar thing – in / outcrop, harvest, hammer, beast' (6). In 'Civil Elegies' his list of treasures is equally humble: 'water, copout, tower, body, land' (57). This is a poetry of immanence, not transcendence.

In reply I suggest that if we take Lee at his word and accept that poetry is indeed written under the sway of an impersonal cadence, then there is no reason to suppose his poems will behave as he directs them. 'I write to find out what the poem wants to do ... The only target, the magnet, the one thing that exists for you is the thing that is trying to get itself into words, and isn't there yet,' he told Twigg (244). Whatever his protestations in prose, his poetry has a life of its own. It obeys an inner dynamic resonating with a universal vitality that Lee finally calls 'the godforce' (*The Gods* 7). He confesses that he worships cadence because it provokes 'awe, astonishment, delight, trepidation' before the grandest mystery of all ('Polyphony' 95, 96). In other words, both individual poems and poetry as a whole subside into their own inwardness in order to blossom forth magnificently. Once again, the way up is the way down. They sink contemplatively into the particulars of 'the real world' only so that they can eventually attain a vision of transcendent unity. Each familiar thing is a grain of sand that discloses a world:

> once brought to the pitch of itself it longs to
> rest in the after-hum of its own being
> and it resonates with every other thing that is (*Not Abstract* 2)

The 'longing' in the first line again expresses a trespass of thought venturing through silence into the 'after-hum' of the cosmos.[33] This largest reality, which sings like the holy music of the spheres, is not an abstraction, he insists ('Polyphony' 98), but it sounds sus-

piciously like one. Our modern sensibility is so alienated from it
that we must undergo the disruptive ordeal of art just to catch a
faint metaphysical echo:

> I mean
> the hymn of the fullness of being. This is not
> achieved in our lives but it is
> never wholly absent, for always we are
> buzzing on the verge (*Not Abstract* 2)

As we approach the verge, we are left with the question: What has
happened to the utopian nation prophesied in 'Civil Elegies'? At
the end of the poem, an authentic national home remains a pious
hope, but Lee trusts more in piety than in history. He has already
shown that history, especially when pressured by modernity, cor-
rupts the best intentions by turning them idolatrous. He will clarify
this point in 'The Death of Harold Ladoo,' when he laments that
even a noble dream of salvation

> turns demonic, for it too gets cherished as
> absolute.
> ...
> Even that glorious dream
> of opening space to be in, of saying
> the real words of that space –
> that too was false, for we cannot
> idolize a thing without it going infernal,
> and in this season of dearth
> there are only idols. (23)

In fact, Lee's final embrace of the earth in 'Civil Elegies' should
not even be construed as utopian, if utopia is understood as a summation, rather than a transcendence, of history. If utopia is the
delighted prospect of realizing our most civilized instincts and of
overcoming our nastiest social contradictions, then it remains a
historical concept, however difficult it may be to attain. But Lee's
vision of sociability, expressed in religious terms that he cherishes

yet abjures, exceeds the grasp of history. E.D. Blodgett reaches a
similar conclusion by a different route. He argues that Lee tries to
renounce a Platonic metaphysic of presence but actually reinstates
it through his idiosyncratic ontology of savage fields (111). Moreover, he reinstates it at the expense of history: 'The victim of ontology is history, and what is left is *aporia,* impasse, raised to the level
of a metaphysical principle' (116). Lee gives a glimpse of this
divine impasse at the end of *Not Abstract Harmonies But,* when he
speculates about the inscrutable source of the being of being:

> although
> I do not know for what
> and who tunes us – if it can be
> said that way at all – is an endless confusion. (2)

To mark this final confusion in 'Civil Elegies,' which undermines the affirmative tone of its closing lines, is not to judge the
poem a failure. Failure implies an intention that Lee has not adequately achieved according to a standard by which his shortcomings can be measured. I have tried to show that neither intention
nor measure can be confidently ascribed. If his intent is to give a
disturbing portrait of 'Confederation going' (52), then he is successful. If it is to depict 'the crisis of living in a de-valued real
world' (Twigg 245), then he is successful, although one might
question his notion of reality. If it is to devise a 'saner version of
integrity' (56) by which person, language, and nation might coa-
lesce, then he fails to the extent that he simultaneously demonstrates how integrity is always a delusion, whether noble or feeble.
If his purpose is to explore the paradox of living in a nationless
nation (my final oxymoron), then his poem might be judged both
a success and a failure, since the terms become interchangeable.

4. The Nation as Monster

Michelet's work also presents, however ... an alternate vision of the Other, one that expresses both the urgency of the historian's desire to justify and sanctify the historical process and his fear that it may not be possible to do so, that there may be no way to subsume the discontinuous and incomparable individual manifestations of 'life' in a continuous and intelligible pattern – in a word, that history does not make sense.

Lionel Gossman, Between History and Literature

Romantic historiography sets itself the contradictory task of recapturing the past while maintaining its remote uniqueness. The historian has to 'retain distinctions [between past and present] while at the same time affirming unity and continuity' (Gossman 261), but to succeed at the first would mean to fail at the second, and vice versa. On the one hand, a historical text should provide direct access to the lived past; it should be 'the inmost form of the real, binding, and inescapable' (244). On the other hand, historians must respect a 'residual gap' (274) between past and present by refining 'a process of divination or symbolic interpretation' (244), a process that is indirect and mysterious. Gossman claims that for nineteenth-century writers, this paradox raised the fear that history was inconsistent to the point that it did not make sense. Life is messy; history is neat; but the writing of history raises a disruptive anxiety, which often was figured as 'the chthonic, the unbounded, the unstructured, the lawless' (274), or as 'the untamable female ("Circe," "marâtre") beneath the gentle, suckling mother' (275).

Patriotic and literary histories are haunted by a fear that the nation is not a gentle nurse or fatherly genius, but a monstrosity. The very urgency with which nation building was pursued testifies to a suspicion that, however hard one tries to domesticate it, one's home remains alien territory. Something disrupts the heroic task of nation building, not just in the sense that there are unforeseen obstacles, but that there is something in the very idea of the nation that resists historians' efforts to master it. In Jules Michelet's writing, Gossman finds a 'combination of terror, desire, reverence and an exacerbated need for mastery' (274) in view of the 'dreaded, undecipherable underside' (275) of what is supposed to be a rational discipline. The nation is supposed to make sense of history, but if history does not make sense, then what of its main building block?

At the end of chapter 2, I described the nation's dreaded underside as a demon, summoned by Geoffrey Hartman to explain how the *genius loci* can be a lawless energy that disperses identity, as well as a protective spirit. Nation builders recruited poets in their campaign to legitimize a homeland by giving it a past, a destiny, and a voice, only to discover in dismay that poetry also shows why the nation does not make sense. Literature has always been a vital but unreliable ally of ideology because it weakens the social cohesion that it is supposed to promote. It challenges the nationalism in which it is implicated, because its self-interrogating forms put that ideology on critical display. If a national literature encourages ideological equanimity, it also rouses ideological commotion. If it knits people together, it also shows how the knitting was accomplished and at what cost. This view, which is romantic, Marxist, modernist, feminist, and postmodernist in turn, even charms an ascetic deconstructionist such as Paul de Man. He contends that art is privileged by a 'literariness' that exposes the 'discrepancy between truth and method' (*Resistance* 4), or between what I have called poetic justice and literary justness: 'What we call ideology is precisely the confusion of linguistic with natural reality, of reference with phenomenalism. It follows that, more than any other mode of inquiry, including economics, the linguistics of literariness is a powerful and indispensable tool in the unmasking of ideological aberrations, as well as a determining factor in accounting for their occurrence ... It upsets rooted ideologies by revealing the mechanics of their workings' (11).

Following this view, one might rejoice that 'the disassembling eye' (Sedgwick, *Between Men* 15) of art[1] will always triumph over propaganda, because it sees the truth even in a world of lies. I am not so optimistic,[2] but I do believe that a national literature has a double function in keeping with its historical and literary aspects. One of its effects is to build a consensus about what a nation was, is, and aspires to be. It forges a sense of community by articulating the cultural sociability that sustains, or lamentably has failed to sustain, a nation. A contrary effect, however, is to reveal the shifting, partisan nature of the national consensus, especially when it is subject to all the strains of a pluralist society. To the resisting reader, even the most patriotic writing contests the justice of the public forum by showing that the nation is not only the reward for honest labour (Goldsmith), or cooperative ingenuity (Pratt), or scrupulous, philosophical meditation (Lee). It is also an elaborate artifice, a social imaginary convoking people, place, and time. It is a national dream shared by some and imposed on others, a dream that can become obsessive and therefore monstrous. As a model of personal and communal life, the nation can terrify as well as nurture.

In chapter 1 I noted how Lynette Hunter cleverly expresses this dilemma through the paradox of cultivated amnesia. A national canon issues 'the nervous instruction of remembering to forget, that each private individual must carry out to be a subject true to the nation' (16): we must dutifully forget that our nation is an unstable ideological project rather than a sturdy fact of nature. But ironically, the literary weave of those instructions, as enunciated in poetry, fiction, and drama, also teaches us to 'remember the forgotten' (17): careful reading discloses a nervous subtext, a figure in the carpet that reveals how the national fabric was woven, and at whose expense. I will study the novels *Obasan* and *Ana Historic* as exercises in the unweaving of repressed memories, but first I wish to show how the Canadian ghost has turned into a monster.

National Monsters

Issuing nervous instructions (worrying) is all too common in English-Canadian literary history, from E.H. Dewart's anxiety about founding a national canon to Northrop Frye's elegant metaphysical disorientation, 'Where is here?' Frye became especially influential after he detected the 'stark terror' of Canadian poets bewildered by the 'sphinx-like riddle of the indefinite' as posed by their monstrous land (*Bush Garden* 138). The sphinx is Goldsmith's wilderness, Pratt's lizard, and Lee's Void. Its enticing-but-deadly riddle asks how nature can be unnatural, how one's home can be alien, and why, as a consequence, the boundaries of the self seem so amorphous. The monster is utter exteriority: the outer world receding beyond human mastery. And it is utter interiority: the psyche's undecipherable underside. These paradoxes appear in numerous poetic evocations of sinking and drowning, welcoming disaster, wielding the double hook, and embracing the darkness.[3] Even Dennis Lee's children's verse 'The Coat' offers an example: 'I patched my coat with darkness: / That coat has kept me warm' (*Nicholas Knock* 47).

Granted, these themes and images appear in all literature, ancient and modern, and Frye associates their rhythm of ascent and descent with the generic structure of romance. But in Canada, their uncanny combination of terror and promise[4] is associated specifically with the nation. Confronting the terror and releasing its promise become both national themes and aesthetic rewards. They provide a dour justice to Canadians seeking to identify themselves. According to this national ordeal, readers will know themselves only by losing themselves in the riddle of their country, as it is cryptically expressed in their literature. I suggested in chapter 1 that literary justness is partly a function of genre: different kinds of literature envision different systems of adequacy and redress, which offer different satisfactions to the reader. If we follow the Frygian line of argument, which treats Canada as a monstrosity to be entered in fear and trembling, like Jonah being swallowed by the whale (*Bush Garden* 217), then we would expect to find works that fail to fulfil their generic expectations – works like 'The Rising

Village' and 'Towards the Last Spike.' In this view, however, the fact that they fail to deliver exactly what they promise – selfhood, nationhood – testifies to their authenticity as Canadian riddles. The justice rendered by Canadian literature, so to speak, finds the reader guilty of being Canadian. We heard this verdict delivered in 'Civil Elegies.'

The nation-as-monster serves as a structural motif in literary histories, where it expresses the complex fate of a country never quite at home in its own place. It appears as the bush engulfing the garrison with a saving ferocity in Jones's *Butterfly on Rock* (1970), as the 'ice women' in Atwood's *Survival* (1972), and as the anxious shifting of perspectives and identities in McGregor's *The Wacousta Syndrome* (1985). For all their differences, these studies quite conventionally continue the nationalist tradition of charting the growth of 'the Canadian imagination' in its quest for authenticity. They treat the national imagination as an evolving spiritual/psychological/social form, and never doubt that it is a valid subject of analysis. Disrupting its growth are dangerous forces, at first identified with brutal nature, then with a paralysing puritanical society, and then with neocolonial and patriarchal subservience. To develop authentically, Canada must come to terms with its secret self, although just what those terms are varies from writer to writer. Canadians – that is, puritanical, colonial, English-Canadian settlers – must immerse themselves in what Gossman calls the chthonic, lawless energy that torments yet sustains their national being. Literary history thus serves as a squire assisting Canadian literature on its quest to confront the national monster.

In these three studies, which I treat as more or less the fruition of traditional English-Canadian literary history, literature serves a therapeutic purpose. It diagnoses an infection in the Canadian psyche and recommends a cure through an advance from dejection to courage (Jones), a sequence of victim positions (Atwood), or a growing talent for compromise (McGregor). These psychological, moral, and social progressions may appear within individual works or in the developing corpus of Canadian writing. Its progressive sociability is also aesthetic in character because Canadian literature is supposed to grow increasingly artful by developing 'a new and distinctively Canadian style of writing' (McGregor 75). We are in familiar territory here, where social authenticity, literary merit, and national purpose all vouch for each other. But the Canadian monster, which must be slain in a mythological ordeal, is still 'our' monster. As our national subconscious, it is a persistent and even essential aspect of the country. Therefore to vanquish it would be oddly self-defeating, since we would thereby destroy our distinctiveness. Instead, the monster must be respected and preserved. The physical and imaginative frontier, which it represents, must be kept 'perpetual' (Morton 72), so that writers can continually pit themselves against it in order to confirm their divided identity. They must obsessively re-enact the primal encounter between humanity and inchoate nature: 'As a result of this mechanism, even generations removed from the real wilderness the *form,* if no longer always the *content,* of Canadian consciousness is still derived explicitly from the peculiar relation between the northerner and his environment. The resulting structure, in both graphic and logical variants, permeates Canadian art and literature' (McGregor 77). This quotation illustrates McGregor's debt to the environmentalist 'frontier thesis' developed by Frederick Jackson Turner in the United States and applied with some strain to Canadian history.[5] For many years it dominated English-Canadian literary history and, after a period of disdain in the 1970s and 1980s, it has begun to reappear, suitably revised, in ecological studies such as D.M.R. Bentley's *The Gay]Grey Moose* (1992).

However, many Canadian writers were never shaped by a northern mystique. They have not had to 'cut the umbilical cord to the wilderness,' as Hugh Kenner advised (207), because their national ties lie elsewhere. Himani Bannerji, who was born in Bangladesh (then East Pakistan), in effect replies to Kenner in her poem, 'A Letter for Home.' She, too, seeks a Canadian home, but she faces a different monster:

> I still have a stake on this land
> It is true that I have walked a long way
> carrying an earthen jar
> With the ashes of my ancestors, earth from my land,

some grains and oil, and my cast off umbilicus.
I have buried this urn here
under my hearth, and built a fire
that I feed daily, and watch the shapes
gather and give me the news
from the other world. (*A Separate Sky* 24)

The transplanted umbilicus is a startling reworking of familiar immigrant imagery. It illustrates how themes associated with traditional Canadian literature are radically recast in ethnic writing. The calamities of emigration, exile, and dislocation persist, but they arise from national and racial differences, not from venturing into the wilderness, whether physical or metaphysical. A fearful 'otherness' persists, too, but it has different sources. For example in South Asian–Canadian poetry: 'This outsider is painfully aware of the contradictions that the cement of a homogeneous ideology carefully conceals from a full-fledged member of the dominant group. Consequently, South Asian poets write less about man's response to nature, the woes of age and death, the joys and pains of sexual love, and other such staples of poets through the ages, and more about racism, poverty, discrimination, colonial exploitation, imperialism, and ideological domination' (Mukherjee 53).

I suspect that Canadian ideology is less homogeneous than Arun Mukherjee suggests here, but there is no denying that it can be violently exclusive. Ethnic literature presents Atwood's key theme of survival, but predators and prey are redefined by injustice and racism, so that 'the theme itself now shift[s] from mere survival to something like "survival under oppression"' (Sugunasiri 35). To writers such as Bannerji and Suwanda Sugunasiri, the oppressive terror associated with Canada is found in the city and in civil institutions rather than in the bush. The battles between 'inside' and 'outside' are refigured as family and communal disputes, which arise when immigrants are urged to assimilate yet scorned when they try to do so. Monstrosity appears in the hypocritical way that hatred pervades a bland social setting. Immigrant stories often depict a hellish scene in the midst of mundane reality, a scene revealing the cruelty that underlies official claims of tolerance and liberty. Examples include the infernal boiler-room episode in John Marlyn's *Under the Ribs of Death*, the grotesque cultural mismatches in Mordecai Richler, the sepulchral Toronto of Austin Clarke's stories, and Bannerji's own portrait of an 'alien street' viewed as if through 'the reverse end of a telescope' in 'The Other Family' (141–2). Such horrifying scenes expose two conflicting demands: a 'multicultural ossificatory imperative,' which segregates people in fixed stereotypes, and an 'assimilative imperative,' which obliterates real cultural differences (Bannerji, 'The Other Family' 148). Like a mythological monster, the nation both petrifies and consumes. But it is no longer 'our' monster in the awful but redemptive way that it was for Jones, Atwood, and McGregor. Now there is no way to wear its dark coat.

Exclusion and assimilation are also strategies of containment in literary history. Ethnic writers complain that their work has been either ignored or travestied by mainstream critics, partly because it does not share the frontier mystique, but ultimately because it does not serve what Joseph Pivato calls a 'federalist interpretation of Canadian literary history' (21):

> Both the view of history and the reading of literature have neglected the institutions, ideas, values and folklore that immigrants brought from Europe and other countries.
>
> The search for a single unifying myth in Canadian writing has its counter parts [*sic*] in the federalist quest for national unity, and in the clear anglocentrism of Canadian History and the anglo-conformism of Canadian Studies ... The price for the lack of anglo-conformism is the possibility of being marginalized, or being ignored and forgotten. (26)

Viewed in this way, the obsessive pursuit of national identity is no longer an existential ordeal, but a way of excluding writers who are haunted by different ancestral ghosts, and whose stories depict the nation, not as a precious, public space carved out of the wilderness, but as a battleground of conflicting loyalties. Even when ethnic writers are welcomed into the Canadian canon, they are assigned eccentric roles that render them humorous or harmless. Ethnic humour is often a devious expression of powerlessness, and even multiculturalism, which has been welcomed as democratic by some ethnic and Native writers (Parameswaran 89–90, Agnes Grant 125), is rejected as coercive by others because, however generous its intentions, it eventually rewrites the colonizing discourse that it claims to reject. It welcomes diversity, but only within the old hierarchy. For Donna Bennett, 'multiculturalism does encourage some understanding between cultures, but it also keeps cultures separate and allows them to be identified as Other. By institutionalizing multiculturalism, Canada has encouraged identity through alterity. In doing so, it has effectively institutionalized marginality, an action that is always associated with postcolonialism' ('English Canada's' 193–4). Here, the ethnic is deprived of independent social agency by being relegated, ever so politely, to the sidelines. For Smaro Kamboureli, 'The possibility of ethnicity becoming a compulsory or inescapable label in a state with an official multicultural policy submits familial genealogies, or biologism, as a prerogative for subjectivity, thereby failing to furnish the subject in question with agency, or limiting that agency within an environment that might be exclusively constructed by displacement. Posited that way, ethnicity runs the risk of becoming a master narrative of marginalization that subordinates the subject's present condition to its past roots, which are privileged because of their "authenticity"' ('Canadian Ethnic Anthologies' 27–8). Here, ethnicity is pushed out of history into folklore or myth, where its roots are 'authentic' but petrified. A multicultural environment 'constructed by displacement' is only a more subtle form of control. It enforces a sociability that makes ethnic writers seem ungrateful if they do not accept the rules that define them as subordinate.

National ghost and monster are transformed further in feminist studies, where the tables are turned on the romantic historicist fear of 'the untamable female.' Now the monstrous nation is redefined as patriarchy. The familiar themes of frontiers, borders, victims, and predators still express shifting configurations of power and knowledge, but the terms are all redeployed. Now male-dominated society is 'the engulfing monster,' whereas nature offers refuge, freedom, or renewal to female victims (Annis Pratt

161–2). In this analysis the nation does not disappear, but becomes all the more important as a site of rebellion. Instead of meekly accepting the minor place assigned to them in the civil forum, women contest the nation by reconfiguring it. That is, they vie for control of both the social/literary territory and the discursive means of defining that territory. Susan Jackel reports that '[f]eminist consciousness in Canada grew up side by side with national consciousness, emerging as the social-reformist or maternal feminism that historians see as the norm in this country' (99). Early feminism was well domesticated. As it grew less ladylike, its alliance with nationalism was complicated rather than abandoned. Feminist interests never eclipsed national ones, but became increasingly entangled with them as the critical strategies of exclusion and incorporation, which previously had disqualified feminist views, were turned to ironic advantage. Previously, Jackel advises, 'women in Canada have all too often seen their efforts towards equality and independence swallowed up by "the national interest"' (108). But now feminism displays its own national character, so that women should not 'accept uncritically theories – even feminist theories – evolved elsewhere, without reference to Canadian experience or Canadian texts' (109). Through a strategic reversal, nationality can be recruited in the feminist cause. Lorraine Weir reaches a similar conclusion.

> If women's texts are to the texts of patriarchy as Canada is and was to America and Britain, then it will not surprise us that much of the best writing in Canada exemplifies the strategies, and often the thematics as well, of women's texts – a metonymic polarity which is even more obvious in the relationship of Québécois writing to Anglo-Canadian. Prolonged experience of material and psychic colonization utters itself through textual violence, whether the introjected violence of deflective irony and decentring or the readerly violence of private parallax, partial revelation, the hidden subtext: strategies which demand the shared response of the designated community. (Weir, 'Toward a Feminist Hermeneutics' 68)

Where W.D. Lighthall praised a healthy 'virility' in Canadian writing (xxi), Weir finds a feminized counter-violence that subverts the master-narratives of traditional literary history. Yet her own argument, as illustrated here, employs the same tactics as earlier Canadian studies – the tactic of positioning Canada between Britain and the United States; of tracing the perverse effects of colonialism and violence; of aligning literary merit ('the best writing') with political purpose; of conflating psychological and cultural dilemmas; of distinguishing personal text from social subtext; of fostering a cultural community. All the familiar terms have shifted in accordance with a hermeneutic that criss-crosses feminist and national discourses.[6]

Finally, the metamorphosis of nation-as-mother into nation-as-monster appears in its most distressing form in Native writing. It offers the greatest rebuke to Canadian literary history, whose methods and models have been positively hostile to indigenous nations. It is astonishing that reverence for 'the native,' which inspired the nation building dreams of romantic historicism, was accompanied in the Americas by such contempt for actual Natives. As we have seen, Wilfred Eggleston saw no inconsistency in cultivating a 'strictly *native* literature' (2) whose spirit and philosophy would be 'European, certainly not Indian, or anything else' (30). This cultural eviction repeats Goldsmith's triumphant banishing of Natives from 'The Rising Village,' even though historically they continued to live only a few miles away. From the perspective of the 1990s, this irony is multiplied many times. The familiar lexicon of terms like 'New World,' 'garrison,' 'frontier,' 'settlement,' and 'ordeal' is charged with irony as soon as European colonials are recognized as colonizers. Then the purgatorial ordeal by which they embrace their nation's secret self becomes an elaborate exercise in self-deception. For example, the theme of survival is cruelly reversed in Maria Campbell's *Halfbreed*, where all the traditional sources of terror (nature, the outside, Native families and customs) become precarious refuges for Campbell; whereas all the sources of comfort (city, school, church, government) become oppressive. 'My Cheechum used to tell me that when the government gives you something, they take all that you have in return – your pride, your dignity, all the things that make you a living soul.

When they are sure they have everything, they give you a blanket to cover your shame. She said that the churches, with their talk about God, the Devil, heaven and hell, and schools that taught children to be ashamed, were all a part of that government' (159). From a Métis point of view 'Canadian literature' is itself a blanket covering a dreadful secret. It is an open secret, however, continually disclosed by poets such as Goldsmith and Pratt, who make an imaginative pilgrimage back to the moment of national origin, only to reveal its underlying shame. Even the blurb on the Goodread Biographies edition of *Halfbreed* repeats the displacement of Natives by announcing sympathetically: 'This extraordinary account, written by a young Métis woman, opens the door to a little-known world that coexists alongside Canadian society.' Unfortunately, the wording implies that Métis society is not Canadian.

The Unjust Society

The irony extends deeper. Not just customary themes and attitudes, but the formative principles of nationalist historicism prove to be conceptual blankets. Throughout this study I am drawing on Hayden White's intriguing suggestion that in both narrative form and political content, post-Hegelian historiography is motivated by justice, which serves as the chief principle of intelligibility to assess human affairs, social order, historical causality and advance, as well as artistic form. Histories are written in order to chart social and moral directions, or to express frustration at their misdirection. History is implicitly the story of justice or, more problematically, of injustices that must be corrected according to corrective standards that are themselves historically produced and – an important corollary – that can be artistically interrogated. For cultural theorists of different persuasions, artistic form is a privileged item in the above list because it illuminates all the rest. Literary forms have their own standards of adequacy and satisfaction, their own precarious equilibrium or thrilling imbalance, their own jurisprudence (and imprudence). Such forms are aesthetically pleasing because they feel 'right,' although resisting readers can always refuse their assurance that justice has been done; they can refuse to agree, for instance, that marriage is a happy ending, or that the conquest of the Americas was a glorious exploit. As we have seen, ethnic and feminist criticism appeals to another court for redress, which means that justice is still very much at issue. For both compliant and resisting readers, however, rightness in its aesthetic sense is interfused with rightness in its ethical and legal senses. The degree and complexity with which they are interfused will vary from genre to genre. When readers are enticed to admire a wicked anti-hero, then they may gauge the tension between justice and justness in horror, bewilderment, or delight. When their judgments are split by hybrid, ironic, or parodic forms, then they are entangled in the paradox that literature can be right in one sense by being wrong in another. Oscar Wilde provided my earlier example of this teasing dilemma: 'The good ended happily, and the bad unhappily. That is what Fiction means' (367). What happens if Wilde's moral is applied to *Halfbreed* and to Métis history? Its mischief no longer sounds so playful. It might even be argued that when Campbell employs conventional forms like the memoir or *Bildungsroman*, her use of them must be parodic, because they express notions of personal identity and development derived from a culture alien to her own.[7] Her book displays a continual structural irony because her life does not fit comfortably into the conventional mould of her life-story. The injustices that she has suffered cannot be redressed by the rhetorical comforts of her narrative.

If national literary history is a discourse preoccupied with justice – with the authority, justification, and threat of the law, as Hayden White advises (13) – then reviewing it from a Native perspective turns the settling of Canada into an unsettling experience. For Jeannette C. Armstrong, the invasion of Canada has been a tale of injustice:

> In the 498 years of contact in The Americas, the thrust of this bloody sword has been to hack out the spirit of all the beautiful cultures encountered, leaving in its wake a death toll unrivalled in recorded history. This is what happened and what continues to happen.
>
> There is no word other than totalitarianism which adequately describes the methods used to achieve the condition of my people

today ... With the loss of cohesive cultural relevance with their own peoples and a distorted view of the non-Native culture from the clergy who ran the residential schools, an almost total disorientation and loss of identity occurred. The disintegration of family and community and nation was inevitable, originating with the individual's internalized pain. (208)

For Armstrong, European settlement in Canada prospered only at the expense of her own nation. The injustice is not just that Native culture was suppressed but that it was 'blanketed' in the sense of being effaced from history. Natives were regarded not only as 'primitive' but as prehistoric, as if their lives had not yet attained true historical dignity. Celebrated in myth, they were barred from history. Hegel declared that America was not yet 'in' history, because it had not attained an authentic historical consciousness of its own: 'What *has* taken place in the New World up to the present time is only an echo of the Old World – the expression of a foreign Life' (*Philosophy of History* 87). History begins with Columbus or Cartier, when written records replaced oral traditions. Armstrong argues from the opposite perspective, as does Fanon when he warns that colonized people will remain intellectually and practically immobilized until they write themselves back into history. Specifically, they must recognize their own national history: 'The immobility to which the native is condemned can only be called in question if the native decides to put an end to the history of colonization – the history of pillage – and to bring into existence the history of the nation – the history of decolonization' (Fanon 40). For Armstrong, Canada is an unjust society[8] built through a history of pillage. Literature, too, has been a means of pillaging her culture, whose national integrity she wishes to reassert.

A second principle of nationalist historicism is sociability, which is the power to promote concord and intimacy in a shared national life. This principle is served generously by literature, because it is itself sociable in the sense of convoking a common understanding and response. Reading may be a solitary activity, but it joins readers in interpretive communities. To insist on a point made several times: cultural and rhetorical sociability is only one effect of national literature. It is opposed by a critical counter-current, which unmasks coercive ideologies such as nationalism. If the first effect unifies, the second diversifies. As we have seen, the relative force of these two currents shifts from E.H. Dewart, who trusts 'the subtle but powerful cement of a patriotic literature' (ix), to Frank Watt, who praises literature for articulating Canadians' consciousness of themselves, including their virtues and depravities (236), to Robert Lecker, who worries that the lack of a Canadian canon threatens to deprive the nation of 'consensus, community, social responsibility, and ultimately ethical challenge' ('A Country' 7). A country without a canon – even a temporary canon subject to revision and derision – will lack the sociability even to undergo a genuine identity crisis. From Armstrong's perspective, however, Canadian literature is afflicted by a more fundamental legitimation crisis. It is monstrously unsociable ('totalitarian'), and betrays its own professed goal when it builds one nation by destroying another. White society has always bolstered itself by disrupting Native communities – for example, by taking children from their families and confining them to residential schools, where they were forbidden to speak their own languages or learn about their own cultures. Starting with the earliest travel journals,[9] Canadian literature has either excluded Native society or incorporated it in white mythology.

Exclusion and assimilation are subtly interdependent. In the Americas, the settler culture forcibly excludes Native culture, but then evokes images of the displaced nation in order to affirm its own legitimacy in the 'New World.' I noted how national literatures oscillate between history and myth, usually by dramatizing the transitional moment when myth lapses into history or history rises into myth. Alide Cagidemetrio contends that, in the United States, the agent of this 'translation of myth into national history' (27) is often the Native, who confers an ancestral blessing on the modern nation by dutifully receding into an ancient 'time of nature.' 'The lesson of the past becomes, then, the ahistorical sanction of sameness, [the blessing of myth] which in its turn legitimizes the American nation's historical right to be different: the Indian as alien is turned into Native American, where native stands for the land, a geographical entity, but also for the new nation, as its symbolic natural ancestor. The last of the Mohicans can die ... but only after bequeathing land and culture for the realization of a better nation' (28). The 'vanishing American' confers legitimacy on the new nation, but only by vanishing. As long as the meeting of cultures is played out as an asymmetrical confrontation between history (white) and myth (red), this injustice will be repeated even when it is not intended. For example, English-Canadian writers who clothe the *genius loci* in Native dress aim to blend the two worlds so that both will benefit. Douglas Le Pan envisages a truly Canadian sociability when he pictures Louis Riel in frock coat and moccasins. But in his bicultural emblem, the two cultures are not integrated justly. Riel wore the outfit 'when he would receive official visitors at Fort Garry as the leader of the provisional government of the Northwest in 1869' (Le Pan 4). Since his government was very provisional indeed, and the real seat of power was in Ottawa, the lesson of his symbolic wardrobe is that Native customs must adapt to European institutions. The moccasins are merely decorative tokens.[10] Native society is still being blanketed, even though the blanket bears a Native design.

Non-Native writers who go so far as to reject Canadian institutions and to embrace the Native world as a compensating source of value face the same problem. As Leslie Monkman shows, where white writers once rejected the Native world as depraved or unchristian, now they embrace it with a fervour that can be equally destructive. They claim authenticity for their nation by forging a spiritual kinship with the people they have displaced, but without recognizing that their self-possession as Canadians is the fruit of an ongoing dispossession: 'the Indian is no longer a foil for white culture but rather an indigenous ancestor in a land where the white man is still an immigrant. Red heroes fill the vacuum created by the absence of white aboriginal traditions on this continent, and the dream of a distinctive national literature focuses on the history and heritage of the red man. In Indian myths and legends, white writers find a new understanding of the landscape and its gods and discover rhythms, images, and structures that enable them to communicate in a new and powerful idiom' (Monkman 5). White culture seeks a legitimizing bond with Natives, but only by banishing them to a mythical past that artfully obscures injustices continuing in the present.[11] Ironically, this problem reproduces itself through the very effort through which critics would solve it. To a Native writer such as Kimberly M. Blaeser, even the most self-conscious multicultural studies offer critical restitution only by appealing to theories – from Levi-Strauss, Bakhtin, Derrida, or Deleuze – that remain embedded in the same Western values they would renounce:

> While I believe these theories ... have been helpful, they still have the same modus operandi when it comes to Native American litera-ture. The literature is approached with an already established theory, and the implication is that the worth of the literature is essentially validated by its demonstrated adherence to a respected literary mode, dynamic or style ... [A]lthough they do contribute to an understanding of the native literary character, they actually do proceed from and reinforce an understanding of the dominant position of the Euro-American aesthetic, constructing their own identity as they do by its relationship to that master template (Blaeser 55–6, 57).

To ethnic, feminist, and Native writers, the bourgeois nation is a monster, an ideological aberration to be corrected, rather than a natural habitation. But corrected on behalf of what alternative? What new vision of community and citizenship is to replace it, and what sort of literature will speak for its improved sociability? In order to pursue these questions I will examine two novels that dis-member and re-member the nation, in keeping with Lynette Hunter's maxim that literature teaches us to recall what ideology teaches us to forget. Hunter cites Marx and Freud on cultural amnesia, but she might also have appealed to Ernest Renan, who claimed that nations are unified only by carefully suppressing their formative discord: 'Forgetting, I would even go so far as to say his-torical error, is a crucial factor in the creation of a nation ... Unity is always effected by means of brutality ... Yet the essence of a nation is that all individuals have many things in common, and also that they have forgotten many things. No French citizen knows whether he is a Burgundian, an Alan, a Taifale, or a Visigoth, yet every French citizen has to have forgotten the massacre of Saint Bartholomew, or the massacres that took place in the Midi in the thirteenth century' (11). Error, in the sense of deviation, is not only a theme but a structural principle in *Obasan* and *Ana Historic*, which illustrate Lionel Gossman's paradox that historians must build a coherent nation out of brutal historical incoherence. These unconventional novels remain traditional in at least one respect: they continue to treat Canada as a riddle to be entered imaginatively rather than solved rationally. For both, history is not merely erroneous and so subject to correction. History *is* error, in the sense of *errare*, to wander.[12] Perversely, both works rely on wandering forms to set things right – where rightness again involves a merging of personal self-possession, social justice, and aesthetic satisfaction. Their aberrant styles ensure that error will be unavoidable, because deviation is the norm in which right and wrong are interwoven.

Joy Kogawa, *Obasan* (1981)

> *'Milk and Momotaro?' I asked. 'Culture clash?'*
> *'Not at all,' she said. 'Momotaro is a Canadian story. We're Canadian, aren't we? Everything a Canadian does is Canadian.'*
>
> Joy Kogawa, *Obasan*

What makes a story Canadian? One reason that the nation is such a worrisome topic is that, the more heated arguments about nationality grow, the more quickly they become circular. They define a nation as a group of people who feel they belong to the same nation. A circular account need not be unavailing, however, depending on how the circle is drawn. For instance, Julia Kristeva proposes a national discourse following a 'transitional' (40) or 'serial' (42) logic that never fixes a national essence, but instead circles through an 'identifying space' continually being redrawn in the light of its historical lineaments as they continue to change. The nation confers a '*historical identity* with relative *steadiness* (the tradition) and an always prevailing *instability* in a given topicality (subject to evolution)' (56). Joy Kogawa insists on one such instability until her topic literally explodes at Nagasaki. *Obasan* asks what it mean to be Canadian and how all citizens can be equally Canadian when they have various national origins that, despite Canada's democratic claims, are ordered hierarchically. Some stories are deemed more Canadian than others.

In practical terms Kogawa redraws the national space by rewriting the ethnic novel of immigration and assimilation. This century-old North America genre explores the cultural clash common to all immigrant experience, which it dramatizes as a conflict of generations within a family painfully adapting to a new world. According to convention, this pain is therapeutic: it expresses a loss of self necessary to create a new and stronger national identity. By 1981, when *Obasan* was published, the genre had well-established narrative patterns (uprooting, travel, entry, dispersal), themes (exile, betrayal, metamorphosis), and character types (heroic ancestors, degenerate offspring, rootless grandchildren). The family drama is usually played out in three acts, which present: the grandparents, who venture into an alien land; the parents, who flounder between two worlds; and the grandchildren, who seek a just balance of old and new. Impelling the drama is a quasi-mystical reverence for place (old country, new world) as sustained by memory, kinship, property, and language. Such novels are therefore about self-possession: how the ethnic self knows, situates, and articulates itself in the course of its dislocation.

This genre illustrates nicely how history is read in accordance with a literary typology. History does not fall neatly into generations, since people are being born all the time, and decisions about how to group them by generation depend on various moral, social, or even mythological functions. The chief aim of generational rhetoric, Werner Sollors explains, is to forge national identity out of ethnic diversity. 'It is when Americans speak of generations, numbered or unnumbered, that they easily leave history and enter "the myth of America." Apparently talking about lineage, they are actually inventing not only a sense of communal descendants – the coming generation so much worried about – but also a metaphoric

ancestry in order to authenticate their own identity' (234). As we
have seen, the permeable border between history and myth is the
place of nation building. In that identifying yet mystifying space,
generational rhetoric serves as a 'community-building device' (Sollors 234) through which the so-called third generation become
'true' Americans. Unlike their bewildered parents, they can reconcile ethnic past with American future. They affirm steadiness in the
midst of instability, and vice versa. Since everyone can be viewed as
third generation, however, (just start numbering two generations
back) America itself is validated as the historical fulfilment of a
moral struggle: 'We may thus create an independent self in the
name of America or a modern identity in the name of ethnicity.
Typologically speaking, a self-declared third generation represents
the antitype, the redemptive fulfillment of types, of original ancestors (real or adopted)' (230). Generational rhetoric is thus a
means of ideological control and self-justification. It soothes the
pain of assimilation, which is made to appear historically inevitable, socially just, and morally right.

   The family drama expresses assumptions that perhaps were
stronger in the United States than in Canada, especially the
assumption that assimilation is a good, if painful, thing. It is desirable and, in any case, necessary. If assimilation requires a betrayal
of past ways, then it is an exhilarating betrayal because it secures a
freer world. It legitimizes the new world by making it 'new.'[13] If
ethnicity and nationality offer competing styles of self-possession,
then assimilation offers a sure, if bumpy, path between them.
Resisting such optimism, however, is a more sombre convention.
Ethnic novels frequently criticize America by exposing its grand
promises as false, its values as shallow and materialistic in contrast
to firmer ethnic values. Immigrant literature is usually about disil-
lusionment. According to an old Yiddish pun, America is the home
of 'am reka,' the hollow people. The generational drama is one way
of allaying these fears by confining them to a family setting, where
they can be worked through to a satisfactory conclusion. Representing the nation as a squabbling family is a version of the rhetorical figure that treats the nation as a single person – Uncle Sam or
John Bull. Within a national family, differences can be recognized

and even indulged because they will always rest on the common ground of kinship. However misguided your family/nation might be, it is still yours, and you therefore have the right to correct its course.

Obasan acknowledges all of these conventions, but uses them in unexpected ways. It, too, studies three generations (Issei, Nisei, Sansei) in relation to a protective maternal figure. It uses images of dismemberment to express the fragmenting of identity through a blending of realism and phantasmagoria – a conventional fusion of styles.[14] But *Obasan* does not endorse the optimistic forging of nationality through assimilation. Instead it brings both nationality and assimilation into question, although it does not rule them out. Canadian society is shown to be, among other things, hypocritical, cruel, discriminatory, and racist. What is the virtue of assimilating to such a society, especially if it means betraying the virtues of Japanese culture, which earlier sections of the novel present so lovingly? Seen from a child's point of view, Japanese culture is ruled by decorum, tradition, and community: 'The train is full of strangers. But even strangers are addressed as "ojisan" or "obasan," meaning uncle or aunt ... It is always so. We must always honour the wishes of others before our own. We will make the way smooth by restraining emotion. Though we might wish Grandma and Grandpa to stay, we must watch them go. To try to meet one's own needs in spite of the wishes of others is to be "wagamama" – selfish and inconsiderate. Obasan teaches me not to be wagamama by always heeding everyone's needs' (112, 128). This passage clarifies the difference between self-denial and denial of self. Japanese tradition teaches self-restraint for the benefit of the community, whereas Canadian society, caught up in the propaganda of the Second World War, requires the suppression of all Japanese practices. As the novel proceeds, the Japanese community is dispersed, its generous sociability disrupted by systematic antagonism. Stephen is the character who most clearly pays the cost of cultural self-suppression. He rejects Japanese food (115, 153) and literature (217); he studies only Western music (214); he is 'always uncomfortable when anything is "too Japanese"' (217). He is 'a young man with a future' (214) who is ashamed of his past. *Obasan* asks why an ethnic group should forfeit its own traits when there is so little compensation for the loss. How much conformity is necessary for a nation to remain cohesive?

In traditional immigrant novels, assimilation is both the problem and the solution. It inflicts a wound that is healed by its own suffering. *Obasan* problematizes this cure; or, stated more accurately, *Obasan* illuminates a problematic that is already lodged within, but pacified by, the conventions of classic immigrant novels. Assimilation is demanded of Japanese immigrants yet also made impossible, because they are a visible minority, because they are Asian rather than European, and because of the war with Japan. The younger generation, like Naomi and Stephen, who dutifully learn the lessons of Canada, are still treated as foreigners. The more successfully they acculturate themselves, the more suspicions they arouse. Even though they are Canadian citizens, they are regarded as dangerous outsiders who must be interned within their own country. *Obasan* continually uses the territorial configuration of outside/inside to explore the ideology of assimilation.[15] It speaks of internment, invasion, infection, infraction, intrusion – of the outside breaking in and the inside breaking out. The Japanese are required to assimilate, but mistrusted when they do. Assimilation is not a cure but a punishment. By being interned, they are segregated within and so in effect kept out. Stephen later inverts this process by internalizing Western culture so successfully that he becomes a stranger to himself. 'We won, we won,' he shouts when the war ends (168), not recognizing the multiple ironies of his own words. As I noted at the beginning of this book, the question 'Who are "we"?' haunts Canadian literature, which continually proposes, displaces, and effaces cultural communities. One village rises; another falls; a third is shunted aside. Stephen knows instinctively that he is Canadian like the rest of 'us,' but his instincts are not sufficient to overcome the foreignness that he bears within himself.

Romantic nationalism proclaims that nations are rooted instinctively in a native soil. Place and the spirit of place are essential. Similarly, ethnic literatures evoke a passionate sense of place that sets people within defining communities and grants them self-possession. 'We' know who we are because we know where we belong – in this house, on this street, in this neighbourhood, in this city, in this country. But in *Obasan*, as in other works of Canadian literature, place is continually being displaced (Where is here?) and degraded. As the Japanese community is dispersed, family homes are replaced by hut, shack, and hovel (121, 191, 194). Characters are caught in the riddle of being simultaneously inside and outside their own country:[16]

> The girl with the long ringlets who sits in front of Stephen said to him, 'All the Jap kids at school are going to be sent away and they're bad and you're a Jap.' And so, Stephen tells me, am I.
> 'Are we?' I ask Father.
> 'No,' Father says. 'We're Canadian.'
> It is a riddle, Stephen tells me. We are both the enemy and not the enemy. (70)

The riddle of national identity finds its most disturbing expression in the episode where Naomi is molested and then gives herself willingly to the molester. 'If I tell my mother about Mr. Gower, the alarm will send a tremor through our bodies and I will be torn from her. But the secret has already separated us. The secret is this: I go to seek Old Man Gower in his hideaway. I clamber unbidden onto his lap. His hands are frightening and pleasurable. In the centre of my body is a rift' (64–5). In this instance the inner space is explicitly female. Throughout *Obasan*, Japanese culture is symbolically marked as female through its association with house, water, hot bath, hen, egg, earth, the threatened women in fairy tales, and, of course, Obasan herself. The intrusion from outside is now a rape, corresponding to the violation of Japanese Canadians during the war. But the violation (the tearing of flesh) is also welcome (a tremor of flesh), a source of pleasure and of dreadful self-discovery. The confusion of inside and outside becomes a blending of fear and enjoyment, which I interpret as expressing the secret, painful intimacy of assimilation. Like the sexual infraction, assimilation means to become other while discovering oneself. Wound and cure have become so strangely confused that it is impossible to say if the wound cures itself or the cure wounds itself.

This involuted riddle ensures that energetic, rational Aunt Emily will not dominate the novel to which she supplies so much useful historical information. Emily, who is always identified by her English name, refuses to exhibit the meek patience traditionally expected of Japanese women. She is so thoroughly assimilated that she beats the Anglo-Canadians at their own game. Quoting documents, writing petitions, marshalling statistics, she demands that a democratic society live up to its own precepts of liberalism, justice, and equality. She displays all the virtues that the West likes to ascribe to itself: she is practical, reasonable, orderly, indignant, indefatigable, conscientious. But Naomi – whose name is both Western and Japanese (Goody 160) – senses that these very virtues keep Emily detached, like an aircraft forever 'airborne' (*Obasan* 79). They blind her to the inwardness of things: 'Like Cupid, she aimed for the heart. But the heart was not there' (40). If Emily were the moral centre of the novel, then *Obasan* would be more conventional in the terms I have described. But Naomi's narrative dominance ensures that Emily will not occupy the centre, because the centre is impossible to locate. It is dark and silent, unlike the voluble Emily. 'Write the vision and make it plain' (31) is her biblical motto, with the emphasis on *write*: she trusts in words to remedy the plight of her people. If Emily were in control, then *Obasan* would prove that an assimilated immigrant, by virtue of the skills learned through assimilation, could articulate the injustice she has suffered and point the way to correct it. The pain of dislocation would be worthwhile, because the new nation could be reaffirmed and improved. In contrast, Naomi's motto shifts emphasis to: 'Write the *vision* and make it plain.' Her style, which is increasingly lyrical, evokes the disorientation of visionary experience. Where Emily rises and flies, Naomi sinks into memory, vulnerability, secrecy, and silence. When contemplating this vast 'underground sea' (14) of interiority, her language grows rhapsodic: 'We are going down to the middle of the earth with pick-axe eyes, tunnelling by train to the Interior, carried along by the momentum of the expulsion into the waiting wilderness ... We are the silences that speak from stone. We are the despised rendered voiceless, stripped of car, radio, camera and every means of communication, a trainload of eyes covered with mud and spittle' (111).

Inwardness and silence are familiar modern themes, and it is important to clarify *Obasan's* relation to them. In modernist practice, their aim is to elicit and then negotiate between unimaginable extremes: intimate and cosmic, transcendent and transgressive, being and knowing, pure matter and pure mind.[17] A criticism frequently made of modernist literature is that its infatuation with silence lures it away from action and civility into private worlds where 'truth' is supposed to live, but it is a truth that can have no practical bearing on the public world, which is renounced as irremediably corrupt. The symbolic 'voyage within' has been criticized, first by Marxists such as Georg Lukács for abjuring history in favour of the luxury of personal suffering; then by deconstructionists such as Derrida, who explodes the inside/outside binary by which truth is given a snug, inner home; and now by cultural critics, who show how binary oppositions subtly police a repressive political/sexual field of thought.[18] Inwardness is now associated with irresponsibility, vulnerability, narcissism, and abjection, or with a tyrannical (patriarchal, Eurocentric) notion of truth that must be resisted. In Canada the inward journey has been criticized by Frank Davey, who worries that recent Canadian novels abandon the 'social arena' for 'the shelter of individual salvation' (*Post-National* 253). Their quest is psychological, aesthetic, religious, and even absurdist, but not political.

I believe that *Obasan* does not fit comfortably into any of these categories because its evocation of intimate experience is so strongly national in character that all its definitions, even its definition of privacy, bear a communal sign. 'Everything a Canadian does is Canadian,' including personal reverie. Even renouncing the family, as Stephen so desperately tries to do, reminds the reader how prominently he bears its features in his face and name. The family – and the larger family of the Japanese community – remains part of him, and he of it, as Naomi realizes: 'My parents, like two needles, knit the families carefully into one blanket. Every event was a warm-water wash, drawing us all closer till the fibre of our lives became an impenetrable mesh ... We are one flesh, one family, washing each other or submerged in the hot water, half awake, half asleep' (20, 160–1). Unfortunately, Naomi is mistaken: like all other certainties in the novel, the family is penetrable by alien forces. Nevertheless 'every event,' no matter how private, continues to display a family and communal character. The voyage within always leads Naomi back outward, where she again confronts her overlapping family/ethnic/national communities. Her problem is finding a way to re-emerge.[19]

The riddle that I have been exploring now can be reframed. By its very nature, ethnicity is communal and expresses its intense sociability by celebrating place, tradition, and kinship. To proclaim oneself Japanese, Jamaican, or Jewish is to announce membership in nations that confer and sustain identity.[20] They do so, however, in the face of immigration and assimilation, which are ceaseless historical processes that confound all the places, traditions, and kinships through which ethnic groups assert themselves. The riddle is that ethnicity both relies on and disrupts nationality. It both founds and confounds nations. Naomi knows herself as Japanese Canadian, yet she wants to 'break loose from [this] heavy identity' (183) or, as she calls it when she reappears in Kogawa's second novel, *Itsuka*, this 'hair-shirt of ethnicity we all must wear' (256).[21] In view of this dilemma, William Boelhower argues that 'ethnicity' is a vexatious signifier provoking a perpetual identity crisis. It makes individuals unsure of their sustaining communities; it makes communities suspicious of individuality. In a multicultural society, especially, the continual influx of immigrants ensures that both personal and national identities will always be dissolving through assimilation, but that the ideology of assimilation will itself be subverted by unruly ethnic energies. On the one hand, assimilation resolves ethnic diversity in the familiar figures of melting pot[22] and national mosaic, for example. On the other hand, cultural and generational clashes always promise further dissolution. The United States and its literature are 'hopelessly riddled with the ethnic sign,' Boelhower warns, because 'the energy of ethnic American contact seems to generate the language of identity in the form of an endless production of questions' (85, 27). The ethnic subject is pervasive but alien, authentic yet deterritorialized: 'As such, he is potentially a figure of eruption, a catastrophic subject. His ethnic appearances are spontaneous, aleatory, and shifting, while his "identity" is ambiguous, cryptic, and allotropic ... As catastrophic subject, therefore, the ethnic self is uncodifiable; his ethnicity a mute and virtual language' (137). A walking catastrophe, the ethnic subject deconstructs the discourses of its own ethnicity: the discourses of family origins, memory, genealogy, roots, generations, place, and community.[23] Since these are also the discourses of romantic nationalism, ethnic catastrophe threatens the nation as well. The riddle, according to Boelhower, is that ethnicity is the ground of nationality, yet in the course of history it deterritorializes its native ground.

The more Boelhower glorifies American deterritorialization, the more his nomadic, ethnic subject sounds like a postmodern Huck Finn, perpetually lighting out to the Territory. *Obasan* is not glamorous in this way, because it is more fiercely aware of catastrophe. It is one thing to be a freely floating signifier on a polymorphous frontier; it is another to be a victim of Nagasaki. As Naomi delves into her 'memories and dreams' (25), she discovers a secret that is no secret at all, but the most explosive of historical events. A child in search of her dead mother, she sinks into her obsession until she discovers a mother in search of her dead child (239).[24] This horrifying spiral finally leads her, not away from, but into history. Her obscure quest brings her into the light of day, but of a day lit by the unearthly light of an atomic bomb. She emerges from her private reverie into a public nightmare.

Through this narrative spiral, Kogawa achieves a remarkable fusion of interiority and exteriority. Earlier in the novel Naomi draws daily life into her rhapsody with a passion that turns reality into personal fantasy: events become expressions of her own needs and fears. At the same time, readers are not allowed to forget that Kogawa is using fictional characters to make valid historical claims. She uses Emily to provide documentation, to confirm facts and vouch for their accuracy. The irony that Emily is a fictional character need not invalidate the information that she conveys. Like most ethnic novels (and all historical novels) *Obasan* sets fictional characters in historical settings. It has a practical aim – among others – to educate readers, to arouse indignation at injustice. This does not mean that Kogawa points 'outside' her text, but that she uses Emily to engage in the practical textuality of Canadian political affairs, where government decisions are made and documents are issued.[25] Naomi's retreat into subjectivity is always contrasted with Emily's outwardness, but the book's final effect is not to neatly balance the two. Kogawa does not use Naomi's intuitiveness merely to complement Emily's insistent factuality, and she does not subsume the two sensibilities in some grand, third possibility, such as the artist's overarching vision. At first Naomi claims access to an inner truth that eludes her aunt, but eventually Naomi is forced to return to the history that she has never really left, because it has always swept her along. Then she learns the most shocking truth of all: that historical reality can be far more horrifying than her worst nightmare, that history *is* nightmare. Just before the revelation of her mother's death, she recalls one of her own nightmares, which for all its uncanniness is far more bearable and intelligible than actual events: 'Always, I dream of soldiers eager for murder, their weapons ready. We die again and again. In my dreams, we are never safe enough' (227). Her ritual of suffering is terrifying, but it is still a ritual, a repeated, symbolic design displaying what Kogawa later called 'the discipline of dreams' (Williamson 155). When Naomi's world turns inside out, however, she is forced to contemplate what lies beyond all designation and discipline. Just as her mother's seared face is hardly recognizable as human, so the bombing of Nagasaki and Hiroshima is hardly recognizable as a historical event. Yet it is the culmination of modern history, the final reward of the same deadly, technological expertise lamented by George Grant and Dennis Lee. In *Obasan* history becomes so monstrous that it defies historical discourse.

At this point *Obasan* may justly be compared to Holocaust literature, in which the actuality of the death camps remains indescribable no matter how many documents, pictures, and personal accounts are called to bear witness. At this appalling moral and conceptual extreme, reality shifts its compass, so that the simplest words cannot be trusted to represent the truth, and writers must resort to rhetorical indirection, riddles, and silence.[26] The effect of these styles is to convey, not an ineffable inwardness, but a rupture in history that human thought can barely accommodate. As Kogawa remarked in an interview, the atomic bomb confounds our fundamental notions of what 'reality' is and how we inhabit it (Garrod 141). Nagasaki marks the final split in a narrative marred by fractures, from the alienating intimacy of Naomi's rape, to the fragmentation of family and community, to the splintered ideology of assimilation. These rifts suggest a broken reality that neither Emily's wordiness nor Naomi's moodiness can repair, yet to which they are drawn. '"That there is brokenness," he [the minister, Nakayama-sensei] says quietly. "That this world is brokenness. But within brokenness is the unbreakable name. How the earth groans till Love returns."' (240). The world is broken and never mended in *Obasan*, but the novel persists in offering a redemptive hope associated with love, and later with 'release': 'What the Grand Inquisitor has never learned is that the avenues of speech are the avenues of silence. To hear my mother, to attend her speech, to attend the sound of stone, he must first become silent. Only when he enters her abandonment will he be released from his own' (228). The Grand Inquisitor is the last of the menacing male figures who threaten Naomi yet to whom she is strangely drawn: old man Gower, Rough Lock Bill, Canadian authorities, the frog prince, the wolf at the door. They offer a savage embrace (the Canadian monster) in contrast to the warm maternal bath, but it is an embrace that Naomi finally resolves to accept. In accepting it, however, she is not magically 'saved,' as in fairy tales where the damsel is rescued by her prince. Such a transformation would be another form of assimilation, which she continues to resist. To attend her mother's speech, there must be another kind of 'abandonment,' a self-denial that is not a denial of self.

What does Naomi hear in her mother's silence? In a analysis of Kristeva's notion of the semiotic *chora* – the undifferentiated, presymbolic, 'primordial integration of mother and child' (Silverman 103) – Kaja Silverman argues that, however rich a source it may be, such an enclosure can actually hamper feminism by denying it practical agency. If the 'maternal substratum of subjectivity' (106) remains pre-articulate and pre-rational, then women are rendered mute and powerless even as they are given the place of honour at the rise of consciousness. Only by entering fully into the world (the symbolic, the legal, the political) can they take useful action: 'Furthermore, because Kristeva's account of the *choric* fantasy excludes both mother and daughter from language, it makes it difficult to imagine them participating in the articulation of new discourses, and so keeps their social disruption from being meaningful, in the strictest sense of that word ... Equally troubling, it conceptualizes the integration of mother and daughter in exclusively regressive terms, as a backward journey. In order for the *choric* fantasy to function as an effective political implement, it must point forward as well as backward – accommodate transformation as well as return' (125). To move 'forward' is not to abandon female integration in favour of the fractured male world of law and meaning, but to advance as women already capable of articulating critical discourses, which will share the strengths and flaws of all discourse. The 'amniotic deep' (*Obasan* ii) into which Naomi sinks resembles Kristeva's *chora* (a parallel studied by Robin Potter[27]). It is a blissfully infantile plenitude where needs are instantly gratified: 'When I am hungry, and before I can ask, there is food. If I am weary, every place is a bed' (*Obasan* 56). But it is also an utterly passive condition, 'half awake, half asleep ... like a hazy happy dream' (160–1), in which, as Mason Harris warns, the silent language of the body stultifies rather than sustains: 'Circumscribed by a family womb, this language can deal neither with the relation between the self and the outside world, nor with conflicts within the self' (46). For Kogawa, too, the integration of mother and daughter must lead forward into effective discourses, of which Emily's lectures and *Obasan* itself are examples.

Emily warns Naomi that the Japanese-Canadian community was vulnerable precisely because it was so important: 'To a people for whom community was the essence of life, destruction of community was the destruction of life' (186). Through her ordeals of silence and solitude, Naomi discovers that while communities are vulnerable, they are also unavoidable. There is always a public life, even if one hides from it. There is always an unsteady national space to be negotiated through cultural clashes. If in one way the bath scenes are regressive, in another way they celebrate shared and even public events, as Potter observes: 'There is a sense of unification in the public bathing scene that takes place in Slocan, which is comparable to the traditional view of the city squares, where information about members of the community is exchanged' (132). To go forward means to re-engage in the public forum, even though it too has been shattered beyond recognition by war, but to re-engage with it without losing the family and ethnic intimacies evoked by the bathing scene. Or, shifting the imagery, to go forward means to take up the 'thread' that is twisted through the novel and associated with Obasan's ball of twine (*Obasan* 227), with the red string securing Emily's folder (45), and with the Japanese ideogram for 'passionate love' (228). The connecting thread is the meaningful link that, for Kristeva, takes the child from the undifferentiated semiotic into the shared but manifold world of the symbolic, a world that in *Obasan* is menacing but seductive. The thread is associated with all kinds of connectedness, both harmful and healing. It is associated with memory, family bonds, communal ties, and story telling. It is 'the narrative impulse both to search for a particular story and to search for an alternative, potentially redemptive form of telling that resists narrative closure, that both speaks out of historical silences and takes them into its account' (Manina Jones 134).

Such links can be painful and even degrading, as Naomi has discovered, but they can also be soothing when they form what Kogawa calls elsewhere 'a complex therapeutic community of people' (Williamson 148) in which the 'structures of connectedness' (*Itsuka* 4) are just. Without connectedness, there can be no justice. The muted hope with which *Obasan* concludes depends on the healing power of its communities, although the novel never lets us forget that the same communities inflict the wounds to be healed. *Obasan* never proposes a perfect world, only a habitable one. It may be an imperfect home, but home is 'where our stories are' and 'where the struggle for justice takes place' (*Itsuka* 160–1). Accordingly, in the final scene Naomi reaffirms her connection to the land and gains a 'new sense of identification with Canada ... a new sense of rootedness in that hostile outer world' (Harris 51). She envisions a nation in which the self can be abandoned safely, because it will not be assimilated or degraded. Such a nation will not be exclusive, because it will recognize, in Kogawa's words, that '[p]art of our common human condition is a tension between belonging to a people, being at home among them, and being free and at home everywhere' (Garrod 151). *Obasan* does not resolve this tension, which is another expression of the ethnic riddle and the circular national argument. Instead it works within these tensions to redraw a viable national space. 'Oh Canada, whether it is admitted or not, we come from you we come from you. From the same soil, the slugs and slime and bogs and twigs and roots. We come from the country that plucks its people out like weeds and flings them into the roadside ... We come from our untold tales that wait for their telling' (*Obasan* 226).

Daphne Marlatt, *Ana Historic* (1988)

I know that timid breathing. Where
do I begin and end?

Wallace Stevens, 'The Man with the Blue Guitar'

Obasan and *Ana Historic* are about timid beginnings and tumultuous endings. More specifically, they are about finding a way to end – to complete a story, a historical period, a painful stage in one's life – in order to start afresh. The two narrators, Naomi and Annie, refuse to 'repeat history,' because it is a tale of frustration and loss, and look instead to what Annie calls: 'promise: the budding of some secret future in me, little knowing all the eggs were already there, lined up and waiting. promise: letting go, a rhythmically repeated event starting each month from full' (*Ana Historic* 62). As Wallace Stevens illustrates, to start afresh means to be refreshed when one discovers the world and one's place in it freshly.

Say even that this complete simplicity
Stripped one of all one's torments, concealed
The evilly compounded, vital I

And made it fresh in a world of white,
A world of clear water ('The Poems of Our Climate' 193–4)

Renewal of this sort is always a re-newal in which the old world is not abandoned but renovated. Stevens's aim is not utopian but practical; he seeks the vibrancy of felt experience, not transcendence. The 'I' will always remain evilly compounded, as Naomi discovers so painfully, but she can still find ways of affirming her own vitality. Where Stevens appeals to the yearly cycle, Annie's imagery evokes a fertile circularity associated with women – with menstrual and birth cycles, with the succession of mothers and daughters, and with women's writing. These forms requite the vicious circularity associated with men and with history as a self-defeating logic of exploitation. Naomi and Annie embrace the future by obsessively rehearsing the patterns of the past in order to gain release from them. To achieve the sense of an ending requires that they make sense of the beginning whose inciting energy got things going in the first place.

> Ana
> that's her name:
> back, backward, reversed
> again, anew (*Ana Historic* 43)

But if Annie renews herself by breaking 'free of history' with its 'useless baggage' (14), where exactly does that leave her? What is the relation between history and promise, especially when the history at issue concerns a nation that is itself in search of renewal?

For Annie, who works as a research assistant to her historian husband, history is 'husbandry' (142). It is manipulative, intrusive, abusive, and ultimately fatal. It is ruled by a deadly fatality entailed by the first attack of Europeans on a paradisal continent ('a green so green it outgreened itself' [15]), an attack that functions in *Ana Historic* like original sin, tainting all subsequent actions.[28] To the male commentators cited from historical records, these actions are heroic exploits that conquer a new world: '*history the story, Carter's and all the others', of dominance. mastery. the bold line of it*' (25). But to

Annie, nation building – represented as felling the forests, extending the railway, settling British Columbia – is doomed by its beginning, because a nation constructed so violently can only become a monster that turns on its creator. This is one of the lessons that she learns from *Frankenstein*.[29] *Obasan* and *Ana Historic* are threatened by growing catastrophes, whose dehumanizing effects are incalculable and whose sources stretch far into the past, beyond history into legend. For Naomi, the bombing of Nagasaki is the dreadful culmination of a long history of Western, scientific expertise. For Annie, historical mastery is associated with the epic venture of European colonialism to the 'end of the world' (30) in pursuit of glory and wealth. Ironically, the end of things is forecast by a hopeful beginning in which the world is to be 'made new' (30), but only through a logical and technological discipline that inevitably grows tyrannical.

Why inevitably? The question of necessity recurs in *Ana Historic* as the converse of its fascination with kinds of freedom. Marlatt draws on feminist and post-colonial theories according to which Western historical thinking conforms to a dominant paradigm based on the supremacy of the Cartesian *cogito*, which is master of all it surveys, and on the Hegelian appropriation of objects by a voracious subjectivity (see Chatterjee 14–17). According to this paradigm, 'thinking' is never an impartial or objective activity, even when it pretends to be a neutral investigation of facts. Rather, it is the tyranny of mind over matter, and over other minds, which are treated as matter to be known and so subjugated. The invasion of Canada, like the invasion of India and the East (alluded to in *Ana Historic* 136), is impelled by a imperialist logic infusing all aspects of Western culture, many of which appear in the novel: exploration, commerce, science, sociology, medicine, history. All such 'disciplines' are means of subduing reality by knowing it, and what is subdued is life in all its rich contradictoriness. All aim to bring 'the intuitive, emotional Other under the scientistic tutelage of the rational, all-knowing Western Subject' (Trinh 20). Marlatt accepts this paradigm with the qualification that it is also phallocentric and can be countered by a feminist critique, because feminist thought is launched from within the 'intuitive, emotional

Other.' Annie already knows herself to be intuitive and emotional, but she has to learn that these are strengths, not shortcomings. She has to learn to accept the 'upheaval within' her (*Ana Historic* 122) as ground for a fresh life.

To return to my question: why inevitably? The fate against which Annie rebels is so involuted that it threatens to entangle her even when she is about to extricate herself from it. In one respect, her fate is personal and involves her relation to mother and husband. In another respect, it is cultural and involves her role as a woman in a patriarchal society. In a third, it is historical and involves her position in Canada and the West. According to conventional historiography, which *Ana Historic* presents as a monologic, masculine, and monopolistic (Manina Jones 140, 149, 159), the 'bold line' of progress follows an 'incontrovertible logic of cause and effect' (*Ana Historic* 147). Historical advance may be spurred by the resourcefulness of individual men, but ultimately it is enforced by an potent brew of economics, technology, and testosterone. 'Progress,' so determined, is inevitable. In place of these motives, Annie anahistorically discerns a moral necessity in the course of events, according to which heroic advance is refigured as growing corruption. For example, one of her documents advises: '*Think what this mastery over huge, heavy logs means to a man who has been used to coax them in tiny movements by patience and a puny jack-screw*' (25). Annie answers this rhetorical question against its grain. What *does* such mastery mean? It means that the epic story of mastery should (the imperative is moral) be re-read as a tale of domination, enslavement, and sexual bravado, which will eventually exact their due punishment. Both interpretations of history distinguish necessary patterns in it, but they assess the necessity, and the value of human actions within that necessity, quite differently.

At first glance, Annie apparently rejects retrospective, male history in favour of prospective, female promise. While she does suggest this handy opposition of terms, Marlatt, who must be distinguished from her character, quickly shows the complications that beset so oversimplified a schema. When Annie sees history as trespass (assaulting the New World) she assesses it in moral terms. When she sees history as a destructive fatality, she assesses it in dramatic terms. These are precisely the techniques that national historians used to envision a nation and chart its destiny. For all her waywardness, then, Annie continues to rely on established discursive strategies, which, however, she cleverly turns against the nation builders in order to expose the cruelty of their regulations. She wants to subvert their laws (the law of the father), but in so doing she implicates herself all the more deeply in the problematic by which historians continually invoke and infringe legality. True, she is a rebel, but she rebels on behalf of a more generous sense of justice (13). She continues to read history as the story of (in)justice.

My point is that Annie's rebellion does not permit her to escape from history into some antithetical mode of discourse. She must find her promises within history. Although she makes a 'monstrous leap of imagination' (135) that exposes the patriarchal nation as a monstrosity, she cannot leap out of history. Although she enjoys 'imagining herself free of history' (14), she discovers that freedom and justice are always historical. They cannot be found in escapist flights of fancy; or in a private 'luxury of being' (153); or in nature, which she represents as 'the Old Wood' where lost girls play (12). Her response to the prospect of 'standing outside of history' (Marlatt's words in Bowering 102) is to write herself back into it. The word 'anahistoric' does not mean non-historic in the sense of transgressing historical discourse altogether. According to the Greek lexicon, the preposition/adverb 'ana' has a variety of meanings depending on how it is used. It can mean: on, upon, back, towards, up (of place), throughout (of time). All these positionalities reflect Annie's critical relation to conventional historiography, which she reframes in accordance with her own imperatives.[30]

My question, 'Why inevitably?' thus points to competing historical imperatives, but also to competing notions of freedom. Annie cannot rebel against history as such, only against her own small place in it. In her own life, the end of things is an impasse where her private life is so constrained that it loses all public significance: 'impasse: impossible to exit. dead end. when the walls close down. the public / private wall. defined the world you lived inside' (23). She is afraid of being trapped as her mother was: 'no wonder you were afraid. sick with the fear of fate, you walked in a world of disasters ... you wanted it to end, the world i mean, at least the world as it was then constituted. because for you there was no way out' (142–3). Annie's solution is not to end the world, but to renew it and herself: 'i wasn't dreaming of history, the already-made, but of making fresh tracks my own way' (98). My question now becomes: Where do these fresh tracks lead her? When she realizes that she and all women are trapped paradoxically 'in the midst of freedom and yet not free' (54), she raises the hope of liberating herself by seizing a superior mode of freedom. Given the post-structuralist terms of the novel, an alternative freedom will require other forms of discourse, authority, and subject positioning. Many of the studies of *Ana Historic* (by Manina Jones, Dragland, Tostevin, Cooley, Banting) investigate these antithetical forms as composed by Marlatt and lived by Annie. They include fragmentation, citation, interruption, juxtaposition, echoes, and word-play – all the techniques of the modernist avant-garde used to elicit an *écriture féminine*, a rich semiotic idiom in which Annie can express herself freely. Her ana-forms may be radically unstable or provisional in contrast to stern patriarchal laws, but through their very instability they must permit her to redirect her fate: 'to fly in the face of common sense, social convention, ethics – the weight of history, to fly' (146).

Her alternative freedom must involve something better than a determined assertion of self-importance, since both the self and the discourses of self-assertion are problematized in *Ana Historic*. If she proclaims herself free only in aggressive, patriarchal terms, then she will merely be reformulating her servitude. In the most familiar sense, freedom means release from constraint – from unjust social conventions, decorum, and male domination. To 'fly' means to escape. But it also means perfecting one's ability to fly: freedom arises from the enhanced ability and control made possible by release from constraint. To be free in any practical sense, one must have the knowledge, ability, and power to do something with one's freedom. This active aspect of freedom is expressed through word-play: 'what is fact? (f) act. the f stop of act' (31, also 56, 134). The dead weight of fact, which is really historical fiction, impedes independent female action by freezing it as if in a photograph. These two aspects of freedom, which I will call release (from constraint) and increase (of knowledge and ability), are logically connected in that the first is the negative precondition of the second. One must *not* be constrained if one is to exercise one's enhanced knowledge, ability, and power. One important qualification of freedom, so defined, is that it requires a favourable setting to provide the enabling and limiting conditions in which free choice can occur. Freedom always operates within a social setting that restricts or extends possibilities for action. One is free to do only what one's environment makes available. Divine freedom may be utterly unconstrained, but human freedom is always enmeshed in necessity. For example, Annie wants to 'fly,' in the double sense of release and increase, but, even metaphorically, flying means working within the necessary conditions of air, speed, gravity, and so on. Similarly, she can embrace a promising future only by accepting conditions already in place: 'promise ... little knowing all the eggs were already there, lined up and waiting' (62). She cannot choose to be a woman, only to be a free woman.

A further complication of the freedom to which Annie aspires is that release and increase are interconnected but not necessarily complementary. Freedom must be active, but actions are always equivocal, because they arise from unfathomable motives and produce unforeseen results. As I just noted, for Annie freedom involves not just the absence of constraint, but the will, ability, and knowledge to act effectively. But the unrestrained exercise of these powers is precisely what drives the historiography of colonial expansion, and she condemns that expansion as subjugating, not liberating. She discovers that one nation's freedom grows at the expense of another's. One nation's freedom may even increase with a wilful ferocity that contaminates its own social setting by making it alienating and self-destructive. In that case, one freely constructs a world in which freedom diminishes. I have already argued that in opposition to conventional history, Annie advocates the moral responsibility and modesty of a female historiography that will not be manipulative: 'perhaps that explains why our writing, which we also live inside of, is different from men's, and not a tool, not a "pure instrument for getting a grip on the world"'

(133). But she later proposes another kind of freedom, which is gripping in another way.

Ana Historic celebrates the joyful discovery of a freedom expressed, not as flying but as falling – as in free fall, falling in love, and falling apart (150). Instead of gaining control, one releases it in a rapturous *jouissance*. Instead of enlarging one's powers, one abandons oneself to superb forces, which the novel presents as fruitful, although there are sinister versions of this story. The self frees itself of all egotism until it barely persists as a separate entity, as Marlatt expresses through a lyrical conflation of pronouns: 'she who is you / or me / "i" / address this to' (129). Ecstatic freedom is also evoked by a series of dangerously seductive rhetorical figures: the wild woods, dancing, breaching limits, broken syntax, accidents, inwardness, animism, torrents (the name Annie finally chooses for herself). Critically it is associated with the free play of the signifier, semiotic excess, *écriture féminine*, Bakhtinian carnival, the deterritorialized ethnic subject – in short, the dizzy playground of post-structuralist theory. Freedom of this sort is so exorbitant that it can obscure all else, at which point it may become obsessive, narcotic, or mystical. We then encounter the same dilemma that arises in *Obasan* when Naomi's inward flight threatens to engulf her entirely and to divorce her from the practical freedom she seeks. Similarly Annie finds refuge in a blissful female space that threatens to become a world apart. Frank Davey criticizes *Ana Historic* for escaping into utopian fantasy rather than accepting political responsibility: 'What may appear superficially to be a political novel, a novel that challenges from a feminist perspective how society is structured, what discourses and roles it allows to women, is in the end not a political novel at all. For the pre-Oedipal space it both dreams of and realizes as the "home" of woman is yet another utopian plenitude, eternal, natural, before (or at least aside from) the symbolic realm of language and thus apart from the social and political clashes and negotiations that the symbolic enables' (*Post-National* 208). In this view, Annie begins by subverting conventional history but ends by ignoring it. She starts her story in bewildered inwardness and finishes it in ecstatic inwardness but, in either case, remained trapped 'inside.' Her final union with Zoe excludes her from critical discourse by conjuring up an ecstatic state of timeless, undifferentiated, female intermingling.[31] When a fictional character escapes from history into mystery – as in Leonard Cohen's *Beautiful Losers* or Aritha van Herk's *No Fixed Address* – what really shifts is the novel's narrative mode. Davey argues that *Ana Historic* begins as one kind of novel and turns into another.

I resist this interpretation, as I did when considering *Obasan*, and for similar reasons. However, it is important to recognize how far-reaching is this critique of both the personal and national subject. In an essay on Kristeva, Allon White worries that while she dethrones the repressive, transcendental ego of Western metaphysics, she replaces it 'with something far worse, a "new" subject, drifting, dispersed, and as politically impotent as it is ever possible to be. An agent without agency, direction, or cohesion' (87). The same powerlessness threatens post-colonial and indigenous nations, according to R. Radhakrishnan, when they resort to a rhetoric of gender that ultimately nullifies their effort to break with (masculine) Western nationalism. The '*true* nationalist subject' liberates itself by assuming the form of a woman, but 'Woman takes on the name of a vast inner silence not to be broken into by the rough and external clamor of material history ... The locus of the true self, the inner/traditional/spiritual sense of place, is exiled from the processes of history while the locus of historical knowledge fails to speak for the true identity of the nationalist subject. The result is a fundamental rupture, a form of basic cognitive dissidence, a radical collapse of representation' (Radhakrishnan 85).

I contend that *Obasan* and *Ana Historic* do not suffer from 'cognitive dissidence,' although both push their narratives to the limit, where representation threatens to collapse. Nevertheless their evocations of the inexpressible do not divorce them from 'historical knowledge.' Both novels problematize such knowledge, but they do not pretend that their characters can escape from the problem into some 'vast inner silence.' On the contrary, they remain alert to the need for social cohesion, and wary of the (bourgeois/positivist/masculine) individualism that regards people as truly themselves only when they are utterly unique. For Naomi and Annie, subjectivity remains inseparable not just from their families and immediate groups, but from their nation, whose history they 'recount' in the double sense of retell and reassess. This is more obviously true of *Obasan*, where the subject is always an ethnic subject defined by a community that she both embraces and resists. But in *Ana Historic*, too, Annie is in search of a therapeutic community that will secure her position within society at large. Active political engagement is suggested in the closing scene, where the women are preparing a pile of flyers for mailing. Davey considers this a feeble gesture, but it still gestures towards a 'world of connection' (*Ana Historic* 151; the phrase recalls Kogawa's 'structures of connectedness'), which will not be negated by a moment of private passion.

Annie devotes herself to 'untelling the real' (141), not because she prefers fantasy to reality, but because the 'real' as represented in official history proves to be fictional. 'Untelling' it means devising a new grip on reality and a new history – 'a woman's version of history,' as Marlatt said in conversation (Bowering 98). Early in the novel, Annie presents Mrs Richards 'imagining herself free of history' (14), and in the same vein Annie projects herself into a secluded female sanctuary: 'a woman's place. safe. suspended out of the swift race of the world' (24). But she immediately confesses her folly by condemning 'the monstrous lie of it: the lure of absence. self-effacing' (24). She discovers, on the contrary, that no freedom is 'cut loose from history' (81) because history provides all the settings within which freedom operates, including the freedom to abandon oneself to a loved one. There is no practical freedom in absence or self-effacement, although these may be temporary strategies in a larger campaign of liberation.

More specifically, self-effacement is a strategy in writing, since the very act of writing ensures an author's ambiguous presence within a text and absence from it. Authors hide behind the words through which they express themselves. In *Ana Historic* the narrator conceals/reveals her identity by fragmenting herself into Ana, Ina, and Annie. She finds herself by getting lost in the woods/ words. Her tale begins by picturing a solitary woman 'sitting at her kitchen table writing '(45) in order to share her solitude with an attentive reader: 'she was looking for the company of another who was also reading – out through the words, through the wall that separated her' (45). As Marlatt explains elsewhere, 'writing and reading go together like speaking and hearing.' They are avenues that meet in the same labyrinth ('Writing Our Way' 44), and when they meet, a basis for mutual understanding (as well as misunderstanding) is established. In a sense *Ana Historic* is about Annie's search for a reader: by writing, she invites a receptive audience and a larger, sympathetic community. 'Who's There?' (9) she asks in her opening question, which will eventually be answered by the name 'Zoe' (life) – 'in life we go on' (150). Her 'personal history' (55) is painfully intimate, yet it is never solely personal precisely because it is history, which always has public significance. By telling her private story, she finds that she has articulated the 'shared life' (151) of all women confined by patriarchy.

> – the truth is, you want to tell your own story.
> – and yours. ours. the truth is our stories are hidden from us by fear.
>   your fear i inherited, mother dear.
> – the truth is, that's woman's lot. (79)

Having reaffirmed the need for community, neither *Ana Historic* nor *Obasan* is concerned to rebuild the nation, as Pratt had done so boldly and Lee so stoically. No flags are waving at the end, and it would be anti-climactic if they were. Nonetheless, both novels show how personal suffering and redemption always seek their meaning in a social context whose scope is ultimately national because the nation is such a compelling political and representational setting. Annie does not choose to be English Canadian, and Naomi does not choose to be Japanese Canadian. They only choose to be free women within the country that their families chose by immigrating. The nation is not an essential social unit, or a mystical bond, or a spiritual soil. It is a contested, public space within which they must find whatever freedom and justice they can attain; it is an identifying space whose meaning they choose to contest through their subversive narrations. The nation can become monstrous, but both women learn to live with a monster by recognizing its features in themselves. Annie discovers that *Frankenstein* was written by a woman who concealed/revealed herself in its terrifying but liberating wildness: 'and now we call the monster by his name. a man's name for man's fear of the wild, the uncontrolled. that's where *she* lives' (142). Both women find a place to live through an interplay of intimate, public, and discursive spaces. We might therefore apply to *Ana Historic* and *Obasan* a remark that Lorraine Weir makes about Marlatt's poetry: 'Parallel to the obligation to voice things in their terms is the obligation to voice the life of a community ... The condition of imagining a community, of wording its context, is the condition of finding its own words, its history, and respecting that manifold reading of a people in their own terms which is "dream," the reading of Reading' ('Daphne Marlatt's "Ecology"' 62). The terms of community as it is lived, dreamed, and written are the subject of my final chapter.

5. Worrying the Nation

Every nation, every race, has not only its own creative, but its own critical turn of mind ... The poet ... must be aware that the mind of Europe – the mind of his own country – a mind which he learns in time to be much more important than his own private mind – is a mind which changes, and that this change is a development which abandons nothing en route.

T.S. Eliot, 'Tradition and the Individual Talent'

The nation is not only the condition of culture, its fruitfulness, its continual renewal, and its deepening. It is also a necessity. It is the fight for national existence which sets culture moving and opens to it the doors of creation ... National consciousness, which is not nationalism, is the only thing that will give us an international dimension.

Frantz Fanon, *The Wretched of the Earth*

These two descriptions of national culture mark the distance between a modern outlook, which is defensive and retrospective in its purview, and a colonial outlook, which is offensive and prospective. Writing in 1919, just after the First World War (and as he was composing *The Waste Land*), T.S. Eliot invokes the majesty of tradition in order to protect England from a chaotic present. Following Ralph Cohen's example (41–2), we might say that Eliot invokes the 'historical sense' only to embrace a timeless tradition that transcends history, whereas Frantz Fanon seeks to historicize tradition. Speaking in 1959 at the Second Congress of Black Artists and Writers, he cautiously roots himself in an equally chaotic present, beyond which he glimpses a new sense of nationhood as yet undefined. For Eliot, tradition unifies: it ensures that nothing is lost and everything fits, because a mature society is sustained locally by its evolving national spirit, and more broadly by its shared cultural ties. For Fanon, tradition is more ambiguous. It is no guarantee of authenticity; it may hinder rather than enhance cultural growth; it functions within an international context. While he agrees that 'every culture is first and foremost national' in character (174), he warns that 'underdeveloped' African nations must overcome a racist, nationalist ideology that has worked its way into their own traditions, so that it oppresses them even as it defines them. The dilemma is that '[t]he efforts of the native to rehabilitate himself and to escape from the claws of colonialism are logically inscribed from the same point of view as that of colonialism' (170). The solution is to reformulate a national culture that will liberate rather than subjugate, and the artist has the privilege of leading the way: 'The artist who has decided to illustrate the truths of the nation turns paradoxically towards the past and away from actual events. What he ultimately intends to embrace are in fact the cast-offs of thought, its shells and corpses, a knowledge which has been stabilized once and for all. But the native intellectual who wishes to create an authentic work of art must realize that the truths of a nation are in the first place its realities. He must go on until he has found the seething pot out of which the learning of the future will emerge' (181).

Canada has its own seething pot, simmering with its own recipes. If there is a 'mind of Canada,' however, it has long been diagnosed as immature, schizophrenic, or ironic, as if the country just cannot make up its mind.[1] In 1864 E.H. Dewart cooked up a national literature from the scattered ingredients at hand in order to prove that Canada was possible as an 'idea' as well as a political state. I argued in chapter 2 that romantic historicism promised the glory of a national literature, but that its principles proved ill-suited to the heterogeneity of Canadian life. Nevertheless, for years its rhetoric seemed ennobling to both English and French Canadians because of its ability to unify knowledge in a way that is politically respectable and socially uplifting. It made sense of Canada, or it permitted Canada to make sense. Understandably, literary historians have been reluctant to relinquish so effective an interpretative model. One hundred and twenty years after Dewart, W.J. Keith renews a familiar call: 'We still have a mission: to have our literature recognized as an essential reflection of our national life' ('Function' 14). Like Eliot and Fanon, Keith believes that the 'national life' is expressed best in literature, where aesthetic and cultural values (merit and authenticity) reflect each other. Although this reflection is supposed to be 'essential' or instinctive, it proves surprisingly hard to recognize, and keen critical effort is necessary to detect it. Either writers have failed to depict the nation's true image, or readers have failed to recognize that image as depicted in 'our literature.' Perversely, Canada remains an underdeveloped nation, at least in regard to national culture.[2] Nevertheless, Keith never doubts that 'our' literature should accurately reflect 'our' national life.

Other literary historians today are more sceptical. They mistrust Keith's sense of 'mission,' because they fear it will turn critics into missionaries, and missionaries into conquerors. They look not only beyond Eliot's idealism and Fanon's renewed national consciousness, but beyond the nation itself. Ironically, the assault on colonialism, once waged in the name of nationalism by Canadian writers like E.K. Brown and A.J.M. Smith, is now waged in the name of anti-nationalism (Bennett, 'English Canada' 194). But what happens to a national literature when the very idea of the nation has been cast in doubt? In this chapter I want to worry at my original question and its formative assumptions one more time.

Beyond the Nation

The historian's cliché that every period is an age of transition has recently been countered by a *fin-de-siècle* sentiment of perpetual belatedness. To be postmodern is not to set oneself between two ages, but to remain resolutely after the fact, where the 'fact' is any principle defining period or place. Since the *genius loci* is the essence of place, it is doubly vulnerable to the postmodern critique of essentialism. In a world of post-discourses, no *Zeitgeist* or communal ghost can be trusted to define nations or to motivate historical transitions. As well as post-colonial and post-structuralist, we must now be post-national. Frank Davey observes with some dismay that contemporary novels 'inhabit a post-national space, in which sites are as interchangeable as postcards, in which discourses are transnational, and in which political issues are constructed on non-national (and often ahistorical) ideological grounds' (*Post-National Arguments* 259). More hopefully, Robert Kroetsch advises: 'The task of criticism, now, is to examine those changes [in discourse] and those new directions without recourse to an easy version of national definition, and without easy recourse to old vocabularies' (*Lovely Treachery* 66).

According to one new vocabulary, nations are tribal remnants in a postmodern world; to be nationalistic in any way is to be hopelessly reactionary. Even Fanon's assurance that cultures are national in character has been challenged by a critique of the nation as neo-colonial, although nation is sometimes confused with nation-state. The old romantic faith in a handy continuity among language, environment, and culture could not survive the attack on totalizing systems of thought launched by modernist and then postmodern critics who stress infraction, not continuity, as the rule of history.[3] In his cultural elegy, *In Bluebeard's Castle*, George Steiner summarizes the now familiar view that we live in a 'post-culture' that has 'passed out of the major order and symmetries of Western civilization' (56). 'The loss of a geographic-sociological centrality, the abandonment or extreme qualification of the axiom of historical progress, our sense of the failure or severe inadequacies of knowledge and humanism in regard to social action – all these signify the end of an agreed hierarchic value-structure ... It is the collapse, more or less complete, more or less conscious, of these hierarchized, definitional value-gradients (and can there be value without hierarchy?) which is now the major fact of our intellectual and social circumstances' (81–2). Nationality, especially when encoded in philology and blessed by literature, had seemed the sweetest of value-structures. It was the masterpiece of master narratives, celebrating communal life, conferring identity, assuring historical continuity. Now critics reject nationhood as a viable conceptual tool, and ask what lies beyond our obsession with trim categories. Ethnic writers look beyond ethnicity (Sollors); African Americans propose a 'post-Black Aesthetic' (Gates 143); even Quebec writers have announced a 'post-Québécois culture' (Simon 171). We are supposed to live in Marshall McLuhan's global village, or in a planetary economy of multinational corporations, or in a post-national technopolis – all of which render the nation obsolete.

'Is Nationality Obsolete?' asks Gertrude Himmelfarb in the title of an essay about the disenchantment with traditional political history, which relied on suspect definitions of collectivity, causality, and growth, all ruled by the 'tyranny of nationality' (123). Gone is the old faith in national character, the prime force that was supposed to direct history but actually was itself created by tendentious historical analysis (126). Such quaint idealism has been supplanted by structural history, quantitative history, microhistory, and psychohistory.[4] Gone, too, is the futile quest for national identity, which in Canada provoked only what A.B. McKillop calls a 'nationalist fallacy' (5) ensuring that we will never define ourselves satisfactorily because of the inconsistent ways that nationality has figured in our historical thinking. Identity is supposed to either precede and infuse the course of events in Canada (the genetic view), or to emerge as the reward of earnest, historical growth (the teleological view). But looking before and after has proven fruitless, since each view produces a plethora of 'nationalisms' but no consensus, only an obsessive self-questioning that feeds on its own discontent. Why worry about a 'national literature' at all, when it is tied by its very title to an archaic theory?

To accept this argument, however, is to shut one's eyes to what Fanon simply calls 'realities,' in this case the fact that nations do exist and continue to proliferate, often at each other's expense. If theory declares the nation to be dead, then we should re-examine our assumptions. If it proves that nationalism is 'a contradictory discourse,' then especially, R. Radhakrishnan cautions, we must study its contradictions in order to avoid being skewered by them: 'the history of nationalism is not easily bypassed just because it has been the history of a failure' (82), or of a monster. Ironically, the nation is scorned as a conceptual tool because it is judged either too flimsy or too ferocious: either it is nothing but a liberal delusion used to make the bourgeoisie feel safe in their beds; or it is a dangerous ideological weapon used to forge empires. Studies of the nation as an 'imagined community' might lead the unwary critic to suppose that imaginary forms can be imagined away simply by re-imagining them. Hence a title like *Reimagining the Nation*, which seems to promise a clean break from past error. But as one of the editors of this collection warns, our imaginations are not entirely our own. They, too, have a cultural and linguistic provenance, which shapes all private imaginings of public spaces: 'As the language of nationalism fuels contemporary crises, so the concept of the nation emerges through language. The nation comes to life in texts other than those which are ostensibly nationalistic: it is sustained in the discourses of gender and sexuality, in discussions of economics and ecology, in the language of everyday and of theory. Therefore, an analysis of the nation which seeks to do more than feed facts into the already swollen corpus of knowledge on particular nationalist movements must explore how the idea of the nation circulates and regenerates itself through a wide variety of texts' (Lerner 1). Critics sharpen their theoretical knives to slay the dreadful nation, only to discover that the monster cannot be destroyed any more than the ghost can be exorcised, because it revives, suitably transformed, in all discourses of community. Nationalism may be reviled as 'the pathology of modern developmental history' (Nairn 359), but reviling does not cure it. Canada may be declared unsociable in contrast to authentic nations (Québécois, Acadian, feminist, gay), or condemned as unjust in contrast to more compassionate, composite polities (relaxed confederation, sovereignty association, anarchism). Nevertheless, the nation regenerates itself as soon as alternative communities are proposed and arranged in some larger social field. How is that public forum to be represented in a wide variety of texts, including literature?

As Adam J. Lerner indicates in the previous quotation, it is the business of representation that regenerates the nation. Not every community is a nation, but any attempt to represent its political standing and motivation – that is, to explain how it constitutes itself and how it participates in a larger public forum – will invoke a discourse of nationhood. The nation is both a historical reality and a discursive need. We are not free to choose or reject it at will, since it has already helped to define the position from which we speak; it has already infiltrated our 'will,' which cannot detach itself from the world we inhabit. For Eve Sedgwick, 'nation-ness' is an unavoidable, defining condition of modernity: 'every *modern* culture and person must be seen as partaking of what we might (albeit clumsily) call a "habitation/nation system." The "habitation/nation system" would be the set of discursive and institutional arrangements that mediate between the physical fact that each person inhabits, at a given time, a particular geographical space, and the far more abstract, sometimes even apparently unrelated organization of what has emerged since the late seventeenth century as her/his national identity, as signalized by, for instance, citizenship' ('Nationalisms' 239). National identity is a volatile, material, and discursive 'arrangement' that must continually be 'signalized' (represented), for example by invented traditions and national literatures, if people are to know who they are and where they belong.[5] Some nations require more reassurance than others, but all depend on 'the powerful familiarizing effect of nation-ness' (241) to sustain them. Signals are disrupted during social upheavals – revolution, exile, immigration, Quebec referenda – but according to Sedgwick, signals are always getting crossed, since semiotic systems are volatile by their very nature. Nations are continually being constructed and deconstructed. No community is utterly homogeneous; it must always find new ways of recognizing and honouring the differences within it. No community is utterly autonomous; it must find ways of interacting justly with other groups. There are divisions within and without, and the problem in Canada is finding ways to respect these divisions without appealing either to a domineering universalism[6] or to exclusionary politics.

Beyond the nation lie more nations, differently conceived. If we are to reimagine them, however, it is important to appreciate why they have proven so resilient in the face of a legitimation crisis not just in Canada, but in modern theory generally, where the nation frequently serves as the site of whatever has gone wrong. As an epigraph I quoted Phyllis Webb's tantalizing remark: 'I often think that in our search for a Canadian identity we fail to realize that we are not searching for definitions but for signs and omens' (109). Perhaps the problem today is that we have too many signs and too few omens. We have endless diagnoses of the national malaise but too little 'promise,' as it was called in *Ana Historic,* to give confidence in the future.

The Nation in/as Crisis

The quotations from Eliot and Fanon suggest that a nation is never fully present to its citizens but must continually be envisaged by looking backward and forward over its history. It thus acts as a powerful discursive agent to unify a society, articulate its parts, and legitimate its authorities. Each of these functions defends certain social values against rival values, which are viewed as corrupting. Each engages the nation with disruptive ideologies that it seeks to control and that threaten to undermine it. If these forces are perceived as internal (Eliot), they are called heretical or treasonous: hence his study of modern heresy, *After Strange Gods.* If they are perceived as external (Fanon), they are called alien or imperialist. Unity concerns the integrating power of nationhood in view of the fragmentation of competing social interests. Articulation concerns the historical coherence or 'life' of a nation and its literature, in view of the divergent paths taken by different groups and regions. Legitimacy concerns the rule of proper authorities to secure a national life in view of competing claims and improprieties. To borrow Northrop Frye's image: the nation acts as a centripetal force drawing the heterogeneity of historical experience towards an elusive, imagined centre (the national ghost or monster), but such action is only necessary because of centrifugal forces that would tear it apart. The national pot is always seething.

Nationalism is 'primarily a quest for unity,' according to Gordon Smith (199), but the quest only becomes urgent when unity is threatened. 'On what terrain does the nation find unity?' asks Charles Taylor of Canada at a time (1988) when '[u]nity is what one quarrels over; it is the hub of controversy' (*Reconciling* 130). His question could not even have been posed in this way earlier, when the nation was itself regarded as the most secure legitimizing terrain. It did not require a 'prime ground of agreement' (130); rather, it *was* that ground. 'Legitimacy,' as the word's etymology shows, concerns the rule of law and what makes a given rule seem reasonable, defensible, and just. In romantic historicism, the nation is not merely one legitimating value among others, but the very basis of legitimacy, articulating everything that is authentic in the life of a people. The old slogan that Mark Twain found so distasteful, 'My country right or wrong,' expresses a national faith that refuses to be dislodged or even to recognize that its ground might be illegitimate. Consequently, Taylor's attempt to foresee 'a post-unanimist national life' providing for 'the legitimacy of multiple options' (131) would have made little sense to a writer such as Samuel Edward Dawson, who wrote in 1908: 'While the literature of a people is the expression of the genius of that people it is, at the same time, a formative power which moulds and preserves national character. Especially is this true of poetry, for in its poetry the ideals of a people find utterance ... Nations live their lives – they rise, endure, and pass away. Knowledge has no bearing on their duration. Life is spiritual, and the soul of a people is not in what it has or what it knows of the material world; but in the spiritual power of its aggregate personality' (Ballstadt 172).

This is my last example of romantic nationalism in full fig. I quote it to emphasize that its splendid promise – the literary power to formulate and inspire a nation – continues to dazzle cultural theorists, although where Dawson speaks of a people finding utterance, we now speak of subject positions and the difficulty of securing their agency within a shifting, enunciative horizon. Today the nation is not only in crisis, but is itself a form of crisis. Jürgen Habermas argues that social meanings and values are not devised individually, but systematically through legitimating discourses that explain a political order, justify its inequities, and obscure its iniquities (*Legitimation* 36). A national literature accomplished exactly this function, and, appropriately, Dawson sees the *genius loci* as a poet who writes the nation into being. Legitimation crises occur when the validity claims of these discourses fail to secure social bonds or to confer identity.

> Social systems too have identities and can lose them; historians are capable of differentiating between revolutionary changes of a state or the downfall of an empire, and mere structural alterations. In doing so, they refer to the interpretations that members of a system use in identifying one another as belonging to the same group, and through this group identity assert their own self-identity. In historiography, a rupture in tradition, through which the interpretive systems that guarantee identity lose their social integrative power, serves as an indicator of the collapse of social systems. From this perspective, a social system has lost its identity as soon as later generations no longer recognize themselves within the once-constitutive tradition. (*Legitimation* 3–4)[7]

Legitimation crises occur not just because entrenched authorities lose credibility, but because the way in which those authorities were constituted is no longer perceived as meaningful. Incompetent authorities could easily be replaced. But when the very grounds of competence are in doubt, there is a fundamental crisis exposing social contradictions that previously had gone unnoticed or seemed unimportant. What looked like a harmonious culture suddenly appears chaotic.

Habermas and Jean-François Lyotard follow Marx in dividing history into social formations whose inherent tensions are subdued by systems of control and their legitimating discourses. Both writers regard the present age as particularly volatile because it is saturated with unreliable ideologies. According to Lyotard, with the loss of consensus comes an erosion of the intellectual disciplines – such as literary history – that interpret society. They lose sight of their objects and their missions because they seem either too disciplined (narrow, reductive, self-confirming) or too undisciplined (pursuing phantoms like the national ghost). 'The classical dividing lines between the various fields of science are thus called into question – disciplines disappear, overlappings occur at the borders between sciences, and from these new territories are born ... The old "faculties" splinter into institutes and foundations of all kinds, and the universities lose their function of speculative legitimation ... The social subject itself seems to dissolve in this dissemination of language games' (Lyotard 39–40). The social subject is also the national subject, which dissolves at times of crisis.

Lyotard's explanation of how neat disciplinary borders become blurred is itself suspiciously neat, at least when applied to Canadian studies, which have not had to wait for a postmodern trauma to question their own integrity. They have always worried. English-Canadian literature has rarely provided a safe home for the 'social subject,' not because homes are unimportant, but because they have always seemed so isolated and vulnerable, like the town of Horizon in *As For Me and My House*. Historians have drawn 'dividing lines' back and forth over the literary landscape so often that it has become an obsessive theme about a country too vast and undifferentiated to fall into neat patterns. For instance, D.M.R. Bentley proposes one configuration by contrasting a social and imaginative 'baseland,' associated with authority and enclosure, with a 'hinterland' associated with openness and escape. Each zone has its own attractions and dangers.[8] Each envisages an appropriate field for sociable activity: one secures freedom *within* a just society; the other seeks freedom *from* unfair constraints (we have seen both situations in Marlatt and Kogawa). Each offers a basis for legitimacy both in the social order and in authentic literary styles. However, poets and critics have continually tried to draw a line between the two zones, only to discover that the opposition between them keeps breaking down. 'It probably needs to be emphasized that, though antithetical in their extremes (like good and evil), the baseland and hinterland orientations of Canadian poetry are not rigid categories, but rather the poles between which poets and poems exhibit greater or lesser dispositions towards one or the other. At different times, in different degrees, and in different poems (or parts of poems), a given poet may reveal both dispositions, perhaps even to the point of inconsistency' (84–5). Bentley is no deconstructionist, yet he freely reveals an inconsistency that threatens to undermine the legitimacy of his own system, which originally set baseland against hinterland. This does not mean his system is useless. On the contrary, it offers a productive way of analysing individual poems and of fitting them and their authors into literary history. But it is a system openly in crisis, acknowledging the inconsistencies of Canadian cultural aspirations. When used sensitively, it confesses the ambiguity of matter and method that besets all literary histories.

National literary history is a tripartite discourse in the sense that it uses the nation to secure both social and literary legitimacy. Its traditional goal is to harmonize social and literary values, but, as we have seen, the Canadian case shows that they can also be discordant. In chapter 2 under the heading of merit and authenticity, I suggested that Canadian literary history is often split between its rival aims and that writers keep stumbling over the split. T.D. Mac-Lulich is another critic who sees this ongoing crisis as productive rather than detrimental, because it has become 'almost the defining feature of Canadian life': 'I am asking, yet again, whether there is a "distinctively Canadian" aspect to our collective existence. Canadian literature, like Canadian culture generally, exists in a state of permanent crisis, always on the verge of being overwhelmed by outside forces. The term "Canadian literature" identifies a mixed category, whose specifications are partly literary and partly political. Whatever the literary purists among us may like to think, the justification for isolating Canadian literature as a separate field of study is linked with a conviction of our cultural divergence from the United States' (27). The phrase 'mixed category' may suggest illegitimacy to purists who consider the mixture unholy, but literary history is always a contaminated (hybrid) genre, while national + literary + history is a *ménage à trois*. This domestic arrangement may produce a fractious Canadian family, but its very multiplicity can have the virtue of guarding against extreme forms of intolerance. A demand for purity, whether made by literary formalists (for whom poetry should be purely poetic) or by cultural nationalists (for whom culture should be purely national), always conceals an ideological imperative that would exclude all contaminants, but covertly maintains their presence through repeated rituals of expulsion. If the easiest way to love one's country is to hate the stranger within the gates, then an alien presence must continually be found and feared in order to defend national purity. *Obasan* (or the racism of an Adrien Arcand)[9] shows that Canada, too, has succumbed to xenophobia, and Native writers such as Maria Campbell or Jeannette C. Armstrong will not likely be satisfied with my reassurance that living 'in a state of permanent crisis' has its advantages. But finding satisfaction in Canada, or finding what will make Canada satisfactory, is one of the aims of this chapter.

In view of MacLulich's final remark about the United States, it is ironic that American critics have become troubled by the illegitimacy of their own literature. Lawrence Buell calls literary history a 'hybrid genre' that 'negotiates between a model of interpretative criticism and a model of empiricist historiography' (216). Negotiations between the two models, that is, between texts and contexts, are conducted through what he calls 'sociograms.' Individual works are interpreted as social parables or 'symptomatic ideological artifact[s],' which can be read both socially and parabolically (221–2). In this way, historical conditions are used to furnish literary structures while, conversely, literary typologies illuminate history. Sociograms in English-Canadian literature are: the garrison, bush garden, baseland, and hinterland. Buell further notes that the social and literary aspects of a work are supposed to chime harmoniously, but when circumstances and attitudes change sufficiently, established parables no longer seem legitimate and must be replaced by others. The sequence of new sociograms marks the course of literary history. At times of crisis, however, the entire procedure becomes suspect. Then unsettling questions are asked about the strategy. Who writes sociograms? How are they composed? What makes them valid only at certain times? A split develops, not just between the literary and historical duties of literary history, but within each category as well. National histories then appear to be obsolete; national literatures lose their bearings.

Although he acknowledges the risks of codifying literary history, Buell does not push his argument to the point where American literature itself is threatened by his unmasking of ideological codes. Perhaps this threat has been unimaginable – at least until recently – to American critics who believe that no matter how often they reinvent their country, 'America' itself is too spacious and compelling a reality to fail as a legitimating historical/literary category. Through political controversy and civil unrest, they feel that their national character is tested but, apart from the Civil War, not threatened fundamentally. Only outside the American orbit, or within American subcultures where people feel less secure in their citizenship, is nationality felt to be problematic. Contrast the scene further south, where we find a precarious sense of national legitimacy. Jean Franco says that in Latin American fiction 'the nation' has become 'a complex and contested form' because 'it is no longer the inevitable framework for either political or cultural projects' (204). It no longer satisfies political or literary thinking, which must contend with militarism and modernization, two ideologies that thrive on nationalism. To criticize the army or its modernizing projects, one must challenge the nationalism that sustains them, but this leaves Latin American writers with a precarious sense of identity. Franco follows Fanon in ascribing to Third World countries a radical scepticism about nation-ness as a political force, as a system of meaning and belief, and as a literary allegory (sociogram). Their literature testifies to 'the dissolution of a once totalizing myth which is now replaced by private fantasies lived out amid public disaster' (208). She suggests that hybrid literary styles like magic realism, for which Latin American writers have become famous, express a crisis in nationhood: 'In place of an identifiable microcosm of the nation, such novels offer a motley space in which different historical developments and different cultures overlap' (205).[10]

Similar attitudes and styles are found in disaffected subcultures within well-established nations, for example in African-American writing and even in Britain. According to Tom Nairn, now that the imperial sun has set, British historians cannot rely on totalizing myths to provide national definition. I noted how for the Leavises 'Englishness' was a flexible critical tool, because it enabled them to organize the ensemble of English writing, to judge the character of individual writers and assess their works. Now, says Nairn, because such tools can no longer do their job, the national subject has begun to dissolve: 'It is quite true that the English need to rediscover who and what they are, to reinvent an identity of some sort better than the battered cliché-ridden hulk which the retreating tide of imperialism has left them' (259).[11] As for Canada, it has managed to thrive 'as a crisis,' according to E.D. Blodgett, who echoes Jacques Godbout's cryptic remark: 'Pas de crise, pas de pays' ('Is a History' 3, 1). French Canadians are confident that they exist as a nation, but they have made an art of feeling threatened; whereas English Canadians have lamented that they hardly exist in their own right (E.K. Brown), or are barely surviving against all odds (Atwood), or are on the brink of extinction (MacLulich, Robin Matthews), or have just ceased to exist (George Grant).

Commonweal

This tour of the Americas shows that many writers consider the nation contestable and even contemptible. Why then does it persist? What does it offer that we cannot resist?

First, the nation persists because it is protean. Nationalism is so deeply ingrained in modern thinking that it can hardly be considered just one dispensable ideology among others (Orridge 52–3, Ahmad 37–9). Instead it requires some grander name such as 'macropolitical discourse' to dignify its role as 'the binding and overarching umbrella that subsumes other and different political temporalities' (Radhakrishnan 78). As a meta-ideological principle, it performs a series of interrelated functions: it unifies a given collectivity, articulates its parts, and legitimizes its authority. But the specific forms of political unity and control can be remarkably different. '[R]endering visible the nationalism that forms the overarching ideology of our age is difficult to the extent that one or another nationalism tends to become the form of last resort for *every* legitimizing political appeal – whether right or left, imperialist or anti-imperialist, religious or secular, elitist or populist, capitalist or anti-capitalist, cynical or utopian, and whether or not on behalf of an ideology that has any account whatsoever to offer of the status of the "nation" as such' (Sedgwick, 'Nationalisms' 238). If romantic nationalism seems passé, there are always other forms to take its place. If in a pluralistic country like Canada, liberal nationalism threatens to paralyse citizens in futile, multicultural antagonism, then other forms of 'nation-ness' will emerge in any community that offers itself as a liberatory alternative. Benedict Anderson notes ironically that the nation is said to be in greatest crisis just when nationalism is most fervent:[12] 'since World War Two every successful revolution has defined itself in *national* terms ... and, in so doing, has grounded itself firmly in a territorial and social space inherited from the prerevolutionary past ... The reality is quite plain: the "end of the era of nationalism," so long prophesied, is not remotely in sight. Indeed, nation-ness is the most universally legitimate value in the political life of our time' (12).

Second, the nation endures as a sacred object. Nationalism is not just a belief or a program, but a passion. Even as modern critics have desacralized the world by turning theology into politics or psychology or rhetoric, the nation has continued to inspire religious devotion. As Anderson and Jean Bethke Elshtain insist, no other social form is so successful, for good or ill, in arousing a '[c]ommunal ecstasy' that makes people eager to sacrifice themselves for the common good (Elshtain 164). Traditionally, the nation is born in bloodshed and sanctified by suffering, which turns historical nastiness into national destiny. Thus John Richardson's *Wacousta* tries to give Canada a good, gory baptism to ensure the well-being of the new country. My point is that when the nation is revered as a 'sacred imagined community' (Anderson 44), it allows people to conceive of a public good, a higher justice worth dying for; yet a sustaining vision of the public good is precisely what current cultural theory finds so hard to articulate. The difficulty in discerning such a vision is the subject of 'Civil Elegies.' Surely the success of *Obasan* and *Ana Historic* is due partly to their tragic and rhapsodic passions, which summon an energy equal to the older kinds of communal ecstasy that Kogawa and Marlatt denounce as destructive. Because no earnest commitment to a social cause (Aunt Emily), and no scrupulous historical accuracy (the younger Annie) could possibly offer the gratification of the old devotions (self-sacrifice, national destiny, the masculine ordeal), Naomi and Annie have to find other ways of envisaging, however imperfectly, an exhilarating fusion of personal joy and public good. I have claimed that neither novel is escapist, because their heroines realize they cannot fulfil themselves without accepting a wider affiliation. Their personal satisfaction is only possible within an enabling social satisfaction, that is, within a vision of justice. This is what makes them heroic, since reimagining a nation is as grand a project as raising a village or constructing a railroad.

Third, the modern politics of identity means that the nation will continue to be the prime forum for justice, because only a national setting can confer legitimacy on communities seeking to articulate their social distinctiveness and power (Parker et al. 8). I agree with Elshtain that: 'The nation-state is a phenomenon that cannot be imagined or legislated out of existence. Needing others to define ourselves, we will remain inside a state/nation discourse of war and politics, for better or worse, as long as states remain the best way we have devised for protecting and sustaining a way of life in common' (170). Risking a gross generalization, I would say that current cultural theories are extremely skilful at disclosing the injustices committed on behalf of the nation, but less successful in portraying what used to be called the commonweal – the public good. All the contentious literary topics over the last twenty years are sites where justice is debated: the canon, racism, equity issues, appropriation of voice, subaltern studies, patriarchy, homophobia, *écriture féminine*, political correctness. In each case a strong sense of systemic injustice provokes a critique that is compromised by its own deconstruction of moral agency. Traditionally, moral authority stems from a secure epistemological subject or psychological ego, which makes informed decisions in order to act responsibly in a shared social setting. Now, when all these conditions are in crisis,[13] an honest critique must find a fairer way to judge worth and share authority, a way that will reshape all cultural practices from reading poetry, to writing literary history, to designing a university. For example: 'This new [feminist] criticism deconstructs patriarchal monolithism by introducing variety and multiplicity in thought and expression, by being resolutely eclectic and interdisciplinary in nature, thus attacking the very monocentrism on which power is founded ... This new feminist literary criticism would not be a meta-language like patriarchal discourse, but would remain open, an assimilated reading, a true intertextuality in which, through shared characters, quotations, or languages, the reader is intimately touched by the other's text' (Godard, 'Mythmaking' 3). Eclectic and assimilated readings, intertextuality, shared characters, intimacy – recast in these terms, the crisis of the nation expresses a resolutely hesitant search for the sociability that justice permits or that injustice frustrates.

If the discourses that I lump together as 'current cultural theory' have difficulty envisioning a genuine commonweal, they are nevertheless eager to articulate such a vision, because they are so sensitive to injustices that are perpetrated in the name of the nation yet are rectifiable only within a national setting. They excel at remembering all that ideology exhorts us to forget, by sounding a wake-up call to the cultural amnesia that, Renan claims, is necessary to nationhood. But this same deconstructive skill, which incisively discloses historical infractions, makes it difficult for them to specify a compensating sociability that will not, in its turn, be exposed as equally unjust. Deconstruction is like the sorcerer's apprentice: eventually it turns on its master, since its task is to undo all mastery. Humanism, liberalism, pluralism, multiculturalism, and even feminism – all have been proposed as just and sociable responses to Canada's colonial past, but later have been condemned as subtly oppressive or as exhibiting at best a 'repressive tolerance' (Herbert Marcuse's phrase used by Spivak 112). They call for tolerance, but only in ways that benefit certain classes of people at the expense of others: Riel's moccasins, but not his politics, are tolerated. They politely welcome everyone to a neutral public forum but ignore that the rules of civility governing the forum are never neutral. By dictating what counts as sociable behaviour and what lies beyond the pale, they ensure that 'we never really hear from the "other" except in the terms already assigned to it by the hegemonic culture' (Gunew 38). Taylor criticizes liberalism on this account, but his remarks apply to more radical ideologies as well: 'Liberalism is not a possible meeting ground for all cultures, but is the political expression of one range of cultures, and quite incompatible with other ranges ... All this is to say that liberalism can't and shouldn't claim complete cultural neutrality. Liberalism is also a fighting creed. The hospitable variant I espouse, as well as the most rigid forms, has to draw the line' (*Philosophical* 249). Even creeds that strive to obliterate 'the line' by renouncing all 'binary logic' that would mark odious distinctions between self/other, male/female, public/private, straight/queer – all are forced to make distinctions of their own, if only to put liberals in their place. They, too, become fighting creeds as soon as they distinguish an incivility (colonialism, patriarchy, homophobia) in need of redress. For instance, Donna Haraway wants to learn

> how to craft a poetic/political unity without relying on a logic of appropriation, incorporation, and taxonomic identification.
>
> The theoretical and practical struggle against unity-through-domination or unity-through-incorporation ironically not only undermines the justifications for patriarchy, colonialism, humanism, positivism, essentialism, scientism, and other unlamented -isms, but *all* claims for an organic or natural standpoint. (157)

Since the nation once provided the most natural and organic of standpoints, Haraway seems to be renouncing nationhood as both a philosophical error and a moral disaster.

I cite Godard and Haraway to illustrate the scope of theories seeking nothing less than a heroic new paradigm, which will not merely transform but redeem the cognitive economy of Western thinking. Haraway's effortless pairing of poetry and politics shows how ardently the latest critiques denounce injustices both in literature and by means of literature, which is one of the most subtle agents of sexist, racist, nationalist, and Eurocentric values, yet is also able to detect and correct (or at least offer a corrective to) those same injustices. I just chided colonialism as an 'incivility' because I want to keep the civil forum in view, but the word will seem absurdly prim to Jeannette Armstrong, who bitterly denounces the crimes committed against Native peoples in the name of civilization:

> Pioneers and traders
> bring gifts

Smallpox, Seagrams
and Rice Krispies

Civilization has reached
the promised land. ('History Lesson' 203)

She is confident that literature has a moral mission, and her task is
to awaken cultural memories that will heal her nation by reaffirming its own notions of civility: 'healing can take place through cultural affirmation ... The dispelling of lies and the telling of what
really happened until *everyone,* including our own people understands that this condition did not happen through choice or some
cultural defect on our part, is important. Equally important is the
affirmation of the true beauty of our people whose fundamental
co-operative values resonated pacifism and predisposed our cultures as vulnerable to the reprehensible value systems which promote domination and aggression' ('Disempowerment' 209). The
'reprehensible value systems' correspond to Western thinking,
which must be combated by 'fundamental co-operative values' arising from a Native commonweal, to which Armstrong is passionately devoted. Far from being obsolete, the nation offers the only
legitimate ground for her people to protest what they have suffered and to grow in accordance with their own cultural values.

The religious devotion inspired by nationalism can therefore
still be salutary. One of the most remarkable features of contemporary theory is the fervour with which it has rediscovered a moral
motive that was always essential to literary criticism. Dr Johnson
could not imagine a just criticism that was not aligned with divine
justice. By contrast, a subtle post-structuralist such as Homi
Bhabha has no faith in an absolute ethical standard, let alone that
it should concur with a universal aesthetic standard. On the contrary, he protests that all such absolutes are not just philosophically
misguided but morally and socially dangerous, and to oppose
them requires strict 'conceptual vigilance' (*Location* 27) lest the
unwary critic be seduced by the solaces of idealism. Yet his objection is strongly ethical and sociable: 'Denying an essentialist logic
and a mimetic referent to political representation is a strong, *prin-*

cipled argument against political separatism of any colour, and cuts through the moralism that usually accompanies such claims' (27, my emphasis). A principled objection to moralism – the careless assumption of an ideology's superiority – is itself moral. Bhabha is something of a puritan: he prefers a morality that is difficult, diffident, and deferential, through which to imagine a just society.

Poetic Justice

Throughout this study I have used the words 'justice' and 'justness' to distinguish competing principles of adequacy and redress as they inform history, literature, and criticism. I have argued that such discourses, no matter how subversive, could not function without faith of one kind or another: faith in rational scrutiny and moral worth; trust in authorities; fidelity to literary genres and conventions. I have hastened to add that lapses in faith are also integral to these discourses. Wherever there is faith, there can be doubt and heresy. Resisting readers may expose moral codes as hypocritical; they may view authorities with systematic suspicion; they may take greater pleasure in aesthetic infidelity than in classical rigour. Nevertheless, they must launch their resistance from their own (wavering) faith. Literature can be right or wrong in many ways, and can provide many kinds of satisfaction. It may be more rewarding when it dissatisfies – when it scorns the expected compensations (laughter, marriage, truth, death), when it baffles rather than consoles, when it reduces to absurdity rather than raises to certainty. A cultivated dissatisfaction can be very satisfying; it has its own justness. Literature may even be right according to one standard by being wrong according to another. We rejoice in seeing the wicked punished as they deserve, precisely because we know what they *do* deserve, and we realize that in reality they often go unpunished. As long as the balance between the two judgments is clear, then this paradox is a source of pleasure, not distress. Of course, a really good, distressing ending is satisfying too. My favourite example is the 'happy' conclusion to Shakespeare's *Measure for Measure,* where Isabella finds herself rewarded with marriage to a stranger. The actress playing Isabella has only to quiver an eyebrow to cast doubt on the meaning of the final scene. Similarly, as critics we feel secure in our judgment when we can confidently assess the relative merits of justice and justness. My example in chapter 1 concerned Jane Campion's film *The Piano,* which according to bell hooks should have sacrificed historical accuracy to the nobler cause of feminism and antiracism. bell hooks justifies her verdict on the basis of genre. Because the film is not a documentary but a fantasy, it should – the obligation is ethical as well as aesthetic – exercise its imaginative liberty to satisfy a feminist, poetic justice (hooks 121).

The justness of justice is the adequacy of art to represent social and moral (in)adequacies. The (im)balance between justness and justice is also displayed as a temporal vector, because justice promises redress or restitution, and in that 'promise' is a temporal disposition linking past to future, and future to past. Redress gives justice both its temporality and its semiotic density. If one act (or sequence of actions) redresses an earlier one, which has been judged culpable, then the relation between the two acts is both temporal and symbolic. For instance, several years of confinement in prison 'equals,' or answers for, a serious crime; fifty dollars is commensurate with a traffic violation; for some other transgressions a sincere apology will suffice. Traditionally, justice provides a significant, moral, redemptive temporality expressed, for example, in the series: crime, arraignment, judgment, punishment, restitution, social reintegration (a convict released from prison). This dramatic order has great aesthetic appeal, which satisfies not just because of its fateful, soothing rigour, but because it provides enough ('satis') to both logic and conscience. Just as hunger is satisfied when we have eaten enough, so justice is satisfied when there has been enough evidence, reward, punishment, remorse, and so on. There is also enough time: a chronological pattern is fulfiled as the future atones for the past. And there is enough narrative: a plot achieves closure. The proportions are just right, as in a classical work of art. Goldilocks could be the Muse of Justice.

The cumulative satisfactions of judicial redress are easily upset, however, especially by post-structuralist criticism, which, in a sense, is committed on principle to being dissatisfied. Instead of endorsing a system of adequation that offers 'just enough' to satisfy our moral and semantic appetites, it finds 'too much': it looks for excess, surplus, supplement. It disrupts the smooth temporality of conventional judgment by deconstructing each term in the causal chain outlined above, so that justice becomes a disjunctive array of enigmas instead of a coherent progression. Or it discloses a 'deadly space between' the links in the chain, so that the redemptive progress falters just when it should advance. Or it detects 'a *time-lag* – a contingent moment – in the signification of closure' (Bhabha, *Location* 183), a hesitation in thought that makes room for critical intervention.[14] Thus Conrad confutes the temporality of justice by viciously conflating it, when one of the 'pilgrims' in 'Heart of Darkness' passes judgment on an African who may or may not – his guilt hardly matters – have started a fire: 'Serve him right. Transgression – punishment – bang! Pitiless, pitiless. That's the only way' (41). Since Marlow as narrator hopes to render to Kurtz 'the justice which was his due' (94), the reduction of justice to an outburst of vengeance casts doubt on Marlow's competence to deliver a satisfactory verdict on his own story. 'Heart of Darkness' provokes so much controversy because the justness of justice is so murky. This example illustrates briefly what we saw at greater length in Marlatt and Kogawa: that to disrupt the justness of a narrative is to subvert its narrative of justice.

Critics dispense their own justice when they appraise a work and assign it a place in literary history, and the stormy climate of current theory has produced some controversial decisions. What makes recent critiques so devastating is their insistence that literary and social injustice is not an unfortunate lapse in judgment but a systemic directive in Western thinking, which proceeds differentially by identifying an 'other,' and subjugating it in the form of 'nature,' 'matter,' or 'woman.' All are passive, mute materials until shaped by an imperial, male will. Likewise, nationalism flourishes in hateful opposition to foreigners. In this view, knowledge is the fruit of domination: it is an intellectual appropriation of objects that in themselves are improper and meaningless until dignified by Western science. What gives current theory its moral fervour is the conviction – here is its faith – that this appropriation is a crime against other cultures, conducted not just through force of arms but through an 'ontological imperialism,' or a 'mode of knowledge as a politics of arrogation' (Young, *White Mythologies* 13, 3). Consequently, injustice stains all aspects of cultural life, from writing novels to selling soap to devising sciences like anthropology and sociology.[15] Even classics like 'Heart of Darkness' and *Huckleberry Finn* are tainted because, although they denounce colonial and racial injustice, they launch their protest from assumptions that remain tacitly imperialist and racist. Conrad and Twain illustrate a misfortune that is the mirror image of Balzac's good luck. He unwittingly condemned the bourgeois ideology that he intended to endorse (according to Engels), whereas they are mired in the racism that they claim to reject.

I have already indicated that I find this line of argument compelling but reductive, since its account of Western thinking fetishizes both 'the West' and 'thinking' according to a simplistic paradigm – roughly equivalent to saying that Westerners are incapable of conceiving of life except as a football game. Nevertheless, great force of argument can derive from great limitation, and it would be a mistake to underestimate the subtlety with which the theory can be deployed or the cogency of its insights.

Consider what happens to the Hegelian assumption that justice is the hidden dynamic of historiography, both in its causal analysis and its narrative practice. Bill Ashcroft recasts this view from a postcolonial perspective:

> Imperial/empirical history is a story of development towards a particular end. This is one meaning of the term 'historicism.' But its teleological impetus is one which is centripetal, that is, it constantly moves towards the center, and establishes an order which is the essential aspect of the imperial – it orders reality ... Such history is grounded on the imperial telos of progress and civilization, the telos of order. The idea of a *telos* [*sic*] – an end or goal to which the great transcendent movement of history is directed, is implicated in the idea of the sequential itself. For out of the notions of contiguity and temporal sequence emerges the principle of cause, which can, in turn, be seen to be a product of narrative structures once the world is considered as a text. (202)

For Ashcroft, the proviso that the world be considered as a text opens the door to a counter-discourse, a rewriting of history in accordance with a new mode of representation. The problem is not just that European imperialists were hypocrites who, as 'Heart of Darkness' shows, enriched themselves by betraying their own ideals of compassion and fairness. The injustice is far deeper and, consequently, more difficult to recognize, let alone correct. The problem lies in Western thinking and how it represents events as historically significant. To 'order reality' – to make sense of things – is judged culpable not because one particular order (imperial history) has been cruelly unjust, in contrast to other, fairer orders, but because all such teleological designs will be exclusive and tyrannical. They impose themselves in the name of truth and fairness but at the expense of other cultures, which are denied any political or moral agency of their own. Therefore, there is no point in colonized people inserting themselves into the standard histories that have ignored or abused them, or even in writing their own histories, because 'history' – and its representation of human affairs – is itself the problem. To employ the master's tool would be to strengthen the instrument of oppression. 'But the problem here is that in history, as in other discursive formations, [science, literature, literary history] the post-colonial exists outside representation itself. The remedy is not "re-insertion" but "re-vision"; not the re-insertion of the marginalized into representation, but the appropriation of a method, the re-vision of "history." This is crucial to the political interpretation of post-colonial experience because it is an attempt to assume control of the processes of representation' (Ashcroft 204). Ashcroft treats Western thinking much as Michael Ondaatje treats his character Pat Garrett in *The Collected Works of Billy the Kid.* Garrett is a 'sane assassin' (29) who feels compelled to discipline everything unruly: instinct, body, criminal activity, the wildness of the American West. But if his goal is neat teleological certainty (justice, history, science), his compulsion to attain that goal is manic and bloodthirsty. Similarly, the deeper significance of Western historiography is not its professed aim to civilize the primitive, but its rage for order, a rage so fierce that it is uncontrollable. In a sense, Garrett is a Hegelian historian who would write the story of the nation neatly, but in blood.

Ashcroft's cure for the wound of imperial history is a Nietzschean transvaluation of values achieved through a transformation of historical representation. This solution sounds superb, almost magical, and it recalls the ecstatic freedom, foreseen in *Ana Historic* and *Obasan*, that I compared to the quasi-religious passion aroused by the nation. Similarly, at the end of chapter 1 I noted a utopian cast to recent theory, evident in Henry Giroux's desire to configure 'a pluralized public space' (115) that would replace the liberal forum with a 'third space' (104), free from the domineering dialectic of self and other, a true commonweal in which joy and justice might commingle. After such splendid promise, who could be content with history-as-usual?

Third Space

The pluralized public space joins a series of models of sociability through which the nation has been imagined, found wanting, and then reimagined: as bourgeois public sphere, domestic village, cooperative privacy, joint venture, shared public space, neutral forum, liberal mosaic, and Canadian community of communities. The phrase 'third space' comes from Homi Bhabha,[16] who contends that the vertigo of post-colonial identity requires an antithetical discourse to express the perplexity of living 'in the disjunctive, liminal space of national society' (*Location* 162). Unlike the liberal forum, with its antagonistic (hierarchical) 'cultural diversity,' the third space is an agonistic (dramatic/enunciative) site of unreconcilable yet companionable 'cultural difference.'[17] Like Ashcroft, Bhabha accepts the post-structuralist proviso that because the world must be considered as a text, it can be changed by being reinscribed as a 'hybrid national narrative' (*Location* 167) that conveys the 'jarring of meanings and values' in 'the uncanny moment of cultural difference that emerges in the process of enunciation' ('DissemiNation' 312).[18] The national ghost lurks in the word 'uncanny,' which is, of course, a term of deconstructive approval. To be 'third' (Third World, third space) is to inhabit an unstable cultural locale, but through a sly reversal (to which Bhabha gives various names: hybridity, mimicry, splitting, sly civility, colonial non-sense) this shaky position offers a firm moral footing, because freedom – coincidentally, the 'third' freedom in *Ana Historic* – requires instability and risk. 'Hybridity is the perplexity of the living as it interrupts the representation of the fullness of life; it is an instance of iteration, in the minority discourse, of the time of the arbitrary sign – "the minus in the origin" – through which all forms of cultural meaning are open to translation because their enunciation resists totalization ... In the restless drive for cultural translation, hybrid sites of meaning open up a cleavage in the language of culture' ('DissemiNation' 314).

This account of a sociability so radically heterogeneous that it is always on the boil turns politics into a kind of surrealistic poetry. I confess that it leaves me wondering if a vote for the New Democratic Party will really make much difference. Nevertheless, Bhabha offers a sophisticated argument, and I do not pretend to do justice to it in a few sentences. Instead, I want to suggest that through the intricacy of his argument, he displays an intellectual daring that takes on existential value, because in a textual world where texts are worldly, passionate theorizing amounts to an intensity of being. Because the popular distinction between theory and practice is another false binary,[19] 'history is *happening* – within the pages of theory, within the systems and structures we construct to figure the passage of the historical' (*Location* 25). This means that the theoretician has great power, but also great responsibility. The communal ecstasy of nationalism, which sanctions self-sacrifice for the common good, here becomes an assiduous theoretical ferment – a trespass of thought, in Pratt's words – which also aims at a fractious vision of sociability. It turns the literary historian, once the obedient squire of national literature, into a disobedient, intellectual hero who foresees the disjunctive destiny of the nation and becomes its exemplary citizen. We have already met this hero in William Boelhower's portrait of the deterritorialized ethnic subject who twists nationality into catastrophe but, by doing so, becomes a sacrificial figure, a true American who is willing to suffer the continuous identity crisis of his nation: 'His ethnic appearances are spontaneous, aleatory, and shifting, while his "identity" is ambiguous, cryptic, and allotropic' (Boelhower 137). He is at home in the third space, even though home is *unheimlich* (unhomely, uncanny).

One more example: the critic as exemplary citizen and sacrificial hero also appears in Trinh T. Minh-ha's portrait of the feminist multicultural artist. She, too, begins by renouncing the liberal public forum in favour of an 'interstitial ground' (229) of cultural upheaval:

> To make a claim for multi-culturalism is not, therefore, to suggest the juxtaposition of several cultures whose frontiers remain intact, nor is it to subscribe to a bland 'melting-pot' type of attitude that would level all differences. It lies instead, in the intercultural acceptance of risks, unexpected detours, and complexities of relation between break and closure. Every artistic excursion and theoretical venture requires that boundaries be ceaselessly called to question, undermined, modified, and reinscribed ... To maintain the indeterminacy of art, criticism is bound to test its limits, to confront over and over again the legitimation of its own discourse, hence to bring about its own indeterminacy. (232)

Here again, art, theory, and politics are interwoven, since theory is creative, creativity is critical, and both are dangerous. By daring to live freely in the midst of indeterminacy, the artist-critic bears in her imagination and on her body the burden of cultural multiplicity. The more closely theory and practice merge, the greater the sacrifice: 'The difficulty, naturally, is to live out a theory fully. How is it possible not to slip or skid when one has to walk along an abyss and at the same time measure its depth?' (120). The artist as solitary rebel is a familiar romantic, avant-garde, and existential hero, and there are theorists (Foucault is one) whose transgressions sometimes push them into dangerous, delicious solitude. But Bhabha and Trinh insist that their goal is always communal; they respect 'collective agency' (Bhabha, *Location* 229), not personal daring. They are describing social experiences in real historical settings, not private flights of fancy or polemical bravado.[20] This *is* the world – with the proviso that the world is happening 'within the pages of theory' – which means that it is shared. Consequently, Trinh offers an invitation that also appears in *Ana Historic*: 'The space of creativity is the space whose occupancy invites other occupancies ... It is thus the space of an activity in which everything takes on a collective value in spite of skepticism' (187–8). Bhabha expresses a desire, which we saw in *Obasan*, to formulate 'other articulations of human togetherness, as they are related to cultural difference and discrimination' (*Location* 191). A just, flexible, and interactive community is the ultimate goal of both writers, although Bhabha states this point a trifle more theoretically: 'Affiliative solidarity is formed through the ambivalent articulations of the realm of the æsthetic, the fantasmatic, the economic and the body political: a temporality of social construction and contradiction that is iterative and interstitial; an insurgent "intersubjectivity" that is interdisciplinary; an everyday that interrogates the synchronous contemporaneity of modernity' (230).

In reply to my analysis, some critics might carp that if I regard the 'third space' as just another reformulation of the consensual public sphere, then I have completely missed the point. No such definition of the nation will suffice, because the process of definition is itself at fault: it relies on a false view of language as instrumental and a false view of meaning as intentional mastery. I will remain caught in the old humanist trap until I admit that culture cannot be 'known' according to a single, clearly delineated model, because it is not an 'epistemological object' to be scrutinized empirically, but 'an enactive, enunciatory site' (Bhabha, *Location* 178) characterized by indeterminacy, contingency, and all the rest. Nations affirm their identity, in the first instance, in opposition to other groups from which they claim to be recognizably different, but ultimately, in defiance of an 'internal otherness' that structures them enigmatically (Siemerling 3, 11). The enigma of alterity collapses both inward and outward: it makes individuals and communities strangely conflicted – different from themselves. The ground of liberal sociability, which would join independent individuals in voluntary groups in a regulated setting that they agree to share fairly, is therefore doubly undermined. On the one hand, 'individuality' is an illusion that ignores how it is always directed by prior ideological motives. On the other hand, 'community' is another illusion that ignores its secret heterogeneity. Individuality is really the projection of an ideological community that, alas, is never truly communal (unified), because it is continually alien to itself. The post-critic must find a home in the midst of all this undecidability[21] by wandering through its labyrinth, not by expecting to draw an accurate map of passages that will continually shift.

I like a good enigma, too, but my concern is with justice and how it inscribes itself in national, social, and literary sites. If knowledge is situated in an 'ungraspable middle space' (Haraway 111), then how is justice to grasp its object? If cultural hybridity requires 'a space in-between the rules of engagement' (Bhabha, *Location* 193), then what becomes of justice, whose job is to define the rules of social engagement? In a pluralist society like Canada, so richly blessed with contradictions and crises, it is especially important for communities to share what Frank Davey calls 'a social sphere to which all human beings have access' (*Canadian Literary Power* 194). It is precisely because Canada has so many conflicting constituencies that we need a national space in which to meet, dispute, and negotiate. To negotiate is to be sociable, even when the interchange is nasty rather than affable, because negotiators must meet on a common ground if only to dispute its terms. As Stanley Fish observes, 'common ground' is usually the most embattled, because it is the greatest prize (35). The winner gets to define what 'common' means: what counts as common sense, common decency, or common fairness. Justice is the contested principle that makes communities sociable.

I hope it is clear that I do not regard justice as unproblematic or transcendent. On the contrary, it is a continual worry, but it is certainly worth worrying about. What could be more problematic than finding justice in an unjust world by means of discourses that perpetuate injustice? (Lucien Goldmann claims that the novel as a genre addresses exactly this question.)[22] Post-structuralists believe in the undecidability of truth, but justice is ultimately obliged to make decisions, flawed though they may be – decisions subject to judicial review that will also be flawed. Post-structuralism teases out disjunctions in narratives that look seamless, but justice is forced to make conjunctions between cause and effect, past and future, guilt and atonement, responsibility and punishment, and so on. Justice is not just speculative but imperative in the sense that it must both make and enforce judgments. Accordingly, I have tossed contemporary critics into one seething pot and argued that they are justifiably indignant about historical injustices still perpetrated today and embedded in the forms of Western surveillance (science, history, literature). For this very reason, they are obliged to articulate a countervailing justice, to which – we all agree – literature offers special insight. Justice, too, must be rethought from an interstitial perspective, but, in a sense, it is located right at the interstice, at the liminal point where rival views confront each other. It, too, can be exposed as enigmatic, but it is not just one contested principle among others, because it is the discourse of contestation itself. It is the discourse through which social and aesthetic contests are conceived, staged, and resolved, for better or worse – and, if worse, they should be corrected by standards that can always be contested anew. A circular argument, perhaps, but not all circles are unavailing. I do not mean that in justice I have luckily stumbled on something that by its very nature resists deconstruction (a secular equivalent of the old ontological proof of God's existence). Obviously it can and should be probed for contradictions – my 'should' registering a moral and intellectual resolve that we do justice even to the notion of justice.

Judgments must be made and enforced. No ideology can avoid imposing its values at the expense of others, even when its values are generous. Even policies whose aim is a mutual respect for diversity cannot avoid becoming forceful when they draw a line between civil and uncivil behaviour. Even a suspended judgment, held in sublime deconstructive deference, is sustained in accordance with its own ideological imperative. To speak of enforcement is to invite the rebuke that, after making a few mollifying gestures, I have reinstated the deadly Law of the Father that underwrites patriarchy and imperialism. But as Barbara Johnson shows in her study of *Billy Budd* (a story that nicely conforms to Goldmann's schema), justice is forceful because it relies on the threat of death not just as its ultimate power but as its paradoxically enabling condition. The union of theory and practice advocated by Bhabha and Trinh is actually attained in Melville's parable, but with mortal results. The union takes the form of a 'sentence' in the double sense of a linguistic statement and a judicial verdict by which reading (interpreting human conduct) becomes killing (executing judgment): 'Judging ... is nothing less than the wielding of the power of life and death through language ... Judgment is cognition functioning as an act' (Johnson 102). The uncanny fate that makes Billy simultaneously guilty and innocent of murder puts his judge, Captain Vere, in the same boat. He, too, is both culpable and blameless, as is the reader who must in turn assume the role of judge. For Johnson, there is no end to this chain of paradoxes, because 'cognition itself becomes an act of violence' (106), which may be directed to noble ends (fairness, equity, restitution), but only by making judgments that are themselves violent, and so subject to the same fate.

This dilemma sounds like the familiar deconstructive *mise en abyme*, but it has practical importance even in writing a nation's literary history, which I can illustrate with an example closer to home. An exchange of articles in the *Globe and Mail* over the 'Writing thru "Race"' conference held in Vancouver (1994), where some sessions were restricted to Native people and people of colour, provides a striking instance of conflicting notions of legitimacy. Those who oppose all restrictions appealed to an ideal of impartial justice: everyone deserves to be heard; discrimination cannot be cured by counter-discrimination. In opposition, supporters argued that a system of justice is never totally impartial, because it is ideologically directed to benefit certain classes of people and to obscure the injustices suffered by other. The aim of the Vancouver conference is fair in the sense that it redresses a historical injustice by creating a public forum beneficial to those who in the past had to play the game by other people's rules. It is time to change the rules. However the issue is judged (and judgment is unavoidable), rules will have to be enforced and conflicting principles will be violated. Injustices will occur in both camps whenever an ideologically loaded idea like 'race' is at stake. The conference's detractors claim the moral high ground without noticing that they thereby relegate other groups to the low ground. Meanwhile, the conference's organizers are obliged to judge who counts as 'coloured' and so is entitled to speak. This is by no means an obvious matter, and people with a just claim may be excluded, although I am not aware that such a problem actually arose. Attempts to classify people by race (or what is taken to be race) always encounter exceptions and oddities, as the old race laws in South Africa illustrated in extreme form, where 'mixed race' was a legal fiction used to justify the violence of the law. The debate over the Vancouver conference replays the politics of inclusion and exclusion that plagues all national literatures, and while the verdict may seem mild compared to *Billy Budd*, for a writer such as Armstrong its outcome is not just a matter of which authors get included in the anthologies. It is a matter of cultural survival.

Worrying the Nation

However different in other respects – in fact, because they are so different – *Billy Budd* and the 'Writing thru "Race"' conference show that justice, like nationalism, with which it is interwoven, is a 'macropolitical discourse' reinforcing all ideologies whose aim is to provide a vision not just of things as they are, but of things as they should be. If ideologies are always self-contradictory, as the Marxist tradition contends, perhaps the contradiction arises in the deadly space between 'is' and 'should,' between things as they are (that is, as our ideology makes them visible to us) and things as they should be. But the second category is divided further. It means things as our ideology foresees their improvement, and things as foreseeable by an improved ideology, the second standard of correction having no secure basis of its own since the 'improved' ideology has yet to be articulated. The final possibility is an interstitial place of signs and omens, interpretations and intuitions, of 'transgressed boundaries, potent fusions, and dangerous possibilities' (Haraway 154) where critics become prophets. Nowadays it is the only place to be. It is also the spot that my own argument has reached, and the problem is how to proceed fruitfully, since I do not claim to be prophetic. Even the most prescient literary history cannot avoid working within a framework of nations and nationalism, because it lingers within even the most rebellious outlook. As Ralph Cohen shows, histories are always complicit with the paradigms they claim to supersede: 'It is thus impossible to generate a new history without being contaminated by the language and genre of the old' (40). No discourse is autonomous or pure, and those that pretend to be brand new have merely mystified their lineage. To propose a clean break from all national literary histories in the hope of devising a unprecedented alternative is to dream of a fresh start, a theoretical Northwest Passage leading around the messy contamination of nation-ness. But to ignore the nation is to fall into the trap of trying to escape from the past by silently reinscribing its forms. Beyond the nation lie more nations, differently conceived.

I confess that through this study my own critical position has tacked back and forth in opposition to whomever I happen to be examining. When considering the legacy of romantic nationalism with its dazzling reward of national identity and destiny, I question its assumptions and applicability to Canada. When faced with today's radical critiques, whose methods and sensitivity to injustice I find compelling, I retreat to the refuge of the public forum where tolerant people can tolerate each other's differences. I am certain, however, that some kind of accommodation, some vision of adequacy and redress is necessary, not just because they are worthy goals, but because they are *a priori* conditions of any literary study. They are ideological imperatives and discursive needs already at work – and always at issue – within any attempt to assess literary works and to configure them socially and historically. A national literature, too, swerves back and forth by marshalling communities, which it shows to be divisive. It invites people to share their experiences, even as it teaches them new ways to disagree. It makes them feel both familiar and strange, by convoking a national family –

Listen, my children, and you shall hear
Of the midnight ride of Paul Revere (Longfellow 45)

Pensez-vous quelquefois à ces temps glorieux,
Où seuls, abandonnés par la France, leur mère,
Nos aïeux défendaient son nom victorieux
Et voyaient devant eux fuir l'armée étrangère? (Crémazie 18)

– and by exposing injustices even when it does not intend to do so. A modest example: the patriotic song 'The Maple Leaf Forever' juxtaposes the 'lily, thistle, shamrock, rose' to celebrate the composition of the nation. In effect, Canada is composed by the song, which provides a model of ethnic diversity as it proclaims a destiny ('forever') sanctioned by a sacrificial past (General Wolfe's death '[i]n days of yore'). However, an alert critic would intervene by noting that an earlier version of the refrain – 'The thistle, shamrock, rose entwine' – excluded the French fleur-de-lys, which was added to make the song more sociable. Unfortunately, this magnanimous gesture is unlikely to make Québécois, who do not want to be entwined in the British family, feel welcome in a song celebrating the defeat of Montcalm. Even this appeal to harmony harbours a threat of death. Literature is called upon to ease the strain of a pluralist society, when in fact the same strains appear within literature and literary history.

My response to this dilemma has not been to resolve it but to inhabit it, not to imagine some magical anti-discourse that will redeem historical trespasses, but to work within social and linguistic conditions that cannot be evaded and must serve as the means of accommodation. If national literary history is a hybrid genre, then it calls upon rival notions of adequacy and redress, which means that it, too, is animated by visions of justice, however conflicted. To regard it in the light of its own ambiguity[23] is to participate in the conflict, to challenge its adequacy, to seek redress. If it is 'contaminated,' then its motley composition is not an imperfection but a strength, because it allows critics to summon 'the contestatory force of an interpretive method whose material is the disparate, but intertwined and interdependent, and above all, overlapping streams of historical experience.' Edward Said goes on to say that because such writing is 'hybrid ... and encumbered, or entangled and overlapping with what used to be regarded as extra-

neous elements,' it gains the critical dexterity to challenge nationalism in the narrow sense, while encouraging a flexible sociability
(*Culture* 312, 317). If the nation is a fractured, contested public
space, then so much the better for literary critics. Whether they
consider themselves squires, heroes, or anti-heroes, they will be
kept busy tracing the fractures and judging the contests. In practical terms this means we must keep working through the idea of
national + literary + history without losing sight of the problemati-
cal interlacing of its three competing discourses. We must continue studying how the nation is imagined: how it defines a body of
writing as national; how it informs and validates that literature;
how its clashing loyalties impassion citizens for good or ill; how it
convokes and disperses communities; how it invokes and subverts
the ideal of heroism; how it foresees a fusion of personal and social
satisfactions (joy and justice); and how it gives a mission to literary
criticism, including the mission to denounce nationalism in its
vicious forms.

If literature shows why the nation does not make sense, it also
shows how it should be improved. I therefore take comfort in discovering that as the deconstruction of the 1980s has given way to
the ethical sensitivity of the 1990s, cultural theorists seek ways of
reaffirming social bonds that will be 'coalitional' rather than coercive. A just public forum is now judged possible provided, first, that
it is maintained 'on the basis of conscious coalition, of affinity, of
political kinship' rather than 'natural identification' (Haraway 156,
see also Fuss 36); and second, that its dialogic freedom is not regulated by some lordly, predetermined plan: 'Clearly, the value of
coalitional politics is not to be underestimated, but the very form
of coalition, of an emerging and unpredictable assemblage of positions, cannot be figured in advance. Despite the democratizing
impulse that motivates coalition building, the coalitional theorist
can inadvertently reinsert herself as sovereign of the process by trying to assert an ideal form of coalitional structure *in advance*, one
that will effectively guarantee unity as the outcome ... Perhaps a
coalition needs to acknowledge its contradictions and take action
with those contradictions intact' (Butler 14). Judith Butler's goal
is not unity (political/cultural/artistic consensus) but sociability,

which here must be understood as 'a permanently available site of contested meanings' (15).[24] She cannot dictate how the contest should be adjudicated, since this would make her guilty of the fault she has just condemned. But she is concerned to keep the site permanently available. I have argued that justice is the discourse of contestation, whether its location be a courtroom, battlefield, novel or literary theory: all are sites of contested meanings. I argued further that because of its disjunctive temporality – its problematic fulfilment – justice must eventually be enforced through a threat (rhetorical or actual) of death. Butler wants to avoid this threat by finding 'a normative ideal relieved of coercive force' (15); but when she admits (above) that a coalition 'needs' to acknowledge its contradictions in order to 'take action,' she is implicitly recognizing the forcefulness of justice. When is a force not coercive? When we accept it as right and just; when it accords with our own values. But in that case, there is some consensus after all, if not about specific political goals or literary judgments, then about the validity of the coalition itself. What is 'normative' is that people must (imperative) agree to disagree.[25]

In elaborating his 'contestatory' method, Said traces a three-part liberating process leading to a coalition of this sort. Following Fanon's advice, he first urges (post-/neo-)colonized peoples to re-establish a 'communal memory' by writing their nations back into history (*Culture* 215). We noted this project in Native Canadian writing. If imperial nationalism was the disease, then local nationalism is the first stage of a cure, because it provides 'a necessary spur to revolt against the colonizer' ('Politics' 197). But the revolt will be self-defeating unless it immediately raises a broader social consciousness, which can envision 'an alternative way of conceiving human history' by 'breaking down the barriers between cultures' (*Culture* 216). This second stage corresponds to the transnational discourses that have proliferated in ethnic and feminist criticism. In the third stage, however, this growing fragmentation must (imperative, hortatory) be checked by 'a more integrative view of human community and human liberation' (216). The 'reintegration of all those people and cultures, once confined and reduced to peripheral status, with the rest of the human race'

('Politics' 198) is only possible through a nuanced articulation of overlapping communities sustained, but not limited, by nationality.[26] Though no humanist, in the pejorative sense in which the term is now used, Said seeks a humane vision that accepts nations by simultaneously acknowledging their interdependence and their diversity: 'There is also, however, a consistent intellectual trend within the nationalist consensus that is vitally critical, that refuses the short-term blandishments of separatist and triumphalist slogans in favor of the larger, more generous human realities of community *among* cultures, peoples, and societies. This community is the real human liberation portended by the resistance to imperialism' (*Culture* 217).

Canadians have aspired to such a commonweal, although they express it differently. I also take comfort in discovering that my vacillation is common in English-Canadian criticism, which has often formulated a sociability so relaxed as to seem irresolute, for instance in Malcolm Ross's 'anti-nationalistic nationalism' (123), or J.M.S. Careless's vision of Canadians sharing common differences ('Limited' 8), or Charles Taylor's definition of national identity as an endless debate 'between a plurality of legitimate options' (*Reconciling* 132), or A.B. McKillop's counsel that 'a more fruitful way of conceiving of an "identity" for Canada is by expanding the term to incorporate within it the potential for contradiction, diversity, and paradox' (6). These national recipes try to secure a workable coherence for the country without imposing homogeneity or hypostasizing a national essence, so that 'Canadianism' (Careless, 'Limited' 11) emerges from them only as a tentative inference continually subject to historical adjustment. Although Canadians have been accused of servile deference to authority (Friedenberg), they have also been loyal to a network of rival, overlapping authorities without worrying about inconsistencies. While this may reflect our inability to make up our minds, it produces some admirable results: a country that awards federal grants to separatists surely invites respect as well as satire. (How is the granting council to judge if the money was well-spent?) Mordecai Richler is fond of noting that Québécois simultaneously supported the separatist René Lévesque and the federalist Pierre Trudeau, who were politically and temperamentally opposed (*Home* 236). More generally, Leslie Armour finds Canadian history marked by a proliferation of competing institutions, which splinter cultural unity (16–20) to the point that 'in conventional terms, Canada, as a nation, is not possible' (137). Yet it has prospered all the same (so far), because different communities find their own ways of endorsing common institutions and contributing to a pluralistic culture.

Now that unconventionality is in vogue, it might appear that Canada was always one step ahead of the game. Like Molière's Monsieur Jourdain, who discovers he was speaking prose all along without knowing it, we have been unwittingly inhabiting an Althusserian nation, a 'decentered whole' in which social coherence is secured not by any ideal or expressive totality (national ghost, myth, or destiny), but only by a presiding contradiction (Jay, *Marxism* 406).[27] George Bowering, Linda Hutcheon, and Robert Kroetsch like to see Canada as bristling with ambiguities, a country that has leapfrogged from a Victorian to a postmodern sensibility: 'Again, all is periphery and margin, against the hole in the middle. We are held together by that absence. There is no centre. This disunity is our unity' (Kroetsch, *Lovely Treachery* 31).[28] While it is flattering to think that we were so avant-garde, it is more likely that we have been struggling with a history that makes pluralism both our problem and our solution. 'Pluralism we have and shall have – or we shall have nothing,' Armour warns (127), although we may end up having both. Canadians have continually tested the limits of pluralism in order to secure a more permissive form of nationality, which would allow for regional and ethnic disparities yet also offer a practical cohesiveness to the country. This condition is sometimes seen as the actual state of affairs that Canadians have failed to recognize, and sometimes as an ideal yet to be accomplished. The former is suggested by Gary Geddes's respect for amicable diversity in his anthology, *Divided We Stand*; the latter by Armour's appeal to 'a new kind of nationalism, a new kind which might actually safeguard cultural pluralism and permit mutual accommodations amongst peoples' (83). The Canadian coalition appears at its most fractious in Herschel Hardin's theory (following Louis Althusser) that a nation derives from a 'central contradiction' whose 'contending forces ... underlie the character of the people' (10); it requires a fruitful-irksome dilemma, which it never solves but only elaborates creatively: 'And when the elaboration occurs on a large scale, or involves important social forces, it constitutes civilization' (27). Hardin regards three formative Canadian contradictions as 'the forcing ground of our identity' (12): English versus French, the regions versus the federal centre, and Canada versus the United States. These ongoing tensions will sustain the nation, as long as we feel they are worth worrying over, by providing a site where meanings can be contested. He concludes that we can live in the midst of paradox as long as it is our own paradox. Canada is still a riddle, but at least it is our riddle: 'Canadians do not assert their nationalism by looking for it, as the historian claims. They assert it by not finding it' (26). Their consistent failure is really a success, because it is consistent and so offers coherence to Canadian life, and because it ensures that no totalizing definition of nationhood will satisfy us.

In the previous section I warned that no model of sociability could adequately delineate the nation's 'third space,' because it is too inchoate a site to be grasped in a single image. Nevertheless, I conclude with such a model taken from a passage that serves as an epigraph to this book:

The meaning of planting this Great Tree is the Great Peace, and Good Tidings of Peace and Power, and the Nations of the earth shall see it and shall accept and follow the Root and shall arrive here at this Tree and when they arrive here you shall receive them and shall seat them in the midst of your Confederacy, and the meaning of placing an Eagle on the top of the Great Tall Tree is to watch the Roots which extend to the North and to the South and to the East and to the West, and the Eagle will discover if any evil is approaching your Confederacy ... This bundle of arrows signifies that all Lords and all the Warriors and all the Women of the Confederacy have become united as one person ... We have now completed our power so that we, the Five Nations Confederacy, shall in the future only have one body, one head and one heart. (Moses and Goldie 10)

To students schooled on Herder and Hegel, this image of a Native confederacy recalls all the grand principles of romantic histori- cism: the organic fusion of nation and nature, the virtue of the soil, the tenacity of roots, the nation expressed as a single person, the threat of death held in abeyance (the bundle of arrows), the eagle vision of art surveying the entire field. But familiar rhetorical fig- ures function differently here, because their meaning and value depend on the cultural context in which they appear. The Five Nations had never heard of Herder and spoke from a different tra- dition, which has to be studied and respected in its own right if it is to be understood. Instead of trying to transplant Herder to the Canadian soil, we have to diversify our sense of what a nation is and should be, and through that diversity find ways of dwelling in Canada. While this approach may sound less glamorous than the uncanny truths prophesied by a transgressive mode of (anti)repre- sentation, I think it shows more promise.

Notes

1: National + Literary + History

1 Fiedler's fourfold division of novels appears in *The Return of the Vanishing American* (New York: Stein and Day, 1969). His comparable fourfold division of poetry appears in *Waiting for the End* (New York: Stein and Day, 1964). For an account of 'deterritorialized' American literature and the revaluation of literary history, see Jules Chametzky, *Our Decentralized Literature: Cultural Mediations in Selected Jewish and Southern Writers* (Amherst: U of Massachusetts P, 1986); Sacvan Bercovitch and Myra Jehlen, *Ideology and Classic American Literature* (Cambridge: Cambridge UP, 1986); and Jeffrey N. Cox and Larry J. Reynolds, *New Historical Literary Study: Essays on Reproducing Texts, Representing History* (Princeton: Princeton UP, 1993).

2 For a brief account of the tangle of nationalities and national claims in central Europe at this time see Orridge 45–6, and Anthony D. Smith, 'Nationalism and the Historians.'

3 'All that is irreducibly required for the exisitence [*sic*] of a nation is that the members share an intuitive sense of the group's separate origin and evolution. ... Because its roots lie in the subconscious, rather than in reason, the conviction that one's nation was somehow created *sui generis* and remained essentially unadulterated down to the present is immunized against contrary fact. There is hardly a nation whom historians have not established to be the off-spring of several ethnic strains' (Connor 49).

4 Literary histories of Québécois and French-Canadian writing exhibit all of the features discussed in this chapter, and with less strain than do comparable English-Canadian studies. For a discussion of the relation between nation and state, especially in Quebec, see Charles Taylor's essay 'Why Do Nations Have to Become States?' in *Reconciling the Solitudes*.

5 Marx mocks this self-flattering logic in 'The Eighteenth Brumaire of Louis Bonaparte': 'But unheroic as bourgeois society is, it nevertheless took heroism, sacrifice, terror, civil war, and battles of peoples to bring it into being' (Marx and Engels 320). Carole Gerson studies how Canadian novelists provided themselves with a mythological past in *A Purer Taste: The Writing and Reading of Fiction in English in Nineteenth-Century Canada* (Toronto: U of Toronto P, 1989), especially chs. 7 and 8.

6 For example, Terry Eagleton's *Ideology: An Introduction* (London: Verso, 1991).

7 'The poet, described in ideal perfection, brings the whole soul of man into activity, with the subordination of its faculties to each other, according to their relative worth and dignity ... No man was ever yet a great poet, without being at the same time a profound philosopher. For poetry is the blossom and the fragrancy of all human knowledge, human thoughts, human passions, emotions, language' (Coleridge, *Biographia Literaria*, 173–4, 179).

8 The intimate link between language, history, culture, and nationality appears in a comment made by C. Alphonso Smith, the founder of *Studies in Philology*: '[S]hould not syntax aid in the interpretation of history? History is one: a nation's art, science, architecture, laws, literature, and language are but parts of a larger whole ... Shall we study the evolution of a people's character in the way they build their bridges and highways and homes, and not in the way they build their sentences?' (quoted by Graff 76). For another account of the power of philology to construct national literary histories, see Hans Robert Jauss, *Toward an Aesthetic of Reception*, trans. Timothy Bahti (Minneapolis: U of Minneapolis P, 1982), especially the chapter 'Literary History as a Challenge to Literary Theory.'

9 For discussion of romanticism as a basis of periodization, see Perkins ch. 5, as well as Hans Eichner, ed., *'Romantic' and Its Cognates* (Toronto: U of Toronto P, 1972), and Mark Parker, 'Measure and Countermeasure: The Lovejoy–Wellek Debate and Romantic Periodization,' *Theoretical Issues in Literary History*, ed. David Perkins (Cambridge: Harvard UP, 1991), 227–47.

10 For example, Geoffrey Hartman treats criticism as a work of art and an 'intellectual poem' (196) in *Criticism in the Wilderness*, especially in the chapter 'Literary Commentary as Literature.'

11 See also Jonathan Culler's essay, 'Literary Criticism and the American University,' in *Framing the Sign*: 'Early statements are concerned to demonstrate that there *is* an American culture, and influential literary studies were often those that tried to identify its quintessential traits, thus providing an overall theory of American literature' (8).

12 For a brief summary of English-Canadian literary histories, see McCarthy. For

French Canada, see Larry Shouldice's collection, *Contemporary Quebec Criticism* (Toronto: U of Toronto P, 1979), and Simon.

13 These inconsistencies were spotted by George Woodcock in his review of the *Literary History of Canada*. The review is reprinted as 'The Long Day's Task' in *Towards a Canadian Literature: Essays, Editorials, and Manifestos*, vol. 2, *1940–1983*, ed. Douglas M. Daymond and Leslie G. Monkman (Ottawa: Tecumseh P, 1985), 416–25.

14 Of the many influential studies of historicism, I have drawn on Hayden White's *The Content of the Form*, and Linda Hutcheon's *A Poetics of Postmodernism: History, Theory, Fiction* (New York: Routledge, 1988), as well as Fredric Jameson, *The Political Unconscious: Narrative as a Socially Symbolic Act* (Ithaca: Cornell UP, 1981); Murray Krieger, ed., *The Aims of Representation: Subject/Text/History* (New York: Columbia UP, 1987); and Robert H. Canary and Henry Kozicki, *The Writing of History: Literary Form and Historical Understanding* (Madison: U of Wisconsin P, 1978).

15 For examples of polyphonic literary histories, see Emory Elliot, ed., *The Columbia Literary History of the United States* (New York: Columbia UP, 1988), and Denis Hollier, ed., *A New History of French Literature* (Cambridge: Harvard UP, 1989).

16 The other side of this coin is a resurgence of British romantic conservatism, which laments the betrayal of English nationality by modernism and the liberal establishment. See Ian Buruma, 'Action Anglaise,' *New York Review of Books* 41.17 (20 Oct. 1994): 66–71.

17 The native–cosmopolitan debate is documented by Dudek and Gnarowski. Leon Surette gives a new reading of the debate by distinguishing between 'Guelph' and 'Ghibellene' critics in his essay, 'Creating the Canadian Canon.' Robert Lecker's collection of essays *Canadian Canons*, gives a sample of alternative readings of literary history, while Frank Davey challenges Lecker's version of the literary canon in *Canadian Literary Power*. Smaro Kamboureli presents the ethnic challenge in 'Canadian Ethnic Anthologies.' Further discussion of these points will appear in chapters 4 and 5.

18 Dermot McCarthy discusses Dewart's and Lighthall's fusion of historicizing and moralizing.

19 Robert Lecker makes this final point slightly differently in 'A Country without a Canon' (8–11).

20 'Interpretative community' is Stanley Fish's well-known phrase. For 'standpoint epistemology,' see Linda Alcoff and Elizabeth Potter, eds., *Feminist Epistemologies* (London: Routledge, 1993).

21 For American, French, and English feminisms, see Toril Moi, *Sexual/Textual Politics* (London: Routledge, 1985), and Janet Todd, *Feminist Literary History*

(London: Methuen, 1985). For African- and white-American feminisms, see bell hooks, *Ain't I a Woman* (Boston: South End, 1981). For American and Canadian feminisms, see Weir, 'Toward a Feminist Hermeneutics,' and Susan Jackel.

22 For further discussion of 'queer nationality,' see Eric Savoy, 'You Can't Go Homo Again: Queer Theory and the Foreclosure of Gay Studies,' *English Studies in Canada* 20.2 (June 1994): 129–52.

23 'Cultures are not impermeable; just as Western science borrowed from Arabs, they had borrowed from India and Greece. Culture is never just a matter of ownership, of borrowing and lending with absolute debtors and creditors, but rather of appropriations, common experiences, and interdependencies of all kinds among different cultures. This is a universal norm' (Said, *Culture and Imperialism* 217).

24 Nikos Papastergiadis elaborates on this paradox: 'Within liberalism the conventional response to the demands for ethnic difference is to privatize them, that is to preserve them purely within the personal space. When individuals seek to make this as [*sic*] the basis of their public and political self-image, then liberalism is faced with a dilemma. The public sphere, in a liberal democracy, allows for no space for heterogeneity, and the politics of difference become equated with the threat of fragmentation. The nation state has always been poised over a precarious paradox: it has sought to defend the rights of minorities and to preserve the right to dissent, while at the same time insisting that the nation must be inspired by unifying themes' (181).

25 Giroux quotes from Nancy Fraser's *Unruly Practices: Power, Discourses, and Gender in Contemporary Social Theory* (Minneapolis: U of Minneapolis P, 1988), 29.

26 '[I]t is the Justice of *human* law which brings back into the universal the element of being-for-itself which has broken away from the balanced whole, viz. the independent classes and individuals; it is the government of the nation, which is the self-affirming individuality of the universal essence and the self-conscious will of all.' (Hegel, *Phenomenology* 277).

27 'A creature is operating in the linguistic dimension when it can use and respond to signs in terms of their truth, or descriptive rightness, or power to evoke some mood, or recreate a scene, or express some emotion, or carry some nuance of feeling, or in some way to be *le mot juste*. To be a linguistic creature is to be sensitive to irreducible issues of rightness' (Taylor, *Philosophical* 84).

2: The National Ghost

1 I grant that Q.D. Leavis's apparently secure position is actually unstable. She and F.R. Leavis often regarded the critic as culturally peripheral rather than

central, an outcast antagonistic to industrial society. According to Francis Mulhern in *The Moment of Scrutiny*, the Leavises became withdrawn and idiosyncratic in their attitudes. See also David Gervais, *Literary Englands: Versions of 'Englishness' in Modern Writing* (Cambridge: Cambridge UP, 1994).

2 'Herder's central political idea lies in the assertion that the proper foundation for a sense of collective political identity is not the acceptance of a common sovereign power, but the sharing of a common culture. For the former is imposed from outside, whilst the latter is the expression of an inner consciousness, in terms of which each individual recognizes himself as an integral part of a social whole. To the possession of such a common culture Herder applies the term nation or, more precisely, *Volk* or nationality. The principle source of both its emergence and perpetuation is language. It is through language that the individual becomes at once aware of his selfhood *and* of his nationhood. In this sense individual identity and collective identity become one ... A *Volk*, accordingly, is not a substantive entity in any biological sense, a *thing* with a corporate existence of its own over and above, or separate from, the individuals who compose it, but a relational *event*, a historical and cultural continuum. An individual's consciousness of belonging to a distinct community, likewise, is not a biological fact, but a derivative social and cultural process, the result of the continuous interaction – in both a temporal and a spatial sense – between the self and the socio-cultural setting of its environment. The individual, far from being enclosed within himself or genetically constituted to be a German, or Italian, or Greek *a priori*, derives the awareness of himself as a member of a particular national community from the social milieu into which he is born, from his contact with the world around him' (Barnard 7, 31).

3 'The general principle which manifests itself and becomes an object of consciousness in the State – the form under which all that the State includes is brought – is the whole of that cycle of phenomena which constitutes the *culture* of a nation. But the definite *substance* that receives the form of universality, and exists in that concrete reality which is the State – is the Spirit of the People itself. The actual State is animated by this spirit in all its particular affairs – its Wars, Institutions, etc. ... In history this principle is idiosyncrasy of Spirit – peculiar National Genius. It is within the limitations of this idiosyncrasy that the spirit of the nation, concretely manifested, expresses every aspect of its consciousness and will – the whole cycle of its realization. Its religion, its polity, its ethics, its legislation, and even its science, art, and mechanical skill, all bear its stamp. These special peculiarities find their key in that common peculiarity – the particular principle that characterizes a people' (Hegel, *Philosophy* 50, 63–4).

4 Weir argues that 'the lexicon of maturation' has been central 'to our understanding of the condition of literature in this country. In this teleological
reduction of texts to "stages," of literature to the "growth" of the country, of
individual production to the norms of the marketplace, lies the crucial move
within the strategy of containment which has been characteristic of the critical
discourse in English Canada for more than a century' ('Discourse' 24).

5 For a post-colonial account of the contradictions in nationalist theories claiming to be universal, see Partha Chatterjee's *Nationalist Thought and the Colonial
World,* especially chs. 1 and 2.

6 'Herder's idea of the nation was deeply nonaggressive. All he wanted was
cultural self-determination. He denied the superiority of one people over
another. Anyone who proclaimed it was saying something false. Herder
believed in a variety of national cultures, all of which could, in his view, peace-
fully coexist. Each culture was equal in value and deserved its place in the sun'
(Isaiah Berlin in Gardels 19). Hegel's view was less cheerful, but even more
insistent on the independent standing of the state.

7 In a more recent formulation, organic processes are reinterpreted as 'cultural
ecology,' as in Bentley.

8 Eggleston is influenced more immediately by Van Wyck Brooks's *The Flowering
of New England* (New York: Dutton, 1952) and by Frederick Jackson Turner's
The Frontier in American History (New York: Holt, Rinehart and Winston, 1962),
but Turner's theory of the spirit of the frontier (the 'environmentalist thesis')
clearly follows in the line of romantic historicism.

9 For discussion of the romantic genius in native dress, see Margery Fee,
'Romantic Nationalism and the Image of Native People in Contemporary
English-Canadian Literature,' *The Native in Literature,* ed. Thomas King,
Cheryl Calver, and Helen Hoy (Toronto: ECW, 1987), 15–33; and Monkman:
'Red heroes fill the vacuum created by the absence of white aboriginal traditions on this continent, and the dream of a distinctive national literature
focuses on the history and heritage of the red man. In Indian myths and legends, white writers find a new understanding of the landscape and its gods
and discover rhythms, images, and structures that enable them to communicate in a new and powerful idiom' (5).

10 For example, in *The Secular Scripture* (Cambridge: Harvard UP, 1976),
Northrop Frye studies romance as the loss and regaining of an original identity; in *Beginnings: Intention and Method* (New York: Basic Books, 1975), Edward
Said analyses 'transitive' narrative beginnings and endings as a perpetual
beginning again; and Jacques Derrida attacks conventional interpretation as a
means of deciphering a true origin that escapes the play of *différance.* For an
account of 'the bottomlessness of origin' as a preoccupation of literary history,

see Ernst Behler, 'Problems of Origin in Modern Literary History,' *Theoretical Issues in Literary History*, ed. David Perkins (Cambridge: Harvard UP, 1991), 9–34. E.D. Blodgett finds the same bottomlessness in Canadian literary histories in 'Is a History of the Literatures of Canada Possible?' 6–7.

11 For a different account of the competing claims of merit and authenticity, see Donna Bennett's essay 'Conflicted Vision.' Peter Uwe Hohendahl finds the same inconsistency in Germany, and by extension in all literary histories that attempt to reconcile national goals with aesthetic perfection (158–9).

12 'All dualisms, all theories of the immortality of the soul or of the spirit, as well as all monisms, spiritualist or materialist, dialectical or vulgar, are the unique theme of a metaphysics whose entire history was compelled to strive toward the reduction of the trace. The subordination of the trace to the full presence summed up in the logos, the humbling of writing beneath a speech dreaming of its plenitude, such are the gestures required by an onto-theology, determining the archeological and eschatological meaning of being as presence, as parousia, as life without differance: [*sic*] another name for death, historical metonymy where God's name holds death in check' (Derrida 71).

13 A summary of Lower's views appears in his essay, 'Canadian Values and Canadian Writing,' *Mosaic* 1 (Oct. 1967): 77–93. For idealist historiography in Canada, also see A.B. McKillop's chapter 'The Idealist Legacy' in *Contours of Canadian Thought*.

14 Three southern authors who pursue the Canadian ghost into an unimaginable Arctic are Rudy Wiebe, *Playing Dead* (Edmonton: NeWest, 1989), Aritha van Herk, *Places Far from Ellesmere* (Red Deer, AB: Red Deer College, 1990), and John Moss, *Enduring Dreams* (Concord, ON: Anansi, 1994).

15 For example, Linda Hutcheon remarks in *The Canadian Postmodern*, 'What [Stanley] Fogel sees as important to postmodernism in America – its deconstructing of national myths and identity – is possible within Canada only when those myths and identity have first been defined' (6).

16 For a detailed study of the way Kroetsch reinstates 'meaning,' history, and the national genius, see Tiefensee, especially chs. 5 and 6: 'The "temptation of meaning" has proved itself stronger than Kroetsch's power to resist, and he has posited for us exactly that which he means to abjure – a prophetic Presence, the prophetic Voice he claims to have rejected for the voices of Babel' (85).

17 For a defence of thematic criticism and a reappraisal of its role in literary history, see Werner Sollors's collection, *The Return of Thematic Criticism* (Cambridge: Harvard UP, 1993).

18 'Although it would not be entirely fair to identify thematicism with federalist ideology, the cohesiveness, the uninterrupted plenitude it stood for accords

well with an optic that had the nation and all its concomitant apparatus as its unit of measure' (Loriggio 63–4).

19 'Places, like people, are subject to often abrupt changes in social and cultural perception; moreover, the relativity and impermanence of the codes through which places come arbitrarily to be defined belie the geometric regularity of the map or town-plan. "Place," like "identity," reveals itself not as a fixed or coherent entity but as an unstable metaphorical construct' (Huggan 122).

20 It is discussed in their book *Kafka: Pour une littérature mineure*, part of which has been translated as 'What Is a Minor Literature?' *Mississippi Review* 11.3 (Spring 1983): 13–33.

21 'The problem in contemporary Canada is not just how to react to the lack of national ghosts (to the ghost story *manquée* that is Canadian literature) but also how to react to the superabundance of unmonumentalized, nondescript, small-time, small-space ghosts hidden in every household or under our skin' (Loriggio 65).

3: Nation Building

1 For a detailed account of building a national literature to assist in building a nation-state, see Peter Uwe Hohendahl, especially chs. 5, 6, and 7.

2 '"Invented tradition" is taken to mean a set of practices, normally governed by overtly or tacitly accepted rules and of a ritual or symbolic nature, which seek to inculcate certain values and norms of behaviour by repetition, which automatically implies continuity with the past. In fact, where possible, they normally attempt to establish continuity with a suitable historic past' (Hobsbawm, Introduction 1). For criticism of Hobsbawm's account of invented traditions, see Anthony D. Smith, 'The Nation: Invented, Imagined, Reconstructed?' *Reimagining the Nation,* ed. Marjorie Ringrose and Adam J. Lerner (Philadelphia: Open University Press, 1993), 9–28. For a discussion of nationalism as an ongoing performance or 'fetish spectacle,' see McClintock, 368–78.

3 Edward Said reaches the same conclusion by a different route: 'Paradoxically, the United States, as an immigrant society composed of many cultures, has a public discourse more policed, more anxious to depict the country as free from taint, more unified around one iron-clad major narrative of innocent triumph. This effort to keep things simple and good disaffiliates the country from its relationship with other societies and peoples, thereby reinforcing its remoteness and insularity' (*Culture* 314–15).

4 In *Beyond Ethnicity,* Werner Sollors discusses this conflict of nationalities as a dialectic of consent (national choice) and descent (national heritage).

5 Habermas quotes a proclamation from the 1670s that illustrates the important

role of such locales: 'Men have assumed to themselves a liberty, not only in coffee-houses, but in other places and meetings, both public and private, to censure and defame the proceedings of the State, by speaking evil of things they understand not, and endeavouring to create and nourish an universal jealousie and dissatisfaction in the minds of all His Majesties good subjects' (*Structural* 59). A succinct history of the public sphere, neatly poised between privacy and politics, appears in Charles Taylor's essay 'Invoking Civil Society' in *Philosophical Arguments*.

6 For a favourable estimate of Goldsmith's poetic skill, see Kenneth J. Hughes, whose judgment is challenged by W.J. Keith and David Jackel.

7 For a detailed examination of order, and how Goldsmith defines and defends it, see Gerald Lynch's Introduction in *The Rising Village*.

8 I cite the 1834 version of the poem.

9 Charles Taylor presents this dilemma as a conflict between two versions of romantic individualism, which stress the spiritual value of material productivity, but then have trouble coping with prosperity. See *Reconciling the Solitudes*, 74–7.

10 K.P. Stich regards Goldsmith as more sophisticated than I do. He sees the inconsistencies and ironies in the poem as deliberate and the village idyll as 'dubious' (49).

11 Tranquilla proposes a different solution to the ideological inconsistency that I have discussed. He subsumes all social and sociable views within a cyclical theory of history prevalent in the eighteenth century. According to this theory, nations inevitably rise and fall following the 'moral imperative' of a 'universal law' (49). Tranquilla distinguishes intricate rising and falling movements throughout 'The Rising Village.' These patterns suggest that Goldsmith recognized the inconsistencies I have noted, but that he appealed beyond them to a grander, moral law. As described by Tranquilla, however, the historical cycles are neither moral nor laws. They are inflexible, universal, and perhaps providential conditions, but they are not moral in the sense that they can be affected by moral choices or actions. People may hasten or delay the fatal process, Tranquilla adds at the end of his argument (60), although Goldsmith gives no indication that they can, but ultimately human conduct makes no difference. Furthermore, the historical cycles are laws only in the rough sense that invariable natural forces like gravity are said to be, or to obey, laws. But the point about laws in morality, justice, or any regulated activity is that they can be broken. They presuppose the freedom to be disobedient. Gravity does not obey a law, and is not itself a law, and in the terms of Tranquilla's argument, neither are historical cycles.

12 *Towards the Last Spike* 'never quite catches fire, never fuses into a fully satisfying work of art' (Pacey, *Ten Canadian Poets* 192).

13 But contrast Frank Davey's judgment: 'A careful reading of Pratt's work, in fact, suggests very strongly that Pratt was much more straightforward as an artist than most of his sophisticated critics care to admit' (*Surviving* 14).

14 'As always, Pratt has researched the historical documents carefully. Like Van Horne, who is shaped in his own image in this sense, Pratt loved facts, the harder the better, regarding them as the source of poetry for the physical world' (Collins 141).

15 Foucault's essays on transgression appear in *Language, Counter-Memory, Practice*.

16 'Unlike a holocaust or a slaughter, a sacrifice is part of a larger design within which the death is meaningful' (Redekop 50).

17 An earlier version of 'Civil Elegies' appeared in 1968. I use the 1972 version. After I wrote this chapter, Lee's poetry became more readily available in a new edition: *Nightwatch: New and Selected Poems, 1968–1996* (Toronto: McClelland and Stewart, 1996).

18 Lee's poetic career is marked by elegies, from Muskoka and Annex elegiacs in *Kingdom of Absence* to nostalgic children's verse to *The Death of Harold Ladoo*.

19 There are varieties of romanticism to suit every occasion, but for a discussion of the conflict between aesthetically pure and ideological committed romanticisms, a conflict that I will consider in 'Civil Elegies,' see McGann.

20 The importance of voice appears almost every time Lee talks about the craft of poetry, notably in his essay 'Polyphony: Enacting a Meditation.' Even in his brief statement in *Storm Warnings,* he emphasizes voice: 'I wanted the voice of the poems to say things directly, concretely, with as much simplicity as is granted by (say) clear eyesight. But the voice itself I wanted to be a rich organic manifest of being human' (96).

21 In his article on Al Purdy, Lee claims that any Canadian poet must begin by being truly local: 'A poet who merely wrote from sea to sea would merely be a bore in motion' ('Running' 16).

22 In his MA thesis, 'Negative Nationalism and the Poetry of Dennis Lee,' Robert Stuart Grant, following a hint from Louis Dudek, calls this alienated attitude 'negative nationalism.' A.M. Klein devises a similar existential puzzle in *The Second Scroll* to express the plight of the Jews.

23 But what does 'true' mean in an alogical system that conflates truth and falsehood? I criticize the modernist dream of alogical logic in *Poetic Argument: Studies in Modern Poetry* (Kingston: McGill-Queen's UP, 1988). By contrast, Ann Munton's essay on simultaneity in Lee's poetry endorses what I take to be the (faulty) modernist argument.

24 Contrast Michael Valdez Moses: 'The rhetorical appeal to one's *own* literary history, to one's *own* culture is a powerful one, but it is based on little more than prejudice and provinciality. Moreover, it merely transforms the question

of what is objectively best for one's own culture into the question of what actually is or should be the character of one's culture' (225).

25 In view of Lee's antagonism to modernism, this is a nice irony. Sean Kane (122–3) argues that Lee opposes modernism and its pernicious ideology, that he is neither modernist nor postmodernist, but something else; while E.D. Blodgett ('Authencity' 104) suggests that Lee is so pre-modern as to be medieval. One might reply that Kane's history of the fall from an Orphic unity of word and world is really a modernist myth. It recalls Yeats's unity of being and Eliot's dissociation of sensibility.

26 'And sure, I write the poem; and that means hard work. But I don't *invent* the cadence I hear; I sit and play in the midst of it. Do you think I can boss it around? Most of the time I can't even keep up' (Lee, 'Polyphony' 94–5).

27 For the poetry of meditation, see Louis L. Martz, *The Poetry of Meditation: A Study in English Religious Literature* (New Haven: Yale UP, 1954). The double hook comes, of course, from Sheila Watson's novel, whose mysteries are plumbed by Marilyn Bowering in *Figures Cut in Sacred Ground: Illuminati in 'The Double Hook'* (Edmonton: NeWest, 1988).

28 The difference between Lee's adult and children's poetry is hazy, doubtless as their author intended. Many 'children's' poems are about 'adult' themes; conversely, some 'adult' poems employ a 'childish' style, for example, '1838,' with its refrain, 'Mackenzie, come again' (*Nicholas Knock* 44).

29 Lee's passive self-denial is quite different from Chatterjee's active, political criticism, but it is not so different from the example set by one of Chatterjee's main subjects: Mahatma Gandhi.

30 For the orphic tradition in poetry, see Elizabeth Sewell, *The Orphic Voice* (New Haven: Yale UP, 1960).

31 'What is "stark heraldic form" that it could be more real than "great art?" Is it that great art, art period, draws away from the chaos (void) that never ceases to be a fact of existence, making a human order profoundly satisfying *because* it distances the chaos?' (Dragland, 'On *Civil Elegies*' 180–1).

32 Eliot offers his own equivalent of Henry Moore's sculpture in 'Burnt Norton': 'The stillness, as a Chinese jar still / Moves perpetually in its stillness' (*Collected Poems* 194).

33 In his children's poem 'The Bard of the Universe, ' Lee mocks the grandiose pretensions of visionary poets 'Who crave to summarize in verse / The meaning of the universe' (*Difficulty* 22).

4: The Nation as Monster

1 'It is also important that the sutures of contradiction in these ideological nar-

ratives become most visible under the disassembling eye of an alternative narrative, ideological as that narrative may itself be. In addition, the diachronic opening-out of contradictions within the status quo, even when the project of that diachronic recasting is to conceal those very contradictions, can have just the opposite effect of making them newly visible, offering a new leverage for critique' (Sedgwick, *Between Men* 15).

2 Neither is de Man, for whom literature tells the 'truth' only about its own 'literariness,' that is, about its linguistic production and subversion of meaning, not about 'natural reality.' Therefore literature can show us why nationalism is an 'ideological aberration,' but not what the nation 'really' is. The same qualification appears in Julia Kristeva's praise of poetic language, which criticizes social order but cannot articulate a truer or more just order, since 'order' is precisely what it subverts: 'Then, in this socio-symbolic order thus saturated if not already closed, poetry – let us say more precisely, poetic language – recalls what always was its function: to introduce, across the symbolic, [i.e., rational, ideological] that which works on it, crosses it and threatens it. What the theory of the unconscious looks for, poetic language practices, within and against the social order' (Quoted by Allon White 83).

3 Examples could be cited from, among many others, Dorothy Livesay, Ethel Wilson, Margaret Avison, Jay Macpherson, P.K. Page, and Phyllis Webb.

4 Fear and temptation are Terry Goldie's terms for the same paradox in *Fear and Temptation: The Image of the Indigene in Canadian, Australian, and New Zealand Literature* (Montreal: McGill-Queen's UP, 1989).

5 J.M.S. Careless describes the frontier thesis as follows: 'The frontier, where man came most immediately into contact with the North American physical environment, was the great seed-bed for the growth of a truly North American society. From the start as the United States and Canada had spread across the continent, environmental influences that first began on the frontier had worked to shape a native American character different from that of the Old World, left far behind ... [T]hanks to the continuous process of adaptation to the environment, an American content had steadily grown in Canada within external forms of government, society, or culture inherited from Britain or France' ('Frontierism' 5–6). I have written about the environmental thesis as it affects Canadian literary history in 'Historical Literary Criticism in English Canada: Within, Beyond and Back Into the Past,' *100 Years of Critical Solitudes: Canadian and Québécois Criticism from the 1880s to the 1980s*, ed. Caroline Bayard (Toronto: ECW, 1992), 98–121.

6 For a recent study of how feminism and nationalism intersect, see Lois A. West, ed., *Feminist Nationalism* (New York: Routledge, 1997). For a survey of theories of historical justice, see Bruce Mazlish, The *Riddle of History: The Great*

Speculators from Vico to Freud (New York: Minerva, 1966). For a detailed account of the *aporias* in historiography, see Robert Young, *White Mythologies*.

7 According to Barbara Godard, this transcultural disruption appeared as a conflict between Campbell's writing and her editor's revisions of *Halfbreed*. See Godard, 'The Politics of Representation,' 204, 225.

8 I borrow the title from Harold Cardinal's criticism of Canadian history: *The Unjust Society: The Tragedy of Canada's Indians* (Edmonton: Hurtig, 1969).

9 For an account of the way that exploration literature treats Native society, see Parker Duchemin, '"A Parcel of Whelps": Alexander Mackenzie among the Indians,' *Native Writers and Canadian Writing*, ed. W.H. New (Vancouver: UBC P, 1990), 49–74.

10 Gayatri Chakravorty Spivak describes the 'scenario of tokenism' as follows: 'you are as good as we are ... why do you insist on emphasizing your difference? The putative center [in this case, Ottawa] welcomes selective inhabitants of the margin in order better to exclude the margin. And it is the center that offers the official explanation; or, the center is defined and reproduced by the explanation that it can express' (107).

11 Monkman shows how self-reproach quickly becomes a means of self-exculpation for the nineteenth-century educator George Munro Grant, who wrote in 1873: 'Who, but they, [Canadian Natives] have a right to the country; and if "a man may do what he likes with his own," would they not be justified in refusing to admit one of us to their lakes and woods, fighting us to the death on that issue? But it is too late to argue the question; the red man, with his virtues and his vices, – lauded by some as so dignified, abused by others as so dirty – is being civilized off the ground' (Monkman 66). Margery Fee discusses this strategy in 'Romantic Nationalism and the Image of Native People in Contemporary English-Canadian Literature,' *The Native in Literature* (Toronto: ECW P, 1987), 15–33.

12 The endlessly wandering form of error is the subject of Patricia Parker's study, *Inescapable Romance: Studies in the Poetics of a Mode* (Princeton: Princeton UP, 1979).

13 For a defence of the painful/desirable/necessary process of assimilation in America, see Arthur Schlesinger, Jr, *The Disuniting of America: Reflections on a Multicultural Society* (New York: Norton, 1991).

14 On generational conflict in *Obasan*, see Mason Harris, 41–4, 52–3. On the importance of protective maternal figures in ethnic literature, see Sollors, 231. For a study of realism and phantasmagoria as characteristic styles in ethnic novels, see Murray Baumgarten, *City Scriptures: Modern Jewish Writing* (Cambridge: Harvard UP, 1982).

15 A classic account of interiority appears in Gaston Bachelard's *The Poetics of Space*, trans. Maria Jolas (Boston: Beacon P, 1969).

16 Erika Gottlieb discusses riddles and puzzles in *Obasan* in 'The Riddle of Concentric Worlds in *Obasan*,' *Canadian Literature* 109 (Summer 1986): 34–53. She offers a single answer to all the riddles – love – but admits that the answer is a 'central mystery' (52) and so, in effect, another puzzle.

17 Of the voluminous literature on silence in modern culture, see Ihab Hassan, *The Literature of Silence* (New York: Knopf, 1967); Jerzy Peterkiewicz, *The Other Side of Silence* (London: Oxford UP, 1970); Susan Sontag, *Styles of Radical Will* (New York: Farrar, Straus and Giroux, 1966); and George Steiner, *Language and Silence* (London: Faber and Faber, 1967). On the role of silence in *Obasan*, see A. Lynne Magnusson, 'Language and Longing in Joy Kogawa's *Obasan*,' *Canadian Literature* 116 (Spring 1988): 58–66.

18 See Georg Lukács, *The Meaning of Contemporary Realism*, trans. John and Necke Mander (London: Merlin, 1962); Derrida deconstructs the inside/outside binary in many works, such as 'The Law of Genre,' *On Narrative*, ed. W.J.T. Mitchell (Chicago: U of Chicago P, 1980), 51–77. See also Diana Fuss, ed. *Inside/Out: Lesbian Theories, Gay Theories* (New York: Routledge, 1991), and Silverman.

19 In *Itsuka* the dangers of inwardness are represented by the failed artist, Min: 'Min of the interiority, of the too much seen and unseen' (236).

20 In her interview with Janice Williamson, Kogawa acknowledges that she must accept as well as create her ethnic identity. It is both a 'burden' and a 'calling': 'I too feel burdened by an identity because it was foisted on me, but on the other hand I chose it inasmuch as I started to talk about it, and by that act got doubly burdened by it. So there's no escaping my identity, which I cannot tear off at night any more, although I would like to escape it' (Williamson 153).

21 'Everyone, from time to time, is fed up with it all – the hair-shirt of ethnicity we all must wear. But by now we know that, however much we may wish to flee, our ethnicity will thud after us. That's the way things are in this country' (*Itsuka* 256).

22 There is a fine chapter on the ambiguous significance of the melting pot in Sollors.

23 E.D. Blodgett gives a comparable account of ethnic catastrophe in Canada: 'Ethnicity's text, by articulating and presenting itself as other, is at once perceptible as boundary, and the texts it employs are paratextual in that they interfere with canonical or central texts ... Thus, its discursive practice is one of continuous equivocation' ('Ethnic Writing' 15).

24 Ila Goody discusses Kogawa's treatment of the maternal quest.

25 For a discussion of the discursive interweaving of fact, fiction, history and fabrication, see Manina Jones; and Coral Ann Howells, 'Storm Glass: The Preservation and Transformation of History in *The Diviners, Obasan, My Lovely*

Enemy,' *Crisis and Creativity in the New Literatures in English: Canada,* ed. Geoffrey Davis (Amsterdam: Rodopi, 1990), 87–97.

26 For an introduction to the Holocaust and the literature of silence, see Stephen Langer, *The Holocaust and the Literary Imagination* (New Haven: Yale UP, 1975) and *Holocaust Testimonies: The Ruins of Memory* (New Haven: Yale UP, 1991).

27 Potter shows at length how Naomi's mother can be aligned with the *chora* – 'the M/mother is safely imbued with the semiotic' (134) – but she does not share Kaja Silverman's concern (124–6) that, as formulated by Kristeva, such safety is debilitating. On the contrary, Potter treats the 'semiotic current' (137) as redemptive. Nevertheless, she too sees Naomi as debilitated: she is rendered abject by her situation as a Japanese in Canada and as a woman, and by her misunderstanding of her mother.

28 'Everywhere Marlatt seeks the essential self, unadulterated by the wrong structures of knowing. Her dream is Edenic. She dreams of return, imagines she will be restored' (Cooley 78).

29 For further discussion of Marlatt's use of *Frankenstein* to deconstruct 'the gothic circle of patriarchy,' see Stan Dragland's essay 'Out of the Blank: Daphne Marlatt's *Ana Historic*' in *The Bees of the Invisible.*

30 Marlatt makes this point in her interview with George Bowering: 'And as a prefix, it's very contradictory. It means upwards and forwards as well as backwards. It has a whole cluster of meanings associated with it' (102). And Stan Dragland observes: 'This is not "ahistoric," not a blank' (*The Bees* 178).

31 Similarly Lola Lemire Tostevin finds the ending of *Ana Historic* 'unexpectedly conventional in its utopian vision' (38). For a reply to Tostevin, see Pamela Banting, *Body Inc.: A Theory of Translation Poetics* (Winnipeg: Turnstone P, 1995).

5: Worrying the Nation

1 Of the many accounts of Canada as an ambiguous nation, see especially E.D. Blodgett's essay 'After Pierre Berton What?' and Linda Hutcheon's study of irony, *Splitting Images.* For an account of how Canada's situation differs from other post-colonial societies, see Hutcheon's essay 'Circling the Downspout of Empire' in *Splitting Images.*

2 For criticism of the ideology of 'under-developed' nations, see Tom Nairn, *The Break-up of Britain,* ch. 9; Brennan; and Radhakrishnan.

3 'For history in its classical form, the discontinuous was both the given and the unthinkable: the raw material of history, which presented itself in the form of dispersed events ... the material, which, through analysis, had to be rearranged, reduced, effaced in order to reveal the continuity of events. Disconti-

nuity was the stigma of temporal dislocation that it was the historian's task to remove from history. It has now become one of the basic elements of historical analysis' (Foucault, *Archaeology* 8).

4 Himmelfarb's answer to her own question is that while nationalism may sometimes be a 'pathological, tyrannical, even murderous' ideology (141), nationality is a historical fact: 'If everything else has a history – if dynasties, regimes, and political systems rise and fall, if modes of production and consumption, class attitudes and relations, social mores and cultural values change over the course of time – then nationality too, which partakes of all these and much else, must have a history. And changes in the character, spirit, or strength of nationality do not negate the idea and reality of nationality any more than economic changes negate the idea and reality of the economy, or political changes the idea and reality of the polity, or sexual and domestic changes the idea and reality of sexuality and the family' (130).

5 Anne McClintock makes the same point: 'As such, nations are not simply phantasmagoria of the mind but are historical practices through which social difference is both invented and performed. Nationalism becomes, as a result, radically constitutive of people's identities through social contests that are frequently violent and always gendered' (353).

6 Domineering universalism that presents itself as benign is the subject of Arun Mukherjee's *Towards an Aesthetic of Opposition*.

7 Habermas cautions that the subjective judgments and feelings described here are not sufficient to account for legitimation crises, because these same judgments and feelings are caught up in the historical change that they are trying to assess. He therefore requires an objective basis of analysis, which he finds in 'social integration' (the functioning of institutions) and 'system integration' (the self-regulating powers of a social order).

8 Robert Kroetsch's inventive essay on horse and home, motion and stasis, develops the same social/rhetorical configuration through different imagery. See 'The Fear of Women in Prairie Fiction: An Erotics of Space' *The Lovely Treachery of Words*, 73–83.

9 See Lita-Rose Betcherman, *The Swastika and the Maple Leaf: Fascist Movements in Canada in the Thirties* (Toronto: Fitzhenry and Whiteside, 1975).

10 See also Doris Sommer's article on the nation in Latin American fiction in Homi Bhabha's *Nation and Narration*, 71–98. Frank Davey briefly compares Canadian and Latin American literatures in *Reading Canadian Reading* (Winnipeg: Turnstone P, 1988), 119; and David M. Jordan discusses nations and regionalism in Latin American, American, and Canadian literature in *New World Regionalism: Literature in the Americas* (Toronto: U of Toronto P, 1994).

11 Louis A. Montrose also describes how British 'cultural materialist' critics dis-

rupt the once decorous field of English studies by treating it as 'the site of a struggle over the definition of national problems and priorities, a struggle to shape and reshape national identity and collective consciousness' (27).

12 Leonard Tivey's collection of essays, *The Nation-State*, provides a good survey of the nation in crisis. Frank Davey's *Post-National Arguments* and *Canadian Literary Power*, which I have found useful, explore the Canadian situation.

13 In *Force Fields*, Martin Jay neatly sums up the post-structuralist critique of moral agency. This includes the deconstruction of the moral subject and its decision-making ability, the impossibility of trusting moral narratives directed by 'virtue,' and the dismissal of 'intersubjectively generated communities' that would permit a shared ethical life (38–9).

14 The phrase 'deadly space between' comes from Herman Melville's *Billy Budd*, and is used by Barbara Johnson in her deconstructive study of it in *The Critical Difference* (92). Homi Bhabha explains the post-colonial 'time-lag' as follows: 'The process of reinscription and negotiation – the insertion or intervention of something that takes on new meaning – happens in the temporal break in-between the sign, deprived of subjectivity, in the realm of the intersubjective. Through this time-lag – the temporal break in representation – emerges the process of agency both as a historical development and the narrative agency of historical discourse' (*Location* 191).

15 See Anne McClintock on the semiotic of cleanliness, and Robert Young's *Colonial Desire* on racist sciences.

16 'The act of interpretation is never simply an act of communication between the I and the You designated in the statement. The production of meaning requires that these two places be mobilized in the passage through a Third Space, which represents both the general conditions of language and the specific implication of the utterance in a performative and institutional strategy of which it cannot "in itself" be conscious. What this unconscious relation introduces is an ambivalence in the act of interpretation' (Bhabha, *Location* 36).

17 'Cultural diversity is an epistemological object – culture as an object of empirical knowledge – whereas cultural difference is the process of *enunciation* of culture as "knowledge*able*," authoritative, adequate to the construction of systems of cultural identification' (Bhabha, *Location* 34).

18 'DissemiNation' is an expanded version of an essay that appears in *The Location of Culture*.

19 'It is precisely that popular binarism between theory and politics, whose foundational basis is a view of knowledge as totalizing generality and everyday life as experience, subjectivity or false consciousness, that I have tried to erase' (Bhabha, *Location* 30).

20 See also Diana Fuss: 'But the problem with attributing political significance to every personal action is that the political is soon voided of any meaning or specificity at all, and the personal is paradoxically de-personalized ... A severe reduction of the political to the personal leads to a telescoping of goals, a limiting of revolutionary activity to the project of self-discovery and personal transformation' (101).

21 Dianne Tiefensee distinguishes between the dialectic of indeterminacy and the *aporia* of undecidability: 'Indeterminacy is the opposite of determinacy and as such, posits determinacy, just as incompleteness posits completeness. By definition, indeterminacy assumes and requires that there be an answer, or a Truth, even if that answer cannot be known. With undecidability, there is no absolute answer, no absolute Truth, because all the possibilities play off one another in an endless chain of substitution and deferral that makes possible all answers of meanings while never allowing one or another of them to become absolute, with the power to control the multitude of meanings Truth would reign over and contain' (113).

22 Goldmann quotes René Girard's definition of the novel as 'the story of a degraded search ... for authentic values by a problematic hero in a degraded world' (*Pour une sociologie du roman* [Paris: Gallimard, 1964], 26, my translation).

23 Robert Weimann advises that literary history must continually resituate itself in order to 'recover both its object and its subjectivity, the works of the historical past and its own consciousness of history, and, most important, the interconnections between them. To be aware of these interconnections is to control, and to make meaningful, the ambiguity of the term *literary history* itself' (*Structure* 89). Similarly Robert Young argues that in historiography there is an 'irresolvable conflict between history as meaning and history as difference, between history as a teleology and eschatology and history as the event, as finitude and mortality. Here we once more encounter the recognition that at a conceptual level, the *idea* of history cannot be taken further: rather it can only be addressed through a tension in the writing itself' (*White Mythologies* 85).

24 I am taking liberty with Judith Butler's words here, since she applies this phrase specifically to the category of 'women' whereas I apply it more broadly to all citizens.

25 Derrida and others cite the French philosopher Emmanuel Levinas as inspiration for this dialogic model of sociability: 'Against the egotism of the preoccupation of being with itself, [Levinas] posits a relation of sociality, whereby the self instead of assimilating the other opens itself to it through a relation with it. In the place of the correlation of knowledge with vision and light, the visual

metaphor by which the adequation of the idea with the thing has been thought from Plato to Heidegger, Levinas proposes language, which in the form of speech enables a kind of invisible contact between subjects that leaves them both intact (Young, *White Mythologies* 14).

26 For an insightful account of Said's changing attitude towards nationhood, see Aijaz Ahmad, ch. 5, '*Orientalism* and After.'

27 'Totality' is the summation of social powers and relations as they contribute to a systematic whole. Martin Jay explains Louis Althusser's view of it as follows: 'Rather than being centered in one original and still effective principle which manifested itself in all its disparate moments, the Marxist totality was a decentered whole which had neither a genetic point of origin [the national ghost] nor a teleological point of arrival [national destiny]. Thus, allegedly "secondary" contradictions in, say, culture and politics were not mere epiphenomena of "primary" ones, as both orthodox superstructure-base theory and Marxist humanist collective subject theory had argued' (Jay, *Marxism* 406–7).

28 The obverse of this attitude, equally questionable, is that Canada suffers from a cultural lag of twenty or thirty years. See, for example, W.J. Keith's *An Independent Stance* (Erin, ON: Porcupine's Quill, 1991), 99–100. More somberly, Northrop Frye feared that Canada 'has passed from a pre-national to a post-national phase without ever having become a nation' (*Divisions* 15).

Works Cited

Ahmad, Aijaz. *In Theory: Classes, Nations, Literatures*. London: Verso, 1992.

Alter, Peter. *Nationalism*. Trans. Stuart McKinnon-Evans. London: Edward Arnold, 1985.

Anderson, Benedict. *Imagined Communities: Reflections on the Origin and Spread of Nationalism*. London: Verso, 1983.

Armour, Leslie. *The Idea of Canada and the Crisis of Community*. Ottawa: Steel Rail, 1981.

Armstrong, Jeannette C. 'The Disempowerment of the First North American Native Peoples and Empowerment through Their Writing.' *An Anthology of Canadian Native Literature in English*. Ed. Daniel David Moses and Terry Goldie. Toronto: Oxford UP, 1992. 207–11.

– 'History Lesson.' *An Anthology of Canadian Native Literature in English*. Ed. Daniel David Moses and Terry Goldie. Toronto: Oxford UP, 1992. 203–4.

Ashcroft, Bill. 'Against the Tide of Time: Peter Carey's Interpolation in History.' *Writing the Nation: Self and Country in the Post-Colonial Imagination*. Ed. John C. Hawley. Amsterdam: Rodopi, 1996. 194–213.

Atwood, Margaret. *The Journals of Susanna Moodie*. Toronto: Oxford UP, 1970.

– *Survival: A Thematic Guide to Canadian Literature*. Toronto: Anansi, 1972.

Ballstadt, Carl, ed. *The Search for English-Canadian Literature: An Anthology of Critical Articles from the Nineteenth and Early Twentieth Centuries*. Toronto: U of Toronto P, 1975.

Bannerji, Himani. 'The Other Family.' *Other Solitudes: Canadian Multicultural Fictions*. Ed. Linda Hutcheon and Marion Richmond. Toronto: Oxford UP, 1990. 141–52.

– *A Separate Sky*. Toronto: Domestic Bliss, 1982.

Banting, Pamela. 'Translation A to Z: Notes on Daphne Marlatt's *Ana Historic*.' *Beyond Tish*. Ed. Douglas Barbour. Edmonton: NeWest, 1991. 123–29.

Barnard, F.M., trans. and ed. *J.G. Herder on Social and Political Culture*. Cambridge: Cambridge UP, 1969.

Benjamin, Walter. *Illuminations*. Trans. Harry Zohn. New York: Schocken Books, 1969.

Bennett, Donna. 'Conflicted Vision: A Consideration of Canon and Genre in English-Canadian Literature.' *Canadian Canons: Essays in Literary Value*. Ed. Robert Lecker. Toronto: U of Toronto P, 1991. 131–49.

– 'English Canada's Postcolonial Complexities.' *Essays on Canadian Writing* 51–2 (Winter 1993–Spring 1994): 164–210.

Bentley, D.M.R. *The Gay/Grey Moose: Essays on the Ecologies and Mythologies of Canadian Poetry, 1690–1990*. Ottawa: U of Ottawa P, 1992.

Berger, Carl. *The Writing of Canadian History: Aspects of English-Canadian Historical Writing, 1900 to 1970*. Toronto: Oxford UP, 1976.

Bhabha, Homi K. *The Location of Culture*. London: Routledge, 1994.

– 'DissemiNation: Time, Narrative, and the Margins of the Modern Nation.' *Nation and Narration*. Ed. Homi K. Bhabha. London: Routledge, 1990. 291–322.

Birney, Earle. 'Can. Lit.' *Poetry of Mid-Century, 1940/1960*. Ed. Milton Wilson. Toronto: McClelland and Stewart, 1964. 37.

– 'Canada: Case History: 1969 Version.' *The Poems of Earle Birney*. Toronto: McClelland and Stewart, 1969. 9.

Birch, Anthony H. *Nationalism and National Integration*. London: Unwin Hyman, 1989.

Blaeser, Kimberly M. 'Native Literature: Seeking a Critical Center.' *Looking at the Words of Our People: First Nations Analysis of Literature*. Ed. Jeannette Armstrong. Penticton, BC: Theytus Books, 1993. 51–62.

Blodgett, E.D. 'After Pierre Berton What? In Search of a Canadian Literature.' *Essays on Canadian Writing* 30 (1984–5): 60–8.

– 'Authenticity and Absence: Reflections on the Prose of Dennis Lee.' *Tasks of Passion: Dennis Lee at Mid-Career*. Ed. Karen Mulhallen, Donna Bennett, and Russell Brown. Toronto: Descant Editions, 1982. 103–17.

– 'Ethnic Writing in Canadian Literature as Paratext.' *Signature* 3 (Summer 1990): 13–27.

– 'Is a History of the Literatures of Canada Possible?' *Essays on Canadian Writing* 50 (Fall 1993): 1–18.

Boelhower, William. *Through a Glass Darkly: Ethnic Semiosis in American Literature*. New York: Oxford UP, 1987.

Bourinot, John George. *Our Intellectual Strength and Weakness*. 1893. Toronto: U of Toronto P, 1973.

Bowering, George. 'On *Ana Historic*: An Interview with Daphne Marlatt.' *Line* 13 (Spring 1989): 96–105.

Bradshaw, Leah. 'A Second Look at *Savage Fields.*' *Canadian Journal of Political and Social Theory* 3.2 (Summer 1979): 139–51.

Brennan, Timothy. 'The National Longing for Form.' *Nation and Narration.* Ed. Homi Bhabha. London: Routledge, 1990. 44–70.

Brown, Russell M. 'Critic, Culture, Text: Beyond Thematics.' *Essays on Canadian Writing* 11 (1978): 151–83.

Buell, Lawrence. 'Literary History as a Hybrid Genre.' *New Historical Literary Study: Essays on Reproducing Texts, Representing History.* Ed. Jeffrey N. Cox and Larry J. Reynolds. Princeton: Princeton UP, 1993. 216–29.

Butler, Judith. *Gender Trouble: Feminism and the Subversion of Identity.* London: Routledge, 1990.

Cagidemetrio, Alide. 'A Plea for Fictional Histories and Old-Time "Jewesses."' *The Invention of Ethnicity.* Ed. Werner Sollors. New York: Oxford UP, 1989. 14–43.

Campbell, Maria. *Halfbreed.* 1973. Halifax: Goodread Biographies, 1983.

Cameron, Barry. 'Theory and Criticism: Trends in Canadian Literature.' *Literary History of Canada.* Ed. W.H. New. Vol. 4. Toronto: U of Toronto P, 1990. 108–32.

Cameron, Barry, and Michael Dixon. 'Introduction.' *Minus Canadian: Penultimate Essays on Literature.* Special issue of *Studies in Canadian Literature* 2 (Summer 1977): 137–45.

Careless, J.M.S. 'Frontierism, Metropolitanism, and Canadian History.' *Canadian Historical Review* 35 (1954): 1–21.

– '"Limited Identities" in Canada.' *Contemporary Approaches to Canadian History.* Ed. Carl Berger. Toronto: Copp Clark Pitman, 1987. 5–12.

Carlyle, Thomas. 'Historic Survey of German Poetry (1831).' *Critical and Miscellaneous Essays.* Vol. 2. London: Chapman and Hall, 1904. 157–90.

Carr, Edward Hallett. *Nationalism and After.* London: Macmillan, 1945.

Chatterjee, Partha. *Nationalist Thought and the Colonial World.* London: Zed Books, 1986.

Coe, Richard M. 'Anglo-Canadian Rhetoric and Identity: A Preface.' *College English* 50.8 (Dec. 1988): 849–60.

Cohen, Ralph. 'Generating Literary Histories.' *New Historical Literary Study: Essays on Reproducing Texts, Representing History.* Ed. Jeffrey N. Cox and Larry J. Reynolds. Princeton: Princeton UP, 1993. 39–53.

Coleridge, Samuel Taylor. *Biographia Literaria.* Ed. George Watson. London: Everyman, 1965.

Collins, Robert G. *E.J. Pratt.* Boston: Twayne, 1988.

Connor, Walker. 'The Nation and Its Myth.' *Ethnicity and Nationalism.* Ed. Anthony D. Smith. New York: E.J. Brill, 1992. 48–57.

Conrad, Joseph. *Heart of Darkness.* Ed. Ross C. Murfin. Boston: Bedford Books, 1996.

Conway, Alison. 'Ethnic Writing and Canadian Literary Criticism.' *Open Letter* 7th ser. 5 (Summer 1989): 52–66.

Cooley, Dennis. 'Recursions Excursions and Incursion: Daphne Marlatt Wrestles with the Angel Language.' *Line* 13 (Spring 1989): 66–79.

Crémazie, Octave. 'Le Drapeau de Carillon.' *The Oxford Book of Canadian Verse*. Ed. A.J.M. Smith. Toronto: Oxford UP, 1960. 18–20.

Culler, Jonathan. *Framing the Sign: Criticism and Its Institutions*. Norman: U of Oklahoma P, 1988.

Davey, Frank. *Canadian Literary Power*. Edmonton: NeWest, 1994.

– *Post-National Arguments: The Politics of the Anglophone-Canadian Novel since 1967*. Toronto: U of Toronto P, 1993.

– *Surviving the Paraphrase: Eleven Essays on Canadian Literature*. Winnipeg: Turnstone P, 1983.

de Man, Paul. *Allegories of Reading: Figural Language in Rousseau, Nietzsche, Rilke, and Proust*. New Haven: Yale UP, 1979.

– *The Resistance to Theory*. Minneapolis: U of Minnesota P, 1986.

– 'Shelley Disfigured.' *Deconstruction and Criticism*. New York: Seabury P, 1979. 39–73.

Derrida, Jacques. *Of Grammatology*. Trans. Gayatri Chakravorty Spivak. Baltimore: Johns Hopkins UP, 1976.

Dewart, Edward Hartley, ed. *Selections from Canadian Poets*. 1864. Toronto: U of Toronto P, 1973.

Djwa, Sandra. '"Canadian Angles of Vision": Northrop Frye and the *Literary History of Canada*.' *English Studies in Canada* 19.2 (June 1993): 133–49.

– *E.J. Pratt: The Evolutionary Vision*. Vancouver: Copp Clark, Montreal: McGill-Queen's UP, 1974.

Dragland, Stan. *The Bees of the Invisible: Essays in Contemporary English Canadian Writing*. Toronto: Coach House, 1991.

– *Floating Voice: Duncan Campbell Scott and the Literature of Treaty 9*. Concord, ON: Anansi, 1994.

– 'On *Civil Elegies*.' *Tasks of Passion: Dennis Lee at Mid-Career*. Ed. Karen Mulhallen, Donna Bennett, and Russell Brown. Toronto: Descant Editions, 1982. 170–88.

Dudek, Louis, and Michael Gnarowski, eds. *The Making of Modern Poetry in Canada: Essential Articles on Contemporary Canadian Poetry in English*. Toronto: Ryerson, 1970.

Duffy, Dennis. *Gardens, Covenants, Exiles: Loyalism in the Literature of Upper Canada/Ontario*. Toronto: U of Toronto P, 1982.

Eagleton, Terry. *Literary Theory: An Introduction*. Oxford: Blackwell, 1983.

Eggleston, Wilfred. *The Frontier and Canadian Letters*. 1957. Toronto: McClelland and Stewart, 1977.

Eliot, T.S. *Collected Poems, 1909–1962*. London: Faber and Faber, 1963.

– *Selected Prose of T.S. Eliot*. Ed. Frank Kermode. London: Faber and Faber, 1975.

Ellmann, Richard. *Oscar Wilde*. Harmondsworth: Penguin, 1988.

Elshtain, Jean Bethke. 'Sovereignty, Identity, Sacrifice.' *Reimagining the Nation*. Ed. Marjorie Ringrose and Adam J. Lerner. Philadelphia: Open UP, 1993. 159–75.

Fanon, Frantz. *The Wretched of the Earth*. Trans. Constance Farrington. Harmondsworth: Penguin, 1967.

Fish, Stanley. *There's No Such Thing as Free Speech, and It's a Good Thing Too*. New York: Oxford UP, 1994.

Fogel, Stanley. *A Tale of Two Countries: Contemporary Fiction in English Canada and the United States*. Toronto: ECW P, 1984.

Foucault, Michel. *The Archaeology of Knowledge and the Discourse on Language*. Trans. A.M. Sheridan Smith. New York: Pantheon Books, 1972.

– *Language, Counter-Memory, Practice: Selected Essays and Interviews*. trans. Donald F. Bouchard and Sherry Simon. Ithaca: Cornell UP, 1977.

Franco, Jean. 'The Nation as Imagined Community.' *The New Historicism*. Ed. H. Aram Veeser. London: Routledge, 1989. 204–12.

Friedenberg, Edgar Z. *Deference to Authority: The Case of Canada*. White Plains, NY: M.E. Sharpe, 1980.

Frow, John. 'Postmodernism and Literary History.' *Theoretical Issues in Literary History*. Ed. David Perkins. Cambridge: Harvard UP, 1991. 131–42.

Frye, Northrop. *The Bush Garden: Essays on the Canadian Imagination*. Toronto: Anansi, 1971.

– *Divisions on a Ground: Essays on Canadian Culture*. Toronto: Anansi, 1982.

Fuss, Diana. *Essentially Speaking: Feminism, Nature, and Difference*. London: Routledge, 1989.

Garber, Marjorie. 'The Occidental Tourist: *M. Butterfly* and the Scandal of Transvestism.' *Nationalisms and Sexualities*. Ed. Andrew Parker, Mary Russo, Doris Sommer, and Patricia Yeager. London: Routledge, 1992. 121–46.

Gardels, Nathan. 'Two Concepts of Nationalism: An Interview with Isaiah Berlin.' *New York Review of Books* 38.19 (21 Nov. 1991): 19–23.

Gardner, John. *On Moral Fiction*. New York: Basic Books, 1977.

Garrett-Petts, W.F. 'Exploring an Interpretive Community: Reader Response to Canadian Prairie Literature.' *College English* 50.8 (Dec. 1988): 920–6.

Garrod, Andrew. *Speaking for Myself: Canadian Writers in Interview*. St John's: Breakwater, 1986.

Gates, Henry Louis, Jr. *Loose Canons: Notes on the Culture Wars*. New York: Oxford UP, 1992.

Geddes, Gary, ed. *Divided We Stand*. Toronto: Peter Martin Associates, 1977.

Gerson, Carole. 'The Canon between the Wars: Field-Notes of a Feminist Literary

Archaeologist.' *Canadian Canons: Essays in Literary Value*. Ed. Robert Lecker. Toronto: U of Toronto P, 1991. 46–56.

Gingell, Susan. *E.J. Pratt on His Life and Poetry*. Toronto: U of Toronto P, 1983.

Giroux, Henry A. *Disturbing Pleasures: Learning Popular Culture*. London: Routledge, 1994.

Godard, Barbara. 'Mythmaking: A Survey of Feminist Criticism.' *Gynocritics: Feminist Approaches to Canadian and Quebec Women's Writing*. Ed. Barbara Godard. Toronto: ECW P, 1987. 1–30.

– 'The Politics of Representation: Some Native Canadian Women Writers.' *Native Writers and Canadian Writing*. Ed. W.H. New. Vancouver: UBC P, 1990. 183–225.

– 'Structuralism/Post-Structuralism: Language, Reality, and Canadian Literature.' *Future Indicative: Literary Theory and Canadian Literature*. Ed. John Moss. Ottawa: U of Ottawa P, 1987. 25–51.

Goldsmith, Oliver. 'The Deserted Village.' *English Prose and Poetry, 1660–1800: A Selection*. Ed. Frank Brady and Martin Price. New York: Hold, Rinehart and Winston, 1961. 306–18.

Goldsmith, Oliver. *The Rising Village*. Ed. Gerald Lynch. London: Canadian Poetry, 1989.

Goody, Ila. 'The Stone Goddess and the Frozen Mother: Accomplices of Desire and Death in Tanizaki, *Tay John*, and *Obasan*.' *Nature and Identity in Canadian and Japanese Literature*. Ed. Kinya Tsuruta and Theodore Goossen. Toronto: U of Toronto and York U Joint Centre for Asia Pacific Studies, 1988. 143–66.

Gossman, Lionel. *Between History and Literature*. Cambridge: Harvard UP, 1990.

Graff, Gerald. *Professing Literature: An Institutional History*. Chicago: U of Chicago P, 1987.

Grant, Agnes. 'Contemporary Native Women's Voices in Literature.' *Native Writers and Canadian Writing*. Ed. W.H. New. Vancouver: UBC P, 1990. 124–32.

Grant, George. *Lament for a Nation: The Defeat of Canadian Nationalism*. Toronto: McClelland and Stewart, 1965.

– *Technology and Empire: Perspectives on North America*. Toronto: Anansi, 1969.

Grant, Robert Stuart. 'Negative Nationalism and the Poetry of Dennis Lee.' MA thesis, University of Windsor, 1971.

Gunew, Sneja. 'PMT (Post Modernist Tensions): Reading for (Multi)cultural Difference.' *Striking Chords: Multicultural Literary Interpretations*. Ed. Sneja Gunew and Kateryna O. Longley. North Sydney: Allen and Unwin, 1992. 36–46.

Habermas, Jürgen. *Legitimation Crises*. Trans. Thomas McCarthy. Boston: Beacon P, 1975.

– *The Structural Transformation of the Public Sphere: An Inquiry into a Category of Bourgeois Society*. Trans. Thomas Berger and Frederick Lawrence. Cambridge: MIT P, 1991.

Haraway, Donna J. *Simians, Cyborgs, and Women: The Reinvention of Nature.* New York: Routledge, 1991.

Hardin, Herschel. *A Nation Unaware: The Canadian Economic Culture.* Vancouver: J.J. Douglas, 1974.

Harris, Mason. 'Broken Generations in *Obasan:* Inner Conflict and the Destruction of Community.' *Canadian Literature* 127 (Winter 1990): 41–57.

Harrison, Dick. *Unnamed Country: The Struggle for a Canadian Prairie Fiction.* Edmonton: U of Alberta P, 1977.

Hartman, Geoffrey. *Beyond Formalism: Literary Essays, 1958–1970.* New Haven: Yale UP, 1970.

– *Criticism in the Wilderness: The Study of Literature Today.* New Haven: Yale UP, 1980.

Hegel, Georg Wilhelm Friedrich. *Phenomenology of Spirit.* Trans. A.V. Miller. Oxford: Oxford UP, 1977.

– *The Philosophy of History.* Trans. J. Sibree. New York: Dover Publications, 1956.

Heidegger, Martin. *Poetry, Language, Thought.* Trans. Albert Hofstadter. New York: Harper and Row, 1975.

Herder, Johann Gottfried von. *Reflections on the Philosophy of the History of Mankind.* Ed. and intro. Frank E. Manuel. Chicago: U of Chicago P, 1968.

Himmelfarb, Gertrude. *The New History and the Old.* Cambridge: Belknap Press of Harvard UP, 1987.

Hobsbawm, Eric. 'Introduction: Inventing Traditions.' *The Invention of Tradition.* Ed. Eric Hobsbawm and Terence Ranger. Cambridge: Cambridge UP, 1983. 1–14.

– 'Mass-Producing Traditions: Europe, 1870–1914.' *The Invention of Tradition.* Ed. Eric Hobsbawm and Terence Ranger. Cambridge: Cambridge UP, 1983. 263–307.

Hohendahl, Peter Uwe. *Building a National Literature: The Case of Germany, 1830–1870.* Trans. Renate Baron Francisco. Ithaca: Cornell UP, 1989.

hooks, bell. *Outlaw Culture: Resisting Representations.* London: Routledge, 1994.

Huggan, Graham. *Territorial Disputes: Maps and Mapping Strategies in Contemporary Canadian and Australian Fiction.* Toronto: U of Toronto P, 1994.

Hughes, Kenneth, J. 'Oliver Goldsmith's "The Rising Village."' *Canadian Poetry* (Fall–Winter 1977): 27–43.

Hunter, Lynette. *Outsider Notes: Feminist Approaches to Nation State Ideology, Writers/Readers, and Publishing.* Vancouver: Talonbooks, 1996.

Hutcheon, Linda. *The Canadian Postmodern: A Study of Contemporary English-Canadian Fiction.* Toronto: Oxford UP, 1988.

– *Splitting Images: Contemporary Canadian Ironies.* Toronto: Oxford UP, 1991.

Iggers, Georg G. *The German Conception of History: The National Tradition of Historical Thought from Herder to the Present.* Middletown, CT: Wesleyan UP, 1983.

Jackel, David. 'Goldsmith's *Rising Village* and the Colonial State of Mind.' *Studies in Canadian Literature* 5.1 (Spring 1980): 152–66.

Jackel, Susan. 'Canadian Women's Autobiography: A Problem of Criticism.' *Gynocritics: Feminist Approaches to Canadian and Quebec Women's Writing.* Ed. Barbara Godard. Toronto: ECW P, 1987. 97–110.

Jameson, Fredric. 'Third World Literature in the Era of Multinational Capital.' *Social Text* (Fall 1986): 66–88.

Jay, Martin. *Force Fields: Between Intellectual History and Cultural Critique.* London: Routledge, 1993.

– *Marxism and Totality: The Adventures of a Concept from Lukács to Habermas.* Berkeley: U of California P, 1984.

Johnson, Barbara. *The Critical Difference: Essays in the Contemporary Rhetoric of Reading.* Baltimore: Johns Hopkins UP, 1985.

Johnson, Samuel. *Lives of the English Poets.* Vol. 2. London: Dent, 1968.

– *Rasselas, Poems, and Selected Prose.* Ed. Bertrand H. Bronson. New York: Holt, Rinehart and Winston, 1958.

Jones, D.G. *Butterfly on Rock: A Study of Themes and Images in Canadian Literature.* Toronto: U of Toronto P, 1970.

Jones, Manina. *The Art of Difference: 'Documentary-Collage' and English-Canadian Writing.* Toronto: U of Toronto P, 1993.

Kamboureli, Smaro. 'Canadian Ethnic Anthologies: Representations of Ethnicity.' *Ariel* 25.4 (Oct. 1994): 11–52.

– *On the Edge of Genre: The Contemporary Canadian Long Poem.* Toronto: U of Toronto P, 1991.

Kamenka, Eugene. 'Political Nationalism: The Evolution of the Idea.' *Nationalism: The Nature and Evolution of an Idea.* Ed. Eugene Kamenka. London: Edward Arnold, 1976. 3–20.

Kane, Sean. 'The Poet as Shepherd of Being.' *Tasks of Passion: Dennis Lee at Mid-Career.* Ed. Karen Mulhallen, Donna Bennett, and Russell Brown. Toronto: Descant Editions, 1982. 121–42

Keith, W.J. 'The Function of Canadian Criticism at the Present Time.' *Essays on Canadian Writing* 30 (1984–5): 1–16.

– '*The Rising Village* Again.' *Canadian Poetry* (Fall–Winter 1978): 1–13.

Kenner, Hugh. 'The Case of the Missing Face.' *Our Sense of Identity: A Book of Canadian Essays.* Ed. Malcolm Ross. Toronto: Ryerson, 1954. 203–8.

King, Bruce. *The New English Literatures: Cultural Nationalism in a Changing World.* New York: St Martin's P, 1980.

Klinck, Carl F. *Giving Canada a Literary History.* Ottawa: Carleton UP, 1991.

Kogawa, Joy. *Itsuka.* Harmondsworth: Penguin, 1992.

– *Obasan.* 1981. Harmondsworth: Penguin, 1983.

Kohn, Hans. *Nationalism: Its Meaning and History.* Rev. ed. Princeton: D. Van Nostrand, 1965.

Kristeva, Julia. *Nations without Nationalism.* Trans. Leon S. Roudiez. New York: Columbia UP, 1993.

Kroetsch, Robert. *The Crow Journals.* Edmonton: NeWest, 1980.

– *The Lovely Treachery of Words: Essays Selected and New.* Toronto: Oxford UP, 1989. 64–72.

Leavis, Q.D. 'The Englishness of the English Novel.' *Collected Essays.* Vol. 1. Ed. G. Singh. Cambridge: Cambridge UP, 1983. 303–27.

Lecker, Robert, ed. *Canadian Canons: Essays in Literary Value.* Toronto: U of Toronto P, 1991.

– 'The Canonization of Canadian Literature: An Inquiry into Value.' *Critical Quarterly* 16 (Spring 1990): 656–71.

– 'A Country without a Canon? Canadian Literature and the Esthetics of Idealism.' *Mosaic* 26.3 (Summer 1993): 1–19.

– 'Privacy, Publicity, and the Discourse of Canadian Studies.' *Essays on Canadian Writing* 51–2 (Winter 1993–Spring 1994): 32–82.

Lee, Dennis. 'Cadence, Country, Silence: Writing in Colonial Space.' *Boundary 2* 3.1 (Fall 1974): 151–68.

– *Civil Elegies and other Poems.* Toronto: Anansi, 1972.

– *The Death of Harold Ladoo.* Vancouver: Kanchenjunga P, 1976.

– *The Difficulty of Living on other Planets.* Toronto: Macmillan, 1987.

– *The Gods.* Vancouver: Kanchenjunga P, 1978.

– *Nicholas Knock and other People.* Toronto: Macmillan, 1974.

– *Not Abstract Harmonies But.* Vancouver: Kanchenjunga P, 1974.

– 'Polyphony: Enacting a Meditation.' *Tasks of Passion: Dennis Lee at Mid-Career.* Ed. Karen Mulhallen, Donna Bennett, and Russell Brown. Toronto: Descant Editions, 1982. 82–99.

– 'Reading *Savage Fields.*' *Canadian Journal of Political and Social Theory* 3.2 (Summer 1979): 161–82.

– 'Running and Dwelling: Homage to Al Purdy.' *Saturday Night* 87.7 (July 1972): 14–16.

– *Savage Fields: An Essay in Literature and Cosmology.* Toronto: Anansi, 1977.

– Statement. *Storm Warnings.* Ed. Al Purdy. Toronto: McClelland and Stewart, 1971. 96.

Lentricchia, Frank. *After the New Criticism.* Chicago: U of Chicago P, 1980.

Le Pan, Douglas. 'In Frock Coat and Moccasins.' *Canada: A Guide to the Peaceable Kingdom.* Ed. William Kilbourn. Toronto: Macmillan, 1970. 3–7.

Lerner, Adam J. Introduction. *Reimagining the Nation.* Ed. Marjorie Ringrose and Adam J. Lerner. Philadelphia: Open UP, 1993. 1–5.

Lewis, C.S. 'Genius and Genius.' *Studies in Medieval and Renaissance Literature.* Cambridge: Cambridge UP, 1966. 169–74.

Lighthall, William Douw, ed. *Songs of the Great Dominion.* 1889. Toronto: Coles, 1971.

Longfellow, Henry Wadsworth. 'Paul Revere's Ride.' *The Oxford Book of Children's Verse in America.* Ed. Donald Hall. New York: Oxford UP, 1985. 45–8.

Loriggio, Francesco. 'The Question of the Corpus: Ethnicity and Canadian Literature.' *Future Indicative: Literary Theory and Canadian Literature.* Ed. John Moss. Ottawa: U of Ottawa P, 1987. 53–69.

Lynch, Gerald. 'Introduction.' Oliver Goldsmith, *The Rising Village.* Ed. Gerald Lynch. London, ON: Canadian Poetry P, 1989. xi–xxvii.

Lyotard, Jean-François. *The Postmodern Condition: A Report on Knowledge.* Trans. Geoff Bennington and Brian Massumi. Minneapolis: U of Minnesota P, 1984.

MacLulich, T.D. 'What Was Canadian Literature? Taking Stock of the CanLit Industry.' *Essays on Canadian Writing* 30 (1984–5): 17–34.

MacMechan, Archibald. *Headwaters of Canadian Literature.* 1924. Toronto: McClelland and Stewart, 1974.

Mair, Charles. 'The New Canada.' *The Search for English-Canadian Literature.* Ed. Carl Ballstadt. Toronto: U of Toronto P, 1975. 151–54.

Manuel, Frank E. Editor's Introduction. *Reflections on the Philosophy of the History of Mankind.* Chicago: U of Chicago P, 1968.

Marlatt, Daphne. *Ana Historic.* Toronto: Coach House, 1988.

– 'Writing Our Way through the Labyrinth.' *Collaboration in the Feminine: Writings on Women and Culture from 'Tessera'* Ed. Barbara Godard. Toronto: Second Story P, 1994. 44–6.

Marx, Karl, and Friedrich Engels. *Basic Writings on Politics and Philosophy.* Ed. Lewis S. Feuer. Garden City, NY: Anchor Books, 1959.

Mathews, Robin. *Canadian Identity: Major Forces Shaping the Life of a People.* Ottawa: Steel Rail, 1988.

McCarthy, Dermot. 'Early Canadian Literary Histories and the Function of a Canon.' *Canadian Canons: Essays in Literary Value.* Ed. Robert Lecker. Toronto: U of Toronto P, 1991. 30–45.

McClintock, Anne. *Imperial Leather: Race, Gender, and Sexuality in the Colonial Context.* London: Routledge, 1995.

McGann, Jerome J. *The Romantic Ideology: A Critical Investigation.* Chicago: U of Chicago P, 1983.

McGregor, Gaile. *The Wacousta Syndrome: Explorations in the Canadian Langscape.* Toronto: U of Toronto P, 1985.

McKillop, A.B. *Contours of Canadian Thought.* Toronto: U of Toronto P, 1987.

Metcalf, John. *What Is a Canadian Literature?* Guelph, ON: Red Kite P, 1988.

Middlebro,' T.G. 'Dennis Lee.' *Canadian Authors and Their Works.* Poetry series 9. Ed. Robert Lecker, Jack David, and Ellen Quigley. Toronto: ECW P, 1985. 189–228.

Monkman, Leslie. *A Native Heritage: Image of the Indian in English-Canadian Literature.* Toronto: U of Toronto P, 1981.

Montrose, Louis A. 'Professing the Renaissance: The Poetics and Politics of Culture.' *The New Historicism.* Ed. H. Aram Veeser. London: Routledge, 1989. 15–36.

Morton, W.L. *The Canadian Identity.* 1961. Toronto: U of Toronto P, 1968.

Moses, Daniel David, and Terry Goldie, eds. *An Anthology of Canadian Native Literature in English.* Toronto: Oxford UP, 1992.

Moses, Michael Valdez. 'Caliban and His Precursors: The Politics of Literary History and the Third World.' *Theoretical Issues in Literary History.* Ed. David Perkins. Cambridge: Harvard UP, 1991. 206–26.

Moss, John. 'Bushed in the Sacred Wood.' *The Human Elements.* 2nd ser. Ed. David Helwig. Toronto: Oberon P, 1982. 161–78.

– *Patterns of Isolation in English-Canadian Fiction.* Toronto: McClelland and Stewart, 1974.

Mosse, George L. 'Mass Politics and the Political Liturgy of Nationalism.' *Nationalism: The Nature and Evolution of an Idea.* Ed. Eugene Kamenka. London: Edward Arnold, 1976. 38–54.

Mukherjee, Arun. *Towards an Aesthetic of Opposition: Essays on Literature, Criticism, and Cultural Imperialism.* Stratford, ON: Williams-Wallace, 1988.

Mulhern, Francis. 'English Reading.' *Nation and Narration.* Ed. Homi Bhabha. London: Routledge, 1990. 250–64.

– *The Moment of Scrutiny.* London: NLB, 1979.

Munton, Ann. 'Simultaneity in the Writings of Dennis Lee.' *Tasks of Passion: Dennis Lee at Mid-Career.* Ed. Karen Mulhallen, Donna Bennett, and Russell Brown. Toronto: Descant Editions, 1982. 143–69.

Nairn, Tom. *The Break-up of Britain: Crisis and Neo-Nationalism.* London: NLB, 1977.

Navari, Cornelia. 'The Origins of the Nation-State.' *The Nation-State: The Formation of Modern Politics.* Ed. Leonard Tivey. Oxford: Martin Robertson, 1981. 13–38.

Neuman, Shirley, and Robert Wilson. *Labyrinths of Voice: Conversations with Robert Kroetsch.* Edmonton: NeWest, 1982.

New, W.H. *Articulating West: Essays on Purpose and Form in Modern Canadian Literature.* Toronto: New P, 1972.

– 'Editorial: The Very Idea.' *Canadian Literature* 135 (Winter 1992): 2–11.

Nietzsche, Friedrich. *The Will to Power in Science, Nature, Society, and Art.* Trans. Anthony M. Ludivici. New York: Frederick Publications, 1960.

Ondaatje, Michael. *The Collected Works of Billy the Kid.* Toronto: Anansi, 1970.

Orridge, A.W. 'Varieties of Nationalism.' *The Nation State: The Formation of Modern Politics.* Ed. Leonard Tivey. Oxford: Martin Robertson, 1981. 39–58.

Orwell, George. 'England Your England.' *Inside the Whale and Other Essays.* Harmondsworth: Penguin, 1969. 63–90.

Pacey, Desmond. *Creative Writing in Canada.* Rev. ed. Toronto: Ryerson, 1961.

– *Ten Canadian Poets: A Group of Biographical and Critical Essays.* Toronto: Ryerson, 1958.

Pache, Walter. 'Tradition and the Canadian Talent: Dilemmas of Literary History in Canada.' *Carry on Bumping.* Ed. John Metcalf. Toronto: ECW P, 1988. 85–100.

Papastergiadis, Nikos. 'Ambivalence in Cultural Theory: Reading Homi Bhabha's *Dissemi-Nation.*' *Writing the Nation: Self and Country in the Post-Colonial Imagination.* Ed. John C. Hawley. Amsterdam: Rodopi, 1996. 176–193.

Parameswaran, Uma. 'Ganga in the Assiniboine: Prospects for Indo-Canadian Literature.' *A Meeting of Streams: South Asian Canadian Literature.* Ed. M.G. Vassanji. Toronto: TSAR Publications, 1985. 79–93.

Parker, Andrew, Mary Russo, Doris Sommer, and Patricia Yeager, eds. *Nationalisms and Sexualities.* London: Routledge, 1992.

Patterson, Lee. 'Literary History.' *Critical Terms for Literary Study.* Ed. Frank Lentricchia and Thomas McLaughlin. Chicago: U of Chicago P, 1990. 250–62.

Perkins, David. *Is Literary History Possible?* Baltimore: Johns Hopkins UP, 1992.

Pitt, David G. *E.J. Pratt: The Master Years, 1927–1964.* Toronto: U of Toronto P, 1987.

Pivato, Joseph, ed. *Contrasts: Comparative Essays on Italian-Canadian Writing.* Montreal: Guernica, 1991.

Plamenatz, John. 'Two types of Nationalism.' *Nationalism: The Nature and Evolution of an Idea.* Ed. Eugene Kamenka. London: Edward Arnold, 1976. 23–36.

Potter, Robin. 'Moral – In Whose Sense? Joy Kogawa's *Obasan* and Julia Kristeva's *Powers of Horror.*' *Studies in Canadian Literature* 15.1 (1990): 117–39.

Pratt, Annis. 'Affairs with Bears: Some Notes towards Feminist Archetypal Hypotheses for Canadian Literature.' *Gynocritics: Feminist Approaches to Canadian and Quebec Women's Writing.* Ed. Barbara Godard. Toronto: ECW P, 1987. 157–78.

Pratt, E.J. *Complete Poems.* 2 vols. Ed. Sandra Djwa and R.G. Moyles. Toronto: U of Toronto P, 1989.

Radhakrishnan, R. 'Nationalism, Gender, and the Narrative of Identity.' *Nationalisms and Sexualities.* Ed. Andrew Parker, Mary Russo, Doris Sommer, and Patricia Yeager. London: Routledge, 1992. 77–95.

Reaney, James, '*Towards the Last Spike*: The Treatment of a Western Subject.' *E.J. Pratt*. Ed. David G. Pitt. Toronto: Ryerson, 1969. 73–82.

Redekop, Magdalene. 'Authority and Margins of Escape in *Brébeuf and His Brethren.' Open Letter* 6th ser. 2–3 (Summer–Fall 1985): 45–60.

Renan, Ernest. 'What Is a Nation?' *Nation and Narration*. Ed. Homi Bhabha. London: Routledge, 1990. 8–22.

Richler, Mordecai. *Home Sweet Home: My Canadian Album*. Markham, ON: Penguin, 1985.

Ross, Malcolm. *The Impossible Sum of Our Traditions: Reflections on Canadian Literature*. Ed. David Staines. Toronto: McClelland and Stewart, 1986.

Said, Edward W. *Culture and Imperialism*. New York: Vintage Books, 1994.

– 'The Politics of Knowledge.' *Falling into Theory: Conflicting Views on Reading Literature*. Ed. David H. Richter. Boston: Bedford Books, 1994. 193–203.

Scott, F.R. *The Collected Poems of F.R. Scott*. Toronto: McClelland and Stewart, 1981.

Sedgwick, Eve Kosofsky. *Between Men: English Literature and Male Homosocial Desire*. New York: Columbia UP, 1985.

– 'Nationalisms and Sexualities in the Age of Wilde.' *Nationalisms and Sexualities*. Ed. Andrew Parker, Mary Russo, Doris Sommer, and Patricia Yeager. London: Routledge, 1992. 235–45.

Seton-Watson, Hugh. *Nations and States: An Enquiry into the Origins of Nations and the Politics of Nationalism*. London: Methuen, 1977.

Siemerling, Winfried. *Discoveries of the Other: Alterity in the Work of Leonard Cohen, Hubert Aquin, Michael Ondaatje, and Nicole Brossard*. Toronto: U of Toronto P, 1994.

Silverman, Kaja. *The Acoustic Mirror: The Female Voice in Psychoanalysis and Cinema*. Bloomington: Indiana UP, 1988.

Simon, Sherry. 'Culture and Its Values: Critical Revisionism in Quebec in the 1980s.' *Canadian Canons: Essays in Literary Value*. Ed. Robert Lecker. Toronto: U of Toronto P, 1991. 167–79.

Smith, A.J.M. *Towards a View of Canadian Letters: Selected Critical Essays, 1928–1971*. Vancouver: U of British Columbia P, 1973.

Smith, Anthony D. 'Nationalism and the Historians.' *Ethnicity and Nationalism*. Ed. Anthony D. Smith. New York: E.J. Brill, 1992. 58–80.

– *Theories of Nationalism*. London: Duckworth, 1971.

Smith, Gordon. 'A Future for the Nation-State?' *The Nation-State: The Formation of Modern Politics*. Ed. Leonard Tivey. Oxford: Martin Robertson, 1981. 197–290.

Solecki, Sam. 'Some Kicks against the Prick.' *Volleys*. Erin, ON: Porcupine's Quill, 1990. 9–34.

Sollors, Werner. *Beyond Ethnicity: Consent and Descent in American Culture*. New York: Oxford UP, 1986.

Sommer, Doris. Irresistible Romance: The Foundational Fictions of Latin America.' *Nation and Narration*. Ed. Homi Bhabha. London: Routledge, 1990. 71–98.

Spivak, Gayatri Chakravorty. *In other Worlds: Essays in Cultural Politics*. London: Routledge, 1988.

Stallybrass, Peter, and Allon White. *The Politics and Poetics of Transgression*. Ithaca: Cornell UP, 1986.

Stedingh, R.W. 'An Interview with Dennis Lee.' *Canadian Fiction Magazine* 7 (Summer 1972): 42–54.

Steiner, George. *In Bluebeard's Castle: Some Notes towards the Redefinition of Culture*. New Haven: Yale UP, 1971.

– *Language and Silence: Essays, 1958–1966*. Harmondsworth: Penguin, 1969.

Stevens, Wallace. *The Collected Poems of Wallace Stevens*. New York: Alfred A. Knopf, 1978.

Stich, K.P. '*The Rising Village, The Emigrant*, and *Malcolm's Katie:* The Vanity of Progress.' *Canadian Poetry* 7 (Fall–Winter 1980): 48–55.

Sugunasiri, Suwanda. 'Reality and Symbolism in the Short Story.' *A Meeting of Streams: South Asian Canadian Literature*. Ed. M.G. Vassanji. Toronto: TSAR Publications, 1985. 33–48.

Sullivan, Rosemary. 'The Forest and the Trees.' *Ambivalence: Studies in Canadian Literature*. Ed. Om P. Juneja and Chandra Mohan. New Delhi: Allied Publishers, 1990. 39–47.

Surette, Leon. 'Creating the Canadian Canon.' *Canadian Canons: Essays in Literary Value*. Ed. Robert Lecker. Toronto: U of Toronto P, 1991. 17–29.

– 'Here Is Us: The Topocentrism of Canadian Literary Criticism,' *Canadian Poetry* 10 (Spring–Summer 1982): 44–57.

Taylor, Charles. *Philosophical Arguments*. Cambridge: Harvard UP, 1995.

– *Reconciling the Solitudes: Essays on Canadian Federalism and Nationalism*. Ed. Guy Laforest. Montreal: McGill-Queen's UP, 1994.

Tiefensee, Dianne. '*The Old Dualities*': *Deconstructing Robert Kroetsch and His Critics*. Montreal: McGill-Queen's UP, 1994.

Tiffin, Chris, and Alan Lawson. 'Introduction: The Textuality of Empire.' *Describing Empire: Post-Colonialism and Textuality*. Ed. Chris Tiffin and Alan Lawson. London: Routledge, 1994. 1–11.

Tivey, Leonard. 'Introduction.' *The Nation-State: The Formation of Modern Politics*. Ed. Leonard Tivey. Oxford: Martin Robertson, 1981. 1–12.

Tostevin, Lola Lemire. 'Daphne Marlatt: Writing in the Space That Is Her Mother's Face.' *Line* 13 (Spring 1989); 32–9.

Traill, Catharine Parr. *The Backwoods of Canada*. 1836. Toronto: McClelland and Stewart, 1989.

Tranquilla, Ronald E. '"Empires Rise and Sink": *The Rising Village* and the Cyclical View of History.' *Canadian Poetry* 23 (Fall–Winter 1988): 47–61.

Trinh, T. Minh-Ha. *When the Moon Waxes Red: Representation, Gender, and Cultural Politics.* London: Routledge, 1991.

Turner, Margaret. *Imagining Culture: New World Narrative and the Writing of Canada.* Montreal: McGill-Queen's UP, 1995.

Twigg, Alan. *For Openers: Conversations with Twenty-Four Canadian Writers.* Madiera Park, BC: Harbour Publishing, 1981.

Watt, Frank. 'Nationalism in Canadian Literature.' *Nationalism in Canada.* Ed. Peter Russell. Toronto: McGraw-Hill, 1966. 235–51.

Wayman, Tom. *A Country not Considered: Canada, Culture, Work.* Toronto: Anansi, 1993.

Webb, Phyllis. *Nothing but Brush Strokes: Selected Prose.* Edmonton: NeWest, 1995.

Weimann, Robert. 'History, Appropriation, and the Uses of Representation in Modern Narrative.' *The Aims of Representation: Subject/Text/History.* Ed. Murray Krieger. New York: Columbia UP, 1987. 175–215.

– *Structure and Society in Literary History: Studies in the History and Theory of Historical Criticism.* Charlottesville: U of Virginia P, 1976.

Weir, Lorraine. 'Daphne Marlatt's "Ecology of Language."' *Line* 13 (Spring 1989): 58–63.

– 'The Discourse of "Civility": Strategies of Containment in Literary Histories of English-Canadian Literature.' *Problems of Literary Reception/Problèmes de réception littéraire.* Ed. E.D. Blodgett and A.G. Purdy. Edmonton: Research Institute for Comparative Literature, 1988. 24–39.

– 'Normalizing the Subject: Linda Hutcheon and the English-Canadian Postmodern.' *Canadian Canons: Essays in Literary Value.* Ed. Robert Lecker. Toronto: U of Toronto P, 1991. 180–95.

– 'Toward a Feminist Hermeneutics: Jay Macpherson's *Welcoming Disaster.*' *Gynocritics: Feminist Approaches to Canadian and Quebec Women's Writing.* Ed. Barbara Godard. Toronto: ECW P, 1987. 59–70.

Wellek, René. *Concepts of Criticism.* New Haven: Yale UP, 1963.

White, Allon. *Carnival, Hysteria, and Writing: Collected Essays and Autobiography.* Oxford: Clarendon P, 1993.

White, Hayden. *The Content of the Form: Narrative Discourse and Historical Representation.* Baltimore: Johns Hopkins UP, 1987.

Wilde, Oscar. *Plays, Prose Writings and Poems.* London: Everyman, 1967.

Williamson, Janice. *Sounding Differences: Conversations with Seventeen Canadian Women Writers.* Toronto: U of Toronto P, 1993.

Wordsworth, William. *The Prelude, Selected Poems, and Sonnets.* Ed. Carlos Baker. New York: Holt, Rinehart and Winston, 1965.

Xenos, Nicholas. 'Nation, State, and Economy: Max Weber's Freiburg Inaugural Lecture.' *Reimagining the Nation.* Ed. Marjorie Ringrose and Adam J. Lerner. Philadelphia: Open UP, 1993. 125–38.

Young, Robert. *Colonial Desire: Hybridity in Theory, Culture, and Race.* London: Routledge, 1995.

– *White Mythologies: Writing History and the West.* London: Routledge, 1990.

Credits and Permissions

The author wishes to acknowledge the following for use of material in this book:

The Education of Henry Adams, by Henry Adams. Boston: Houghton Mifflin Company, 1927.

'History Lesson,' by Jeannette Armstrong, courtesy of the author. From *An Anthology of Canadian Native Literature in English*, edited by Daniel David Moses and Terry Goldie. Toronto: Oxford University Press, 1992.

'Traditional History of the Confederacy of the Six Nations,' courtesy of Oxford University Press Canada. From *An Anthology of Canadian Native Literature in English*, edited by Daniel David Moses and Terry Goldie. Toronto: Oxford University Press, 1992.

A Separate Sky, by Himani Bannerji. Toronto: Domestic Bliss Press, 1982.

Civil Elegies and Other Poems, by Dennis Lee, courtesy of Stoddart Publishing Co. Limited. Toronto: Anansi, 1972.

'Towards the Last Spike,' by E.J. Pratt, courtesy of the University of Toronto Press. From *Complete Poems*, edited by Sandra Djwa and R.G. Moyles. Toronto: University of Toronto Press, 1989.

Nothing But Brush Strokes, by Phyllis Webb, courtesy of the author. Edmonton: NeWest, 1995.

Index